D0915937

RIDE THE RAZOR'S EDGE

Other books by the same author:

The Complete & Authentic Life of Jesse James
The Day Jesse James Was Killed
Escapades of Frank & Jesse James
Great Gunfighters of the West
Outlaws of the Old West
Great Lawmen of the West
The Bandit Belle
Quantrill and His Civil War Guerrillas
Killer Legions of Quantrill
Date With Destiny: Billy the Kid
The Man Who Shot Jesse James
Badmen of the Frontier Days
Forty Years on the Wild Frontier
Lawmen & Robbers

RIDE THE RAZOR'S EDGE

THE YOUNGER BROTHERS STORY

CARL W. BREIHAN

PELICAN PUBLISHING COMPANY
Gretna 1992

The word "Pelican" and the depiction of a pelican are trademarks of Pelican
Publishing Company, Inc., and are registered in the U.S. Patent and Trademark
Office.

Library of Congress Cataloging-in-Publication Data

Breihan, Carl W., 1915
    Ride the razor's edge: the Younger Brothers story/Carl W.
Breihan.
      p. cm.
    ISBN 0-88289-879-5
    1. United States — History — Civil War, 1861-1865 — Under-
ground movements. 2. Younger, Cole, 1844-1916. 3. Younger,
James, 1848-1902. 4. Quantrill, William Clarke, 1837-1865. 5.
James, Jesse, 1847-1882. 6. James, Frank, 1844-1915. 7. West (U.S.) —
History — Civil War, 1861-1865. 8. Guerrillas — West (U.S.) —
Biography. 9. Outlaws — West (U.S.) — Biography. I. Title.
E470.45.B742   1992
973.7'42'0922 — dc20
(B)
                                                              91-43547
                                                                  CIP

Manufactured in the United States of America

Published by Pelican Publishing Company, Inc.
1101 Monroe Street, Gretna, Louisiana 70053

To
Scott, Sandy, Danny, and Laura Hogberg
and
Hon. Michael Zane and Lora Yates

Contents

Foreword

HAVING KNOWN MR. BREIHAN for many years and being aware of the integrity in his writing about the Jameses and the Youngers and others, I am pleased to introduce this manuscript. As a Missouri farm girl now past 86 years of age, I am aware of the history covered in this book.

My father, Benjamin H. Morrow, joined the Quantrill guerrillas and fought with them throughout the War Between the States. This book covers many incidents that I heard discussed by my father and his old buddies. Sometimes I was permitted to listen to their conversation; at other times I listened by leaving the door open a crack. Of course I heard of many incidents that have never been recorded and that have therefore never been learned by earnest researchers.

Many times Hi George, John McCorkle, Harrison Trow, Bill Gregg, and others came to Father's farmhouse and talked over their experiences. Besides, the fiery Adjutant General Jo Shelby came by often, when he praised the good points of the boys. It was he who wrote and published a scathing editorial against society as a whole after the murder of Jesse James by Bob Ford.

I recall that once John McCorkle told how his only brother, Jabez, was killed. It was in February of 1861 when Quantrill told Jabez to round up some of the men at the time Cole Younger was almost captured at the home of his Grandmother Fristoe. John McCorkle's men were on Cedar Creek, and when his brother came up and accidentally dropped his Springfield rifle, the weapon discharged. The bullet struck Jabez in the right leg below the knee, passing upward. He lingered for thirteen days before dying. He was buried in a country graveyard near the home of his mother-in-law, Mrs. Harris. Frank James later told me that he had helped to bury Jabez McCorkle. I am proud of the letters I have from Frank James, as well as some of the ribbons that the ex-guerrillas wore at their annual get-togethers.

It is good to see that Mr. Breihan has finally told the facts about Cole Younger's sweetheart, Lizzie Daniels, and Jim Younger's sweetheart, Cora Lee McNeill. The stories circulated by Alix Muller were false, for Jim never loved any girl but Cora. Apparently Mr. Breihan did not know that Cole also had a young girl friend during the war. She was Lizzie Brown, who lived several miles northwest of Harrisonville, Missouri. One evening I heard the men talk of how Cole visited her for a week at one time with John McCorkle, George Wiggington, and several other guerrillas who went along to protect him. On the way back to camp, at a high point on the road leading from Kansas City to Lone Jack, they saw the Seventh Kansas Cavalry approaching. These soldiers were outwitted and lured into a wooded area, a plan which the Federal soldiers did not relish.

John McCorkle had tears in his eyes when he related the story of how Captain George Todd died. He said that he had been ordered by Quantrill to go from Bone Hill to Independence in order to contact Todd at that point. En route he was met by John Vaughn who said, "John, Captain Todd wants you. He was badly wounded near Blue Mills and told me to send you to Independence with the boys. He wants to see you all before he dies."

Dave Pool met them on the way and told McCorkle that Todd had already been buried in an Independence cemetery. From what I could gather during the conversation, Todd's last words were something like this: "Boys, we are in a tight place. Where is John McCorkle? We could get out of this if he were here."

Dave Pool was then elected captain of the men remaining from Todd's detachment.

Bill Gregg, who later wrote *The Gregg Manuscript*, was a good fighter from what I heard. Near Johnson County, on the Sni River, Gregg married Lizzie Hook and took her south with him. He wanted McCorkle and some others of the guerrillas to attend his wedding. Some of the men in our house laughed as they recalled how the beautiful young girl was standing beside her lover, a soldier with four Navy revolvers buckled around his waist, while twelve long-haired, heavily armed men stood by as witnesses.

Cole Younger and Frank James visited my father a number of times. I could tell by the way they talked that some of the guerrillas had an axe to grind, while the majority of them had fought with the guerrillas for the country's sake. I learned of how Cole Younger's family was persecuted, how the James family was harassed by the Federals after Frank joined the Quantrill band, and how Bill Anderson became a fiend incarnate after the murder of his sister Josephine and the maiming of his ten-year-old sister Janie.

"Bloody Bill" carried a leather pouch in which was a silken cord. For each Federal soldier that he personally killed he tied a knot in the cord, and there were fifty-three knots in that cord when he was killed in Ray County, near Orrick, in October of 1864.

John Thrailkill, Jesse James' close friend, also became an avenging angel after the death of his sweetheart. Federal soldiers had murdered her invalid father in front of her, and she lost her reason, dying soon afterward.

This book is a valuable addition to the history of the Missouri outlaws during the war years, and I can vouch for the authenticity of both the text and the photos used here. I was born several years after the murder of Jesse James, and I am grateful that I lived through the part of the history which follows.

My father was one of the men who identified the body of Jesse Woodson James to the satisfaction of Governor Crittenden and others. My younger sister and I used to attend the guerrilla reunions at Oak Grove and Independence and often saw Frank James and Jesse's son there. When Frank died I took my father to young Jesse James' office to meet the other men who were to be pallbearers.

As for those who blame the railroads for the Jameses and Youngers joining up with Quantrill, as far as I know the railroads did not even reach to that part of the state then. They ran only to Tipton, from which point the Butterfield stages were used.

MARY B. MORROW
Independence, Missouri

With thanks to my wife Ethel for her collaboration in this work, and with warm acknowledgment for the assistance rendered by Mary and Emma Morrow, daughters of Ben Morrow, guerrilla and life-long friend of the Jameses and the Youngers. Also thanks to Harry Younger Hall, nephew of Cole Younger; Charles Kemper, Clerk of the Circuit Court, and Stella James, Jesse Edwards James, Mae James and Robert F. James, for all their assistance.

COLE YOUNGER

Being an outlaw brought me fame.
    Cole Younger is the name!
It all began 'way back in '61
    When many lawless deeds were done.
Both sides fought with no holds barred,
Leaving Missouri scorched and scarred.

To settle down we tried our best,
    But never would they let us rest.
Ambushed by day, shot at by night,
    Always forced to renew the fight,
We took up arms against those who would
Destroy our home and livelihood.

"Those Younger boys, outlaws!" they cried,
As through the many towns we ride.
When banks and trains fell to bandit guns
The Jameses and Youngers were said to be the ones.
So we rode the lonely and forgotten trail
To clear our name, or forever fail.

                                    Carl W. Breihan

In men whom men condemn as ill
I find so much of goodness still —
In men whom men deem half divine,
I find so much of sin and blot —
I hesitate to draw the line
Between the two where God has not.

RIDE THE RAZOR'S EDGE

Cole Younger's grandparents: Charles and Sarah Younger

CHAPTER 1

A Chilling Experience

THE JUNE SUN HUNG LOW in the sky, its rays, slanting across the miles, splintered like bucket-flung diamonds upon the floor of the forest. As the avenues of light stabbed through the trees, grotesque figures appeared amid the leaves blowing through the aisles of the woods.

On that morning of June 6, 1859, two young boys sauntered through the thick formation of trees where not a bird chirped. Big River, zigzagging across Jackson County, Missouri, went through the farm of Colonel Henry Washington Younger where life seemed to be waiting for some tragedy to occur.

"Bud, I don't like it," said eleven-year-old James Younger to his fifteen-year-old brother Cole. "Things are too quiet."

"Just your imagination," said his brother. "Let's keep going. We still got a few more miles before getting home."

The forest was thick with humidity which hung low to the ground. Then the eerie silence was suddenly broken by the echoes of booming black-powder explosions from a 12-gauge shotgun.

The two boys stopped short. They had heard stories of Kansas raiders and of retaliation forays by men from Missouri, the neighboring state. They were aroused by the sound of fast-moving horses dashing through the underbrush.

Suddenly a bare-footed man hopped out of the brush and raced across a newly ploughed field. He was scratched and

Bob and Jim Younger

bleeding and flushed from panting, his clothing in shreds, his eyes wild with fear. Whether he saw Cole and Jim Younger they were not aware.

"C'mon, Jim," cried Cole. "We got no business here."

"Bud, we'll never make it across the field in time. Dive into the furrows," Jim yelled.

Into a deep furrow the boys dived, feeling it would be a temporary hiding place.

The gleam of the sun bounced off the shotgun barrels as the pursuing men raced into the clearing. Others came from the opposite side of the field, hemming the fugitive into a wedge. Quickly the riders dismounted, grabbed the fleeing man, tied his hands behind his back, and dragged him to a nearby cottonwood tree.

"Good God! You going to hang me? What for?"

A young, slight-built man who was still astride a beautiful ebony horse, laughed out loud, the shrill echo penetrating the air like a sharp sword. "Why not? You're a Kansan. That's reason enough. Hang 'im, boys."

A noose was placed about the young man's neck, and soon he was dangling in the air. It was a gruesome sight for the hidden boys to witness.

At that point another rider reined up. From his vantage point he overlooked the mound of earth in which Jim and Cole were hiding.

"There's someone in the field!" he cried, pointing in the direction of the boys' hiding place.

"Dammit!" the young leader yelled. "We don't want any witnesses to our hangings, not yet anyway."

Later Cole and Jim said that they did not know if the sour, brassy taste in their mouths was fear or what, as they leaped up and dashed for the cover of the forest. They sucked air past clenched teeth, their fists clutched until the tendons ached. Their shoulders hunched as against a raw wind. If they could reach a cave in the hillside they would be safe.

Suddenly the air cracked wide open, musket balls screaming about their heads, but already their distance was in their favor and they saw that they were only a few yards from shelter. The air ripped with yells and curses from the mounted men.

An eternity of hot sweat and cries ricocheted from the field-stone which covered the ground before the boys plunged into the forest. They heard howls of baffled rage while they dashed into the safety of a cave they knew. Not knowing whether they would be pursued, they ran into the cave until they no longer heard any sound but their own breathing.

Even for Cole Younger, large of bone and possessed of great physical willpower despite his awkward youth, the ordeal had been too much. For Jim it had been worse. They flung themselves on the floor of the cave, gasping. They were suffering the aftermath of combat, chest muscles loose and lungs burning for air.

In the darkness Jim said, "I think we're lost now."

"Could be," said Cole. "But there ought to be more than one entrance to this cave. Been in it a few times, but never this far back."

They groped about until they saw a faint ray of light and darted toward it, their hopes renewed. But when they reached the opening they saw that they were on a ledge no more than five feet wide. Below them was a drop of some thirty feet with no outgrowth of shrubbery that could support their weight on the way down. They judged the time to be about three o'clock. Should they hope to discover another means of escape, or should they scale the walls of the cliff?

"Cole, I know we'd never try to scale that wall if we could help it," said Jim. "But I'd rather try that than trust the entrance of the cave again. Those men might just be a-waiting for us."

Cole nodded in agreement.

Fortunately the wall was not too high, and the rock was somewhat seamed and scarred by exposure to the elements. Out of the crevices grew stunted bushes which offered a foothold. Soon they were having to work their way in spots that seemed impossible. Suddenly they noticed a nest on the side of the cliff that was big enough to cover the top of an old tree. They felt a swish of wings like a gust of wind, and they gasped. At this dizzy height they were unnerved to see two golden eagles hovering.

"Hold on!" yelled Cole. "Don't look down and don't pay any attention to the eagles."

As they struggled they had to ignore the flapping wings about their heads. Those eagles seemed to be hideous monsters, growing fiercer every minute. The friendly earth and distant treetops seemed farther and farther below. From the corners of his eyes Cole saw the strong, sharp-cutting beaks, and the long, cruel talons. But fortunately the mother and father eagles had concluded that the boys did not mean to harm their eaglets in the huge nest. Foot by foot the boys at last reached a friendly ledge and were able to rest nearly at the top of the cliff.

At their first move the eagles were in the air again, protecting the scrawny young eaglets in their cluster of twigs and leaves. They circled about the boys' heads, their eyes glaring dangerously.

Cole and Jim had only a short distance to travel now. At last they were able to pull themselves over the ridge of the precipice and feel they were safe. But by now they were almost at the limit of their endurance. They fell on the turf and lay, gasping and shaking. It took a full half hour for them to recuperate.

As new life entered their bodies they struggled to their feet and peered into the far valley.

"Look!" cried Jim. "We can make it easy from here. There's Big Creek, and you can almost see our house."

Finally they did reach home and told their father what they had seen in the forest.

"Boys," said their father, "things are bad enough around here, so it'll be better to say nothing about what you saw. You might even be implicated in the matter if it becomes known that you saw the hanging."

"Do you think the leader we saw could have been Quantrill?" ventured Cole.

"Who knows, son? But from what I hear about his recent actions, I'd not be surprised."

Their mother was shocked at the boys' report. Her sympathetic hands quickly tended to their bleeding hands and sore feet, and the giant supper she prepared for them was compensation indeed.

Cole Younger during the Civil War

But what the boys had seen was just a prelude of what was to come.

"Well, I'll say one thing," Cole said. "I've traveled the mail route many times between Butler and Harrisonville, but I've never had such an experience as that today. I doubt if anybody would believe us if we told about it, Jim. Like Dad said, it's better to just forget all about it."

Cole Younger's birthplace near Lee's Summit, Mo.

CHAPTER 2

Compelled to Join
the Outlaws

THINGS WERE GOING WELL for the Younger family on Big Creek, for the Colonel had accumulated 3500 acres of fertile land, and he was now acting as mail carrier for the Federal government. One route led from Harrisonville to Kansas City, another from Harrisonville to Butler, and that route the young Cole often handled on his own.

The one-room schoolhouse, were Stephen B. Elkins was the teacher, was also situated on Big Creek, and Cole was liked by his schoolmates. But the border wars cast a cloud over that section of Missouri, because of the slavery question. Men from Kansas came into the Show-Me State, stealing horses and cattle, sometimes looting and burning homes. In retaliation bands of enraged Missouri farmers struck out at Kansas.

Colonel Younger felt so strongly about the slavery question that he freed his own slaves, and two of them refused to leave but continued working for him. Though a slave owner, Colonel Younger had never been in sympathy with succession, and was always first to give counsel and advice in opposition to inciting violence against Federal troops. Although a true southerner, Colonel Younger tried to remain neutral in the upcoming struggle between the North and the South. His decision to free his slaves was the result of this conviction and other Missouri farmers did likewise.

One night a band of Kansas Jayhawkers led by Colonel Charles R. Jennison raided the Younger plantation and drove off twenty-five pure-bred animals, including some cows. The loss of his fancy horses preyed heavily on the Colonel's mind. Other such bands, one headed by General James H. Lane, raided Jackson and Clay counties, burning the town of Osceola to the ground and carting off wagonloads of loot.

The Ohio born William Clarke Quantrill appointed himself savior of the Confederacy in Missouri, for he had a personal score to settle with the Kansas anti-slavery militia. He was a cardshark who had been thrown out of Lawrence, Kansas, accused of cheating at the game. His one driving motive was to kill all Kansas people he could, along with any Union soldiers he could find.

Cole Younger was shocked that men from Kansas had attacked his father's farm, and this turned his sympathy toward the South. His father was eager to move his family farther away from the troubled area, so he set up his residence at his plantation at Harrisonville, in Cass County, Missouri. He had resigned his post as county judge of the Jackson County Court, but soon he was in politics again. He was elected Mayor of Harrisonville in 1859.

There Cole attended the Academy which was equivalent to the modern high school. Stephen C. Reagan, the principal, praised him as one of his best students. No doubt Cole would have been successful in the business or political world had not the Civil War interrupted his ambitions. The latch-string of the Younger home was always out, and all visitors, friends and strangers alike, were shown genuine hospitality.

As the war between the states came closer, the adherents of the North formed military companies. One of these was Neugent's Regiment of the Enrolled Militia, and it was quartered near the county seat of Harrisonville. Many people believed the presence of the militia would stir the pro-slavery youth to violence, but it merely stimulated social activities. The Youngers were able to counsel the citizens not to incite acts of violence against the troops. Because of this tolerance the Militia officers attended all the social functions—dances, dinners, and hunts—and this cooled the heat of the war news.

Naturally the dashing manner and the brass buttons of the Federal officers captivated the hearts of the county maidens. However, the Younger girls were not deceived by the glittering uniforms.

Captain Irwin Walley, in command of a company of Union soldiers, was always seen at the local dances. Although he was a married man he showed noticeable attention to the young women. He seemed frustrated when Cole Younger—tall, well-built, and handsome—appeared to outclass him as the social favorite. At any rate, he took a dislike for this young Missourian. His animosity came to a head at a dance given by Colonel Cuthbert Mockbee in honor of his daughter's birthday.

Bent on making this last dance memorable—before volunteers should be called up for one side or another—everyone attended, and of course the elder children of the Younger family were present. One of Cole's pretty sisters, aware of the bad feeling between her brother and Captain Walley, secretly vowed that if the opportunity arose she would embarrass that captain. Therefore when Captain Walley strutted across the ballroom, bowed politely, and asked her to dance with him, in a loud and clear voice she said, "I don't care to dance with you, Captain Walley."

His face flushed. He turned on his heel, motioned for several of his companions to follow him, and approached Cole, who was about to dance with one of the girls.

"Your sister promised this minuet with me!" Captain Walley announced.

"I am not aware of it," said Cole. "It is not my concern with whom she dances."

Thereupon Captain Walley stormed from the ballroom and paced up and down the side veranda until the minuet had ended. He then returned to Cole and said, "Where's that renegade, Quantrill?"

"I don't know and never did," replied Cole.

"You're a liar!" Walley yelled.

It was the wrong remark to make to Cole Younger, and Captain Walley found himself flat on the floor. He made an effort to draw his pistol, but several friends restrained him. Cole and his sisters went home and told their father what had happened.

Fearing that this squabble between supporters of the Union and Cole would inflame Cole's followers against the soldiers, Colonel Younger suggested that his son leave for their plantation in Jackson County.

Drinking heavily after the dance, Walley's hatred grew until he vowed that nothing but the death of Cole Younger would satisfy his honor. All the next day he nursed his wrath and, under cover of night, he gathered six of his men and rode to Colonel Younger's plantation near Harrisonville.

Leaping from his horse at the veranda, he stalked to the door and beat it vigorously with the hilt of his sword.

"Where's Cole Younger?" he demanded of the Colonel.

"What do you want him for?"

"We'll decide that later."

"He's not at home," replied the Colonel, and he closed the door in Walley's face.

"I'll get him! I'll fix that young whelp! I'll report him as an outlaw, riding with Quantrill!" cried Walley, beside himself with rage.

Colonel Younger, alarmed for the safety of his son now that the soldiers knew he was on the plantation at Jackson County, rode into town to reason with Captain Walley, to no avail. The very next day Walley reported to his superiors that Cole Younger had joined Quantrill's raiders. He was therefore ordered to search him out and arrest him.

When this information reached Colonel Younger he hurried to his plantation in Jackson County. After a long discussion the father suggested that Cole should go to some college in an eastern city. Cole agreed. However, it was too late. Back in Harrisonville Cole's father learned that this action had been anticipated and that measures had been taken to prevent his son's departure.

"It's all right, Father," Cole said. "Union soldiers have driven me from my home. Then I'll fight them. I've never met Quantrill personally as yet, but I am sure he was the leader of the band when Jim and I saw those men hang that man from Kansas."

Cole's family tried to dissuade him, but the tiger in the young Missourian had been aroused. Without any arms or supplies, for fear the soldiers would punish his family for siding with him, Cole Younger set out to find Quantrill. It was the winter of 1861.

For days the lad wandered about in the brush, always in hiding, for fear that Walley or his men might spot him and shoot him without provocation. Finally he reached the home of friends where he received food and shelter. He also learned from them that Quantrill was encamped on the Little Blue River in Jackson County, not too far from his place of refuge. Nothing had been heard of these guerrillas since the battle of Carthage, Missouri, on July 5, 1861, where Quantrill and his fifteen followers had served under Captain Stewart.

While Cole was still resting, his brother-in-law, John Jarrette, visited him and informed him that Captain Walley had stolen two prize mares from Colonel Younger.

"I cannot believe that!" exclaimed Cole. "A Union officer a common horse thief? What happened?"

"Walley went to see your father and asked to hire the horses and a buggy. Not wishing to broaden the breach between you and him any farther, as your father's refusal would have done, the Colonel allowed him to take them. After several days, when Walley failed to return them, your father asked for them. Walley just snapped his fingers in the Colonel's face, declaring he intended to keep the horses."

Jarrette had been sent to escort Cole to Quantrill's camp. When the two arrived there Cole noted there were five young men he knew—William Haller, George Todd, Oliver and George Shepherd who were brothers, and Kit Chiles, the three last of whom were soon assigned to Cole's squad.

Quantrill was a strong man, but never robust. His face was round and full, with piercing blue-grey eyes of a strange tint, the upper lids of which fell too low, imparting a peculiar expression which became very marked when he was in a rage. His forehead was high, with hair almost white, and his nose was curved and sinister. He moved with the stealth of a stalking mountain lion, and with some people he was in good repute, while others despised him without being able to explain why.

Cole did not have many idle hours before action erupted. Colonel John Burris had a detachment raiding in the vicinity of Independence, Missouri, and Quantrill's band struck their camp at sunset. The guerrillas numbered 32, the Federals 84. But the raiders were sure shots, and one volley caused the enemy to break in confusion. Twelve of the soldiers died before the remainder of Burris' men reached the safety of the town.

That day Cole's persistent pistol practice paid off, when one of the soldiers fell, seventy-one yards away by actual measure. That was on November 10, 1861.

Because of heavy snows and the difficulty of obtaining supplies, the little band remained in camp throughout the rest of the winter, devoting their time to working out an effective system of espionage and communications among their friends and relatives.

Cole's presence with the band was especially pleasing to Quantrill because of the youth's thorough knowledge of the local topography acquired during his many hunting expeditions. Many times in later days this knowledge saved the guerrillas from annihilation.

CHAPTER 3

The First Encounter

THE LONG WINTER'S BROODING over the trouble which he had brought upon his family changed Cole considerably. It was easy for Quantrill to notice that here was a desperate and efficient man under his command.

It was agreed that their first move should be against "Doc" Jennison's Jayhawkers in Kansas, the party that had raided Colonel Younger's plantation during the previous year and had driven off many horses and cattle. The Jayhawkers seemed to have anticipated such a move. Nothing was seen of them or of the stolen stock as the guerrillas scoured the Kansas hinterland.

No sooner had Quantrill's men ridden back into Jackson County than Captain Albert P. Peabody, with 100 Federal troops, pursued them. On the night of January 3, 1862, Quantrill had failed to post pickets and Captain Peabody trapped the guerrillas in the home of John Flannery, much to the delight of the attacking Federal soldiers.

Peabody placed his men at all egress points. He then boldly walked onto the porch of the house and rapped loudly on the heavy oak door.

Quantrill leaped from his bed, astonished at the sight of the blue uniforms as he peered through a window.

"Damn!" he muttered. "We certainly messed up here."

"We want your unconditional surrender," shouted the captain. "I have the place surrounded by a hundred men."

"I must consult with my men. Give me a few minutes."

"Ten minutes — not a second more."

Quantrill deployed his men on all sides of the house, at the windows from which they could effectively fire into the Union ranks. Cole Younger was assigned the attic window of the loft.

Quantrill then strode to the front door, opened it, and yelled defiantly, "Quantrill and his men never surrender!"

At the same time a blast from his double-barreled shotgun almost tore Peabody's first lieutenant in two.

The entire house erupted with rapid gunfire, and before the soldiers could gather their wits many of them fell dead or wounded. For several hours the fight raged.

"They've set the house on fire," yelled Cole from the high vantage point.

The fire had gained so great a headway that the main part of the building was ablaze, and part of it had already collapsed.

"Get the men together," said Quantrill. "Then gather all the pillows and hats you can find and bring them to me."

Several missing men were found hiding under a bed, and they refused to budge. They were subsequently burned to death.

"Place these hats and pillows at the windows. When the soldiers are reloading, follow me from the house," ordered Quantrill.

Desperate as the plan was, the strategy succeeded, and during a lull in the firing the guerrillas rushed from the door, discharging their guns as they ran, opening a breech among the soldiers and escaping.

To Cole Younger the fight was a terrible experience. Never before had he heard the cries of the mortally wounded or had he seen men writhing in their death throes. Cole had formed a rear guard action to assist the guerrillas in escaping, and in so doing he had become separated from them as they scaled a fence when rushing away from the Flannery house. He was alone when he started his dash across the open field toward a stand of heavy timber.

Several of Peabody's men saw Cole trying to escape. As they came within range Cole stopped and raised his rifle, taking careful aim. The riders paused for a moment, reining in to get out of range of Cole's weapon. Cole noticed this and lowered his rifle, and he dashed away, taking advantage of the halt of his pursuers. The horsemen then renewed the chase. Again Cole stopped and raised his rifle, but this time the cavalrymen did not pause. Perhaps they now thought he was out of ammunition.

Cole fired, and a Jayhawker toppled from his saddle. The other horsemen advanced, and again Cole fired. Another rider fell. By that time Cole had reached the safety of the brush.

It was later learned through friends of the guerrillas that eighteen of Peabody's men were killed and wounded at that encounter.

Quantrill was pleased with the quickwittedness and courage which Cole Younger had displayed in escaping from the soldiers, and he praised him highly.

Quantrill was now without mounts for his men and also in need of guns and ammunition. He therefore dismissed his band temporarily.

"Don't come back until you've got a horse. Don't steal any. I won't have a horse thief among my men. We'll meet near Blue Cut in three days."

Cole managed to see his family for several hours one night and was amazed to learn that the news of the fight at the Flannery

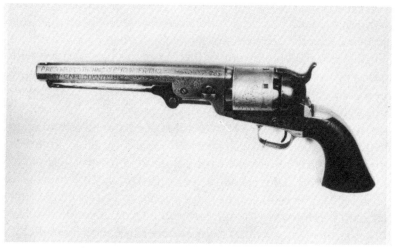

Cole Younger's cap and ball percussion

house had already spread over the county. A state of wild excitement prevailed regarding the ease with which the young guerrillas had outwitted and outfought the soldiers.

In Harrisonville and in Independence, where the Federal
troops were stationed, and across the Kansas border to where the
Jayhawkers had withdrawn, officers and men smothered their
disappointment and eased their feelings by swearing eternal
vengeance against "the damned guerrillas."

Determined to kill or capture Quantrill's band before its ranks
were augmented, Captain E. Neugent sent out many squads to
hunt down the various members. He knew they had been forced
to leave their horses at the Flannery place and, he thought, until
they got new mounts the task of finding them would be easier.

But the country folk simply refused to tell what they knew
about the guerrillas, even when Neugent used threats and force.
He killed young men in cold blood before the eyes of their
parents, dragged aged men and women off to prison, and insulted wives before their husbands. No wonder George Todd,
"Bloody" Bill Anderson, Arch Clements, and others whose families suffered such horrors were fiends in battle against the soldiers.

When the guerrillas met at Blue Cut according to plan, all
brought tales of insult and outrage to their friends and relatives.

Several weeks after the Flannery house ambush, Quantrill
heard that Union troops at Independence had learned that Cole
spent a day at the home of an old friend named Amos Blythe. A
contingent of soldiers went to the old man's place armed with
authority to search, with instructions that, if Cole was not found
there, they should torture Blythe until he revealed Younger's
hiding place.

Cole was livid when he heard of this plan, and he sent word to
Amos Blythe that he should take to the brush until the affair was
settled. Blythe left his twelve-year-old son at home, not fearing for
a lad so young. Then Cole declared to Quantrill: "There is a
defile where the road from Independence to Harrisonville runs
between two hills. The people call it Blue Cut, as you know. The
Federals must come by that road, and we can waylay them there."

Capt. George Todd

Bloody Bill Anderson

John Chatman

John Maupin

Gooley Robertson

Nat Tigue

As Quantrill and all his men knew, it was an ideal spot for an ambush. Thirty feet on each side of the road the earth rose and for 150 yards there was no change. The guerrillas took up their position in the thick woods which topped the rises.

All afternoon the guerrillas waited for the Federals to show themselves. Cole then rode to the Blythe home to see what had happened. He was nearing the farm when an old Negro servant of Squire Moore, a neighbor of Blythe, called to Cole, "Massa Younger, sir, de Feds done been to Massa Blythe's place and done kilt his son."

The excited man told Cole that he came to the Blythe home on an errand and heard that the troops had taken another route, having lost their way. They seized young Blythe and took him to the barn after searching in vain for Amos Blythe. The boy refused to talk, even under threat of being hanged. At an opportune moment he sprang toward the house and ran inside while a hail of bullets struck the door behind him.

Snatching up an old pistol, the boy dashed out another door and darted toward the woods in his effort to escape. One of the Union soldiers spotted him as he climbed a fence behind the house, yelled to him, and fired. The shot struck the boy in the back, and he tumbled to the ground. Raising himself on his elbow, the plucky youngster leveled the old pistol at the onrushing soldiers, waited a second, and then fired.

A Jayhawker fell to the earth, dead. Again the boy pulled the trigger, and a second soldier fell, badly wounded. Before he could shoot again, the brave lad sank to the earth, his little body riddled with bullets.

The horrified Negro had run from his hiding place and had not stopped until he bumped into Cole. Cole asked the man to tell his story to the guerrillas at Blue Cut.

Racing to a small hill, Cole saw the Federals coming up the road from the south. He galloped back to the cut and told Quantrill that the soldiers were heading into the trap.

"Massa Cole, is it all right efen I hit the brush? Ah don't like no kinda fightin'," said the frightened Negro.

"Go right ahead," Cole replied with a smile.

Thomas Little

Sam Hildebrand

"Don't fire until they're all in the pass," Quantrill ordered. "We don't want any of them to escape. Remember young Blythe!"

There were thirty soldiers, riding two abreast in cavalry fashion. When the last couple had entered the Cut, the guerrillas fired a volley. The Federals panicked. Men and horses fell in confusion. Above the rattle of musketry, the shrieks of the wounded, oaths, and hurried commands rose. The middle of the pass was a mass of struggling men and horses.

The high hills of the defile made escape impossible except by riding down the guerrillas in front. As one Jayhawker leaped his horse over a dead comrade and dashed through the obstructing line of guerrillas, Cole Younger seized the animal by the bridle. With an oath the rider lunged at him with his saber. Avoiding the blow, Cole drew his pistol with his left hand, while still holding the bridle with his right hand, and shot the soldier dead.

When Quantrill gave the order to cease fire, only three Jayhawkers were still alive.

CHAPTER 4

Escape from
Indian Creek

ELATED OVER THEIR VICTORY, the guerrillas rode away from the Blue Cut and pitched their camp on the shore of Indian Creek, in Jackson County.

The Jayhawkers and Federal troops quartered at Independence were in a rage. They wanted to wipe out the disgrace of the two successive routs. Their tempers were not mollified by the country folk who lost no opportunity to deride and taunt them with the fact that neither thirty nor a hundred of them could cope with the few men led by Quantrill.

When word reached the Union forces of the whereabouts of the guerrillas there was rejoicing, and it was determined to exterminate them. It seemed that no more favorable opportunity would ever present itself. On all sides of the timber which surrounded Indian Creek were open fields, and by occupying these in force they could prevent the little band from cutting their way to safety. With bands playing and flags waving, the soldiers marched out of Independence, their ranks swelled by every available man. In the rear, with the ammunition wagons, were the two pieces of artillery on their limbers. When they arrived on the shores of the creek the officers lost no time in placing their soldiers. In a lane that led down to the thickest timber they stationed their two brass cannon and a strong force of infantry. On the opposite field, across which it was thought the guerrillas might try to escape, the cavalry was placed.

Quantrill

When all was ready, the artillery opened fire. The shells, shrieking through the trees, were the first intimation that Quantrill and his men had of the presence of Federal soldiers. Without delay Quantrill led his men to a ravine which traversed the woodland, near the field in which the Union cavalry was ready to charge. There the shells could not reach them and, while the rest of his men kept up a galling fire on the horsemen whenever the latter came within range, Quantrill and Bill Haller discussed with Cole Younger the best means of escape.

Knowing every foot of the ground, Younger told them that within the Federal lines were a farmhouse and a barn and many head of stock. These, he suggested, could be stampeded toward the soldiers while they themselves would thus have an opportunity to escape in the ensuing confusion.

"It's a desperate try, but our only one," said Quantrill. "Haller, you and Cole stampede the stock. The rest of us will do what we can. At nine o'clock we'll move."

Moving in his forces as night fell, the Federal commander established a strong cordon around the little band. Later every man who could be spared without weakening the blockade was dismounted and, formed in companies, they were drilled as infantry with the intention of making a determined charge upon the camp when morning should dawn.

At nine o'clock Cole and Haller, their double-barreled shotguns in their hands, their pistols in their belts, set out on their mission of stampeding the farm animals. Carefully they picked their way, advancing with the noiseless tread of men skilled in the craft of the woods, and in due course they reached the horses and cattle. It was the work of but a few minutes to mill the startled beasts, and when the two guerrillas had worked them into a state of maddened fear, Cole cut out a bunch of leaders and drove them toward the Federal lines. Bellowing and snorting, the remainder of the animals followed.

Unswerved by the few shots that were fired at them, the animals continued their wild run, and the soldiers fell back to allow the frenzied cattle and horses to pass. Their sudden and wild appearance left the Federals without order or control. Quantrill and his men crawled in the trail of the beasts, yet not so close but that they could regain the woods if their plan should fail. When they saw its success they dashed silently through the breech and, in the confusion, they were not discovered by the soldiers.

The guerrillas had one more obstacle to surmount — getting by the pickets. This task also was entrusted to Cole Younger. Taking his position at their head, Younger ordered them to drop to their hands and knees and follow in single file. He led them to a nearby stonewall and, in that protecting shadow, the entire band crawled past the pickets to safety.

Quantrill's nine men clamored for some action that would show the Federals they had escaped. It was known that number odds were against them, so they decided to steal the two cannon. If they could capture those two pieces of artillery from the more than a hundred soldiers, that would eclipse their former exploits.

"Cole, take us to some place where we can watch the Federals when light comes," Quantrill suggested.

It was slow work. At last the little group stopped in an old orchard over-grown with hemp. While the rest were getting out their food, Cole told Quantrill that the orchard was directly back of the cannon and that, if he remembered correctly, it ran up to within a few yards of where they were mounted.

Cole was sent on a reconnoitering mission. Coming suddenly upon a large number of horses guarded by a dozen Negro soldiers, he was puzzled. Further investigation revealed that the mounted men had been brought in to serve as foot soldiers. He saw them all fast asleep not far away. At four o'clock, when it was still dark, Cole brought this information to Quantrill, and it was decided to make ready for their surprise attack.

At the flash of dawn Quantrill's lookout reported that the infantry was making preparations to charge the piece of timber and that the cavalry was moving to the opposite side of the belt of trees. Almost at the same time Cole, who had been on another scouting expedition, rushed in with the information that a large body of cavalrymen were approaching from the east.

"Can it be Colonel Hays with his Confederate cavalry?" asked Quantrill. "He's likely to be in the area any day now."

"I don't think so," said Cole. "They don't ride like Southerners. More likely they are Federals."

Clark Hockensmith

David Tate

Dick Kinney

Bud Stary

He was correct, for the approaching men turned out to be Doc Jennison and his Kansas Red Legs, as it was later learned.

"If we're going to do something, now is the time," said Quantrill.

George Todd, an experienced artilleryman, with the assistance of Cole, rammed home shells in the guns and opened a terrific fire upon the dismounted troopers who were hurrying to regain their horses, in view of the approaching cavalrymen. Thrown into confusion by the shells from the cannon, the infantry scattered, and the guerrillas added to their demoralization by sending some shots among the horses, stampeding them and their guards as well.

Jennison, on hearing the cannon, thought the Confederates were present in force, so he commanded his men to wheel and ride away as fast as they could. Todd, meanwhile, turned the cannon against the dismounted Federals again and, as Jennison's men fled in one direction, they retreated on the double-quick toward the Little Santa Fe River.

Quantrill threw the cannon into the Big Blue River, caught the best of the horses which had been abandoned by the Jayhawkers and, after mounting his men, rode in the direction taken by Jennison.

For the third time nine men had routed the Federals, but on this occasion, besides putting them to flight, they had captured two cannon from under their very noses.

At Union headquarters in Kansas City the report was at first received with incredulity which turned to consternation when the rumor was confirmed. The District Commander realized that something must be done to restore the Federal prestige. General Blunt, in charge of the Army of the Frontier, ordered Colonel Thomas Ewing, Jr., to use what tactics were necessary to bring about the destruction of Quantrill's raiders.

In futherance of this plan the authorities sent for Doc Jennison and his dreaded Kansas Jayhawkers or Red Legs. This band was composed of cutthroats and thugs, men who would not hesitate to commit any type of crime. While Jennison's men scourged the

Missouri countryside, the regular soldiers were billeted at Kansas City so that responsibility for what was to occur would not rest upon their shoulders.

With the march of Jennison and his men there was inaugurated a veritable reign of terror. Old men, young girls, boys, and women were tortured , killed, according to the mood of the Red Legs. Ike, Joe, and Bob Hall of Cass County, Missouri, had joined Quantrill's band, and Jennison vowed vengeance on all who did. In the winter of 1862 he made the mother of the Hall boys set fire to her own home and forced her to watch it burn. He once hung a man from the rafters of his own home while the wailing wife watched. But these actions were not condoned by the Missouri people. Jennison was discredited and resigned, but later he returned to duty and commanded the Fifteenth Kansas Cavalry. This group did their best to carry out the terms of Ewing's infamous Order No. 11 — by laying waste great sections of Missouri's finest counties.

Protests rained upon Union headquarters as a result of Jennison's wanton slaughter of the innocents. Every able-bodied man rallied to the support of Quantrill. In several days his band was increased from nine to sixty, and each hour brought more volunteers.

To cope more effectively with the Red Legs, the guerrilla chief formed his men into regular military companies, with William Haller as first lieutenant, Cole Younger second lieutenant, and George Todd third lieutenant. To each officer was assigned a squad of men, and Quantrill took charge of the rest.

At one point Quantrill was presented with a steer horn which gave forth a peculiar tone that could be heard for several miles or more. Acquainting his whole company with its sounds, Quantrill arranged that when he blew a certain blast all who heard it should hasten to his support. For his officers he constructed a code by which he could signal to them what he wished them to do whenever they were within range.

Everywhere Quantrill had his followers, and they reported to him every move of the Federals, even to the arrival and departure of messengers and scouts. As a result, with his four squadrons Quantrill was able to checkmate many of Jennison's moves.

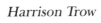
Harrison Trow

T.F. Maupin

Skirmishes were of daily occurrence and, as may be supposed, Quantrill's men usually came out winning, while many Red Legs, Jayhawkers, and soldiers, all of whom actually feared the guerrillas, went to their just reward.

CHAPTER 5

The Tragic Surprise

IN JUNE OF 1862 the plantations were beautiful with their array of flowers, green trees, and wide acres of corn, wheat, oats, barley, and other grain crops. The pursuers of the guerrillas saw no beauty in nature as they lashed out, burning, looting, killing. The sight of burned-out homes and barns was more satisfying to them than a bountiful land. Their raids, instead of impressing the natives with their prowess and holding them in check through fear, only served to make themselves thoroughly hated, so the country folk did all in their power to aid Quantrill in his raids. All the men who could be spared from the plantations flocked to his support.

One day three guerrillas rode down a lane leading to a ford on the Little Blue River to water their horses, little dreaming that surrounded by trees a party of Jayhawkers was watching them. As the horses plunged their noses into the river to drink, a volley of shots rang out. Two of the guerrillas fell dead from their saddles, while the third man was seriously wounded. The Jayhawkers seized the wounded man and dragged him into Independence as their prisoner.

For several weeks after that the guerrillas sought to capture some of those guilty Union men, but without success. Quantrill thought that his man, whom they had in their power, might receive proper care from the enemy if he could take several of the soldiers as his own prisoners. One day word was brought to camp that the authorities at Independence had decided to hang their prisoner at the courthouse within a few days, as a dire warning to all guerrillas in the field.

The garrison at Independence was too strongly manned for a frontal assault by Quantrill, so he decided to try to seize several Union pickets. He ordered Cole and Haller to enter the town from one side, while he and George Todd entered from the opposite side. Haller's mother lived in Independence, and it was decided that he and four of his men should go there at night to learn the whereabouts of the pickets. While Haller was executing this bold plan, Cole took his own man to one of his father's former farms three miles south of town.

Haller learned that four pickets had that very evening been stationed near an old woolen mill to the south of the town, in case the guerrillas should attack from that direction. He therefore decided to personally learn the exact whereabouts of these pickets, and he found them secreted in a dell where their capture could be accomplished with comparative ease. In the realization that, when he should attack the Federals at the woolen mill, the sound of the shots would result in the troops from the barracks being sent there on the double-quick, Haller sent one of his mother's servants to notify Cole Younger to attack the pickets on the opposite side of Independence in order to distract the attention of the soldiers from his own operations.

Cautiously skirting the town Cole felt out the position of the pickets who were near a large one-story building that was used as a wagon factory by Hiram Young. Knowing that there was no floor in that factory, Cole forced open the rear door, dismounted his men, and led them and their horses through the building. The front door of the place opened into the street between the main camp and the pickets whom he hoped to surprise.

Giving command to mount, Cole rode from the wagon factory, closely followed by his men. He saw that the pickets were in total ignorance of their presence. On an old bridge two of them sat talking and smoking, their rifles leaning beside them, while near at hand there were reclining figures. Evidently the rest of the pickets were asleep.

Whispering a hurried command Cole slapped his spurs to his horse and rushed upon the soldiers with his men at his heels, all of them yelling like Indians and discharging their guns right and left. The surprised guards returned the fire, wounding Kit Chiles and killing "Ol" Shepherd's horse. The sleeping pickets awoke with a start, viewed the scene around them, then made a dash toward the town square.

"Don't shoot them," Cole yelled. "We need prisoners!"

Cole's squad managed to cut off five soldiers as they tried to retreat. They thus secured prisoners and horses for them from a nearby stable. His men forming a guard around the prisoners, the guerrillas rode off toward their camp. On the Blue Hill Road they encountered more pickets, who quickly ran toward the main force of soldiers.

At the old woolen mill, south of town, Haller had been equally successful. When he heard Cole Younger's fire he charged the Federal pickets and, taking them completely by surprise, cap-tured all of them without the use of a single shot. He led them away to the guerrilla camp.

Quantrill later wrote Colonel James T. Buell at Independence that if his man was hanged he would shoot every one of his recent prisoners. He offered a proposition to exchange the Federal pickets for the guerrilla and all the aged men, some twenty in number, whom the Jayhawkers had dragged from their homes and thrown into jail.

The commandant was furious when he read this communica-tion. In the end he agreed to the exchange, and the prisoners were sent to their respective friends.

It was after the incident at Independence that Cole went to visit his Grandmother Fristoe. Obtaining a short leave from Quantrill, he rode to her house, tied his mount in the brush, and joined the old lady just as she was sitting down to supper. Joyful was their meeting, and when the meal was finished they talked until long after the moon had risen. Not a lamp was lighted for fear some prowling Federal soldier might discover Cole's pres-ence there.

At last, however, Cole bade his grandmother goodbye and took his departure. As he stepped onto the porch in the full light of the moon, he was startled to see the figure of a Union officer rise above the four-foot side of the veranda. Greater still was his surprise when he noticed that this man was his cousin, Captain Charles Younger of the Enrolled State Militia.

"How are you, cousin?" Cole said, extending his hand.

"Cole Younger, you are my prisoner," replied the captain, ignoring the extended hand.

Astonished, Cole searched his cousin's face for a sign of the smile which would announce the words as a joke. But none did he see. Still unable to believe that one of his own blood would so treat him, he was more astonished by the captain's next statement.

"I mean what I say: you are my prisoner."

No longer doubting his cousin's intentions, Cole whipped out his revolver and shot him in the face. As the body pitched forward, Cole leaped from the porch and dashed up through the yard, when for the first time he discovered that the house was surrounded by Union soldiers.

Bending over, he ran with all his speed toward the brush where his horse was tied. As he neared the spot he tripped over a beehive and fell. Simultaneously the crack of rifles sounded, and a volley of lead passed over him as he lay prostrate, cutting the back of his coat to shreds although not a bullet touched his body. A chill went through him as he realized he would have been killed instantly had he not fallen to the ground.

After that he dragged himself along on his stomach, moving slowly and feeling a pain in his right knee. At first he thought a bullet had reached him, but as he raised himself into the saddle, he was able to ride back to camp. Then an examination of his leg showed that he had dislocated his knee in the fall.

CHAPTER 6

Ambush and Escape

In Accordance With Their Usual Custom, after some unusually bold and daring stroke by the guerrillas, the Federals vented their wrath over the capture of their pickets by turning the Kansas Jayhawkers loose upon the defenseless country folk to murder and pillage.

However, the new commandant at Harrisonville, Major A. H. Linden, accustomed to honorable warfare, did not approve of the atrocities perpetrated by the Union soldiers and Jayhawkers. Calling an assembly of his subordinates, Major Linden told them they were a disgrace to their uniforms.

He said, "Instead of committing crimes which turn the populace against you and drive allies into the Confederate ranks, you ought to endeavor to make friends with the neutrals and by your conduct win their good will."

As may be imagined, such views were not welcomed by Doc Jennison and Captain Neugent and the other cut-throats, who lost no opportunity to denounce Major Linden. Nevertheless the attitude of the Major had its effect, and the Jayhawkers became less brutal. Besides, among the rank and file Linden became respected and feared by the lawless. However, in a thousand ways Captain Neugent and his brother officers harrassed that officer, making life a burden to him. At last, in September of 1862, seeing that the majority of the officers disapproved of honorable warfare and being unwilling to carry on in accordance with their ideas, he resigned his command.

Quantrill, concentrating his men at Lee's Summit in Jackson County, kept his force hidden in the brush while Cole Younger, with the six men of his squad, raided the Union camps at Kansas City, Harrisonville, and Independence, sweeping down upon first one and then another, now surprising and killing some of the pickets, now releasing bands of horses from their guards, all in the vain attempt to entice the Federals to give him chase. He managed to lure them to where Quantrill was secreted with his main force, who fell upon them and decimated them.

The Union men, however, had come to look upon Cole as one with a charmed life, and they refused to go after him. Time and time again, in broad daylight, he rode within range of their pickets, fired a few shots at them and then withdrew, but the Federals never gave chase — merely nursed their wrath behind their own lines. One result was that Younger and his men cut off Federal communications between Independence and Harrisonville. The United States mail was then sent out only once every few days and only under the escort of a strong guard.

A man who claimed immunity from the attack of the guerrillas because of his alleged friendship with Quantrill made several trips between the county seat and Lexington, carrying mail and supplies. But instead of delivering the mail properly to the men to whom it was addressed, he gave the letters to the Jayhawkers who made a jest of the trick. On learning of this deception, Quantrill told Cole to find the man and teach him a lesson. On discreet inquiry Younger learned the day this man was to be in Lexington with letters and supplies. Although the seizure of military supplies was one of the fortunes of war, to seize personal mail was inexcusable.

Concealing himself and his six men between the steep hills where the bushes alongside the road were thick, Cole waited for the mail carrier whose two fine animals were drawing a springboard wagon. Cole jumped his horse into the road, pistol in hand.

"Hands up!" he cried.

The team was jerked to a halt.

"Get down from the seat!" Cole added.

Then the contents of the wagon-mail pouches, boxes of ammunition, and uniforms — were transferred to the men on horseback.

"Give my compliments to the Federal officers at Harrisonville," said Cole. "Tell them that Lieutenant Cole Younger stopped you. Also, tell them you lied when you said you were a friend of Quantrill."

The frightened man grabbed the reins and whipped his horses to a run, while the guerrillas sent pistol shots whizzing over his head.

When this hold-up was reported at Harrisonville, scouting parties were rushed out in all directions in an effort to recover the mail pouches, but they were compelled to return without even an empty ammunition case. Quantrill's next move was to see what would happen if he and his men took the mail from a carrier under escort of the Federal troops.

The mail route lay over Pleasant Hill and through the same Blue Cut where, with his band of nine men, Quantrill had avenged the death of young Blythe. Stationing runners to inform him of the escort's approach, Cole followed the same plan in placing his forces, except that he was accompanied by more men.

One of the lookouts soon arrived with the information that the escort was under command of Captain Long, an old friend of the Younger family.

"I'm sorry to hear that," said Younger. "He's a good fellow."

Singing and laughing, the troops approached the cut, their spirits high from the contents of whiskey flasks they had procured. One of them, however, looked about nervously as he recalled what had occurred there earlier.

"What if Quantrill strikes again?" he asked.

"Aw, he's gone south. No guerrillas here now except that damned Younger and a few of his men," another young trooper returned with a laugh.

At that moment Cole Younger, shotgun to his shoulder, appeared on a large rock alongside the trail.

"Surrender!" he cried.

The reply was a rattle of musketry, answered by a well-aimed shot or two from the entrenched guerrillas. So deadly was the fire from above that the soldiers turned to flee, only to see the guerrillas closing in at each end of the cut. Spurring his horse, Captain Long tried to regroup his men, but Younger shot his mount which fell and held its rider pinned down.

"Are you wounded?" asked Cole.

"No."

"Then sit there until I see what has become of my men," Cole told the captain.

By now Cole's men had taken a score of prisoners.

"Bring them to Captain Long," Cole told them.

Quickly the rest of the injured Jayhawkers pressed forward.

"Now Long," said Cole, "we've got to be going, but I suggest that your men respect this as a field parole. They should go home and work in the fields and not fight further."

The Federals were bewildered at such gracious action by this remarkable young man who, they had reason to believe, was a devil in battle.

Actually Cole's magnanimity served to anger the Union officers more than anything else he could have done. They were angry especially at having been made ridiculous by him, as they had been on more than one occasion. But when it came to ambushing a whole company, killing half of them, wounding others, and capturing a score of prisoners only to release them, that was too much. All their available men were thrown into Jackson County by the Union authorities. Until the middle of July 2000 men were beating over the hills around the Little and the Big Blue Rivers and the Sni Hills, seeking Quantrill and his forces who numbered only seventy men.

Quantrill knew that sooner or later such a large force would drive him to bay. Therefore he planned to leave Jackson County and to attack Harrisonville in Cass County. To his surprise, when nearing the county seat he saw a large body of Union soldiers approaching in hot pursuit. Therefore it would mean certain capture if he should enter Harrisonville. Upon his order to make a quick turn, his men took the road leading to Austin.

"All the Federal soldiers in Missouri seem to be on our trail," Quantrill lamented to Bill Haller. "We've got to get to the hills somehow."

Cole informed him that it was an easy task to find their way to the Blue Hills, for he was familiar with that part of the county. Thus the guerrillas raced along the road to Dayton, where they enlisted the aid of a dozen bushwhackers, and continued along the road to Jackson County.

Arriving at Walnut Creek, Younger ordered the men to take to the brush. By this maneuver they succeeded in throwing the Federals off their trail. After riding for some time through the woods, Cole led them out onto the main road going north, straight for the Sni Hills. After traveling six miles they stopped at an old house, back of which was a heavy stand of timber.

Scarcely had they settled down for a brief meal when the pickets rode in, announcing that several hundred soldiers were approaching from the south. Immediately the guerrillas fell back to the stand of timber, on each side of which there was a steep bluff. They left Cole with a dozen men to stand off the cavalry until he could secure his position.

The guerrillas set to work gathering dead trees from the forest and placing them in such a position at the opening of the small ravine that it would be impregnable to cavalry attack. Only a small opening was left to allow Cole and his men to enter singly. By that time the soldiers had advanced to within a half mile of the old house. Suddenly they halted, forming in line of battle, and sent forth a squad of twelve men to feel out the situation.

As the squad advanced, Cole persuaded the lady of the house to take the blankets of his comrades and hang them upon a fence as though she had just washed them. When she had hung the last one he and his men crawled up behind them to await the approach of the enemy. On came the Union cavalry advance guard. When they were within close range, the guerrillas rose from behind the blankets and fired a volley, killing all but one man.

When the main body of the approaching soldiers saw the slaughter of their men, they made ready to retreat, but before they got in motion they were reinforced by 200 troops arriving from Butler. With their number swelling to 400, the Union men felt strong enough to attack, and they began an advance.

Cole and his group retired to the improvised fort, where Quantrill signaled them how to enter. As the last of them rode inside, the others dropped the prepared trees and closed the entrance. By this time all the horses of the guerrillas had been taken to a ravine out of the way of bullets, and the men were behind the breastworks with their double-barreled shotguns ready for action. Before Cole and his men had dismounted, the Union cavalry charged, only to be met with a deadly volley which forced them to retreat.

Seizing their heavy Sharps rifles, a good supply of which the guerrillas carried for long-range shooting, Cole's men put them to such good use that they compelled the Union forces to withdraw. Three times the Federals charged with no better success than at first.

After their last retreat Quantrill decided to risk a charge in the open field, despite the fact that he had only seventy-five men against 400. He had ordered his men to mount and was leading them through the breech, when several hundred more Federal cavalrymen approached the scene. Naturally, in the face of such over-whelming odds Quantrill gave up the idea of a sortie.

A seventh time the Federals charged, making a desperate attempt to gain the narrow entrance through which the guerrillas had passed. But fire from seventy-five shotguns and rifles was too hot. For the seventh time they withdrew. Feverishly the guerrillas worked to close the entrance to their improvised fort, giving the impression that they meant to keep fighting from that point. But when the night was darkest they stole out through the ravine, Quantrill riding behind Cole's saddle because his own horse had been killed beneath him. The other men whose animals had been shot did likewise with their comrades. Under Cole's guidance the band reached the Sni Hills, where they separated into small bands and completely threw off their pursuers.

CHAPTER 7

The Battle of Lone Jack

TWO EVENTS OCCURRED IN 1862 which served to embitter Cole Younger more than ever. It was also during that year that he fought beside the quasi-military Quantrill group, as well as in Captain Jarrette's company of Colonel Hays' Enrolled Missouri Army of the Confederacy.

The shock that stunned Cole was the deliberate and brutal murder of his father, Colonel Henry Washington Younger. On July 22, 1862, Colonel Younger was returning from Kansas City to Harrisonville, after registering a serious complaint against the Federal soldiers in the field. Captain Irvin Walley knew that the Colonel always carried a large sum of money on his person at all times. Now was the time to rob him.

At one point along the road Colonel Younger saw a number of soldiers ahead of him, and it worried him. Perhaps they had heard of his going to Kansas City to file a complaint against them. Perhaps they were out to get their revenge. He speeded his horses in the hope of passing them unmolested.

As he neared them, the soldiers, numbering ten, wheeled their horses, raised their pistols, and fired at him pointblank. Many of the shots took effect. When the assassins saw the colonel's body, limp and lifeless, sink on the seat of the buggy, they sprang from their horses, ran to him and rifled his body. Owing to their haste and to the colonel's precaution, however, they failed to find the

Henry Washington Younger

money belt which contained several thousand dollars. They took with them only the $400 from his wallet.

So great was the fear of retaliation by the Jayhawkers that well-wishing neighbors permitted the colonel's body to lie in the hot sunlight for hours before Mrs. Washington Wells and her son Sam came along and managed to get help to bring the body to the Younger home. There the agonized wife swooned with grief.

When the dreadful news reached Cole he stared in disbelief. He and his father had always been very close.

Seeking out Quantrill, Cole asked, "With your permission I'd like to go home to see the remains of my father and look upon his gentle countenance for the last time."

"It will be suicide, Cole. The soldiers will be expecting you."

"Regardless, I must go," said the grieving young man.

Cole refused an escort and set out alone on his sorrowful ride. Arriving home, he went to the casket in which the body of his father lay. Not a tear did he shed. Suddenly he placed his right hand upon the beloved forehead and, without speaking, he swore a mighty oath that he would hunt down and kill his father's assassins.

In a short while he returned to the guerrilla camp.

The second incident which incited Cole to extreme anger was the arrest of his sisters and several of his cousins by Captain Walley some time after the murder of his father. The girls — along with Janie, Molly, and Josephine Anderson, sisters of "Bloody Bill" Anderson — were taken into custody for no apparent reason other than — it was learned later — that they had seen Captain Walley in the vicinity of Westport the day Colonel Younger had been murdered. Walley did not wish to hold the girls in custody in Independence. Therefore he sent them to a rickety building at 1409 Grand Avenue, Kansas City. There they were held, pending banishment from Missouri.

When the soldiers discovered that Cole's sisters and Anderson's sisters were among the prisoners, they decided to destroy the old house in order to kill them. Mrs. Duke, who ran a boarding house at Oak Street and Independence Avenue, over-heard the soldiers plotting to kill the girls by undermining the building so that it would cave in rather than burn. She was a cousin of Bill Anderson, so she rushed to military headquarters in Kansas City to explain what she had heard. Her story fell upon deaf ears and, while she was expostulating, the building collapsed. Nan Harris, a cousin of Cole Younger, and Molly Anderson were in the hallway when they heard the crash. One of the guards who did not approve of murder helped them to safety. Janie Anderson, ten years old, had both her legs broken. Josephine Anderson was killed when a pile of bricks fell on her, and Charity Kerr, another cousin of Cole's, was killed by falling timber. Fortunately, none of Cole's sisters were injured.

In August of that year, while Cole was roaming the border seeking any stray bands of Jayhawkers or Red Legs, a runner reached him with orders from Quantrill to come with all possible speed eight miles east of Independence. From his camp on Cedar Creek in Jackson County, near the Thomas Talley plantation, Cole and his forty men left at five o'clock that same evening. By hard riding and taking circuitous routes to bypass any Federals in the area, they arrived at the rendezvous at daybreak. At that time Colonel James Buell was in command of the Federal forces at Independence.

It was on August 7th when Quantrill met with Confederate Colonel J. T. Hughes to discuss the matter of an attack upon Independence where Colonel Buell was stationed with over 600 men. Colonel Upton Hays, who was in Jackson County at the time recruiting a regiment of Confederates, also participated in the attack. In reconnoitering that vicinity Cole took with him Dick Yager, Boone Muir, and one other man, all of Quantrill's command.

Colonel Hughes decided the attack should be made on August 11th, and he wanted more accurate data concerning the enemy forces. Cole volunteered, knowing of course that if he should be captured he would be immediately shot as a spy.

At a nearby farmhouse he found an old gray wig which had been used at parties and stage plays, an old calico dress, a faded bonnet, and a pair of spectacles. Donning these he certainly looked like an old apple woman although the dress hid the solid frame of a six-foot giant, solid muscle and sinew to a total of 170 pounds.

Col. John T. Hughes

With a splint basket laden with apples and other fruits of a country farm, Cole rode into Independence, exciting no suspicion. He had no trouble selling his wares, yelling out in a squeaky voice like an old crone, "Apples, pears, vegetables, come an' buy 'em."

One young private, apparently more alert than his companions, kept watching Cole.

"You know, that old woman sure is getting around town today. Sure looks suspicious to me," he said to his sergeant.

By that time Cole had started for the edge of town, a point he reached just as a mounted picket rode up beside his horse and grabbed the reins. Cole kept riding leisurely along.

"What can I do for you, sonny?" he asked in a scratchy voice.

"Didn't you hear the sergeant yell for you to stop?"

"No sir!"

"Well, dammit, stop!"

A spurred boot under the ragged dress pierced the horse's flank. The hand that came from the apple basket fired a pistol almost before the sentry knew it, and he fell dead.

The reserve squad of six mounted soldiers at the rear sat on their horses as if stupefied. They saw a weird figure dash away down the road, its huge bonnet flapping in the wind, and the trail of an antique dress, split at the shoulders, streaming back like a grotesque Chinese kite. The guards gave a half-hearted chase, but they were outdistanced by Cole's superior horse. His report to Colonel Hughes aided greatly in the day of battle, August 11th.

The forces of Colonels Hughes and Hays, together with Quantrill's men, attacked Independence with devastating effect. A Mrs. Wilson saw these men approaching her home at Blue Springs and rushed into town to warn Colonel Buell. He ignored her warning and did nothing to save the day.

Quantrill and his twenty-five men rode into the town square at 4:00 A.M. on August 11th, closely followed by Hughes and his main group. They encountered no guards or pickets, and it was comparatively easy for them to take the Union forces by surprise. Brave fighting was done by Captain Rodewald's men who rushed into the street and ordered his men to fire at the enemy. Colonel Buell took over the command and ordered his men into his headquarters, a foolish thing to do. The building was surrounded, and he was forced to surrender after Cole Younger and "Ol" Shepherd brought piles of hay from a nearby barn and set fire to the building.

The real fighting was done by Captain Axline and the men he was able to rally around him behind a stone wall which ran for a half mile along the south side of the camp. In a charge upon the right of Axline's position there, in an attempt to flank it, Colonel Hughes was shot in the forehead and killed instantly. In the same rush James "Kit" Chiles of Quantrill's band also died. Twenty-six Union men were killed, thirty wounded, and 256 were reported missing. No Confederate record can be found, and no report on the losses under Hughes' command seems to have been made. Quantrill's command listed eleven guerrillas slain. Prisoners taken were released on field parole.

The Battle of Independence over, Quantrill marched his men to the Ingraham farm, six miles west of Lone Jack. There, on August 15, 1862, Quantrill and his men were mustered into the Confederate service. So, from that day forward, until the end of the war, the Confederate government was responsible for all the acts of Quantrill and his followers. They were regular Confederate soldiers, properly enrolled, with officers regularly commissioned. Quantrill was commissioned a captain in charge of 150 men, with William Haller, first lieutenant; George Todd, second lieutenant; William H. Gregg, third lieutenant, and Cole Younger being made a "captain at large" by Quantrill. Cole's regular commission did not occur until after he had left Quantrill's service to become a part of the regular Confederate army. Nothing seemed to please Quantrill more than to strut around showing off his captain's commission.

Of course, being an egomaniac, Quantrill was never satisfied with being a mere captain, so he tried to convince the Confederate authorities at Richmond to commission him a colonel with full recruiting power. His request was denied. It is just possible that General Sterling Price did grant Quantrill a "field commission" as a colonel, something that was done frequently in the Confederate army west of the Mississippi River. However, he was never given the power to recruit solders into the Confederate service, something he eagerly longed to do.

And on August 16, 1862, the Battle of Lone Jack took place where a lone black-jack tree had stood for many years. Major Emory S. Foster, stationed at Lexington as commander of the Union forces there, rode out with a contingent to avenge the defeat at Independence. Foster had in his command almost a thousand men and two pieces of Rabb's Indiana Battery. He was unaware of the presence of Colonel (later General) Francis M. Cockrell's Confederate forces and Colonel Vard Cockrell (a brother of Francis Cockrell) at Lone Jack until he stumbled upon them.

The residents of Lone Jack were Confederate in sympathy, and Major Foster ordered the Indiana battery to open up on the little town. Colonel Vard Cockrell withdrew to the west, and Colonel John T. Coffee to the south, thus cutting the Confederate command in two. Colonel Upton Hays arrived with his command and agreed to attack Foster the following morning.

It was the firing of the cannon on the afternoon of August 15th that Cole heard when he was about five miles from Lone Jack. With his cavalry he was a welcome sight to the Confederates, and he assumed a position on the left flank, in the brush.

The battle began at daylight on the 16th, an accidental shot having given Foster the alarm. For five hours furious fighting raged, most of it across the road from the town. Rabb's artillery was captured several times. Had Foster known that the Confederates were almost out of ammunition he could have destroyed most of its command.

Cole Younger, waiting for the signal to charge, discovered a company of men to the rear who were not participating in the fight. Wondering at their inactivity, for he knew that Cockrell needed every available man, Younger rode over to them.

"Why aren't you men fighting?" he asked.

"We have no ammunition," was the answer.

Cole recalled having seen a cache of arms at a nearby farmhouse, so he raced there, obtained a large basket, filled it with ammunition, and hurried back to the lines. He then rode up and down the Confederate line distributing ammunition to those in

Col. J. Vard Cockrell

Col. Francis M. Cockrell

need of it. His courage and daring brought a yell of praise from the Union lines, about a hundred yards away.

Quantrill did not fight at the Battle of Lone Jack. However, his squads under Bill Gregg, Cole Younger, and John Jarrette were there. Gregg came up shortly after the fighting stopped and helped to chase the Federals back toward Lexington.

Major Emory of the Union army was shot and captured. He was taken to a house which served as a Confederate hospital. A guerrilla came in and saw that Emory was a Union officer. With an oath of rage he pulled his pistol, stating he was going to kill the no-good Yankee then and there, and also his wounded brother. Cole had just entered the room and, seeing the situation, grabbed the man's pistol, seized him, and threw him out of the house.

While Cole was standing picket guard on one of the roads leading to Lone Jack, a young Confederate soldier came riding up and was stopped. The young man said he was Warren C. Bronaugh, attached to Colonel Vard Cockrell's 16th Missouri Infantry, Company K.

The lad said, "I'm trying to get back to Cockrell's command."

"Well, you'll wind up right in the hands of the Federal troops if you keep going in that direction," Cole informed him with a smile.

"How come?"

"Colonel Cockrell is now on the east side of town. Keep riding down the Chapel Hill road and you'll bump into him."

"Thank you kindly," said the boy with a grin. "You probably saved my life."

Cole Younger was responsible for saving the life of another man too at that time. While some historians claim this incident occurred later that year, actually it occurred that spring.

One day, while Cole and several of his men were camped on Big Creek, several miles from where he had been born, one of his men raced into camp reporting that Stephen Elkins had been captured and was being taken to Quantrill's camp to be hanged. Cole, highly excited at the news concerning his former teacher, leaped upon his horse and dashed toward the guerrilla camp. Cole knew that Elkins was a northern sympathizer, but he also knew he could not stand by to see his friend killed. He reached Quantrill in time and explained about his friendship with Elkins, further stating, "To kill him would be wrong."

"All spies must die," declared Quantrill.

Then Cole tried lying: "He's a good southerner and has chosen not to fight because he is needed to care for his ailing mother."

"Well, all right, Cole. He's yours to handle if you can get by the men who are ready to shoot him."

Late that night Cole and Elkins managed to slip by the guards. Several miles from the camp Cole urged his friend to leave the area post haste before he could be missed. So far as any recorded statement is concerned, the matter was settled with the "escape" of Elkins. In later years Elkins returned the favor by coming to the assistance of the Youngers in an effort to secure their release from prison. At that time Elkins was a United States Senator from West Virginia.

When Quantrill went south for the winter he left Cole and George Todd each with a squad of men to continue their campaign as they saw fit, uniting whenever the occasion demanded. Cole took his guerrillas into camp on Cedar Creek, where they lived in caves and low houses made of mud and straw. From time to time they made forays until the coming of a heavy snowstorm which compelled them to ease their operations because the enemy could easily follow their tracks.

Due to the shortage of food for both man and beast, the guerrillas were compelled to apply to their friends, who always obliterated their tracks by driving cattle over them. In some instances they even cut down trees and dragged them about so as to deceive the Federals and Jayhawkers patrolling the region (especially Jackson and Cass counties).

One day a stranger appeared in camp, claiming that he had served in the Confederate army and wished to join Cole Younger's company. He gave a pathetic report of mistreatment in a Federal prison and how he had escaped. He so played upon Cole's sympathy that he was allowed to remain.

When George Todd heard of this he hurried to the camp and urged Cole to drive the man from camp or shoot him, for Todd had received bad reports of him. Cole again thoroughly questioned the man about his background. All the guerrillas maintained an instinctive dislike for him. John McCorkle said he had served with that man in the Confederate Army, and that put an end to the doubts.

On December 10, 1862, the stranger asked permission to leave camp to visit his wife who was ill. At first Cole refused, in fear that he would fall into Federal hands and disclose the whereabouts of their hiding place. Finally, giving in to the man's pitiful plea, Cole gave him leave for two hours. Immediately at the man's departure most of the guerrillas openly claimed their distrust of him, and this troubled Cole.

"Ol" Shepherd said, "Cole, there's something wrong. Look at my horse. He's a smart one and can smell a Fed a mile away."

"Nonsense. How can that be?"

Actually the animal was tramping and smelling nervously. At that point Cole looked toward a ridge about a quarter of a mile off and saw a squad of men headed their way, an officer in the lead.

When they were within hailing distance Cole yelled, "Is that you, George Todd?"

There was no reply. For a moment Cole hesitated, then he called out, "We've been betrayed! Fall in, and be lively."

As the men took their places, Noah Webster looked behind and saw a sight that caused him to exclaim, "We're surrounded! There are men to the rear."

"It's all right, Cole. We're Todd's men."

"Let into them, men. Give 'em hell!" Cole shouted.

Instantly the guerrillas opened fire at the men in front, and at the same time those in their rear poured in a volley, killing several soldiers. Forming his men back to back, Cole kept up a stubborn resistance. Suddenly, the Federals in front made a desperate charge.

Knowing that he was surrounded, his whereabouts having been betrayed by the man he had trusted against the advice of Todd and his own men, Cole determined to cut his way through the enemy or perish in the effort. He led his men down the ravine on the double quick, shooting as they ran, and by the sheer impetus of their charge they forced their way through the Federals. Turning, the Union men closed in and gave chase.

Clear of the woods Younger found that the sleet had made the snow so slippery that speed was out of the question. He ordered his men to pull off their boots. Despite the rain of bullets, they obeyed and then continued their retreat. For several hours they kept up a running fight. Fortunately the Union horses were having a lot of trouble in the deep snow, while Cole and his men were able to walk on the ice-crusted surface.

Striking the main road to Harrisonville, Cole led his men over it until they came to one which branched to the right, and down this they hastened until they came to a bridge over a creek. Cole commanded his men to spring into the water, and they waded upstream for about a mile until they came to a stone wall on the top of which they continued for half a mile, hoping that the Federals would not be able to trail them in the morning.

Long after dark, their feet bruised and bleeding, the guerrillas reached the house of friends and were given food, clothing, and treatment for their half-frozen feet. As soon as they were rested Younger ordered them to split up into couples and by different routes to go to Todd's camp.

After the last pair had gone, Cole persuaded the men at the house to take a tree, branches and all, and drag it over the snow to obliterate the tracks. This was done with the aid of a yoke of oxen.

Arriving at Todd's camp, Cole found most of his men there, and after several days all of them had arrived except the three who had been killed by the soldiers at the cave. By some stroke of luck the horses milling around after the flight were taken to Todd's camp by friendly farmers who had found them.

CHAPTER 8

All About
George Shepherd

MANY HISTORIANS HAVE RECORDED INCIDENTS which only they thought interesting, but now and then valuable information that remained hidden for years is discovered. In this category falls the story of George Shepherd, the Maddox brothers, Dick and George, as well as George's wife, the former Martha Sanders.

Martha Sanders, a young Bloomfield, Kentucky girl, was noted for her modesty and good looks. When she visited Missouri she met and married George M. Maddox. The Civil War began during their honeymoon and Maddox at first enlisted in the Southern army, eventually riding with Quantrill's raiders along with his brother Dick.

The once bashful Martha donned men's clothing, changed her first name to Matt, and rode beside her husband in several engagements. She was later known as Matt Sanders, a notorious Confederate spy. Her name is still respected along the line between Kentucky and Tennessee, even by families of the northern officers who were duped by this young woman.

After the close of hostilities and the death of her husband Martha Sanders suddenly reappeared among her former acquaintances in Kentucky on her father's farm. She might have forgotten her earlier excitement if George Shepherd had not come along and persuaded her to renew their adventures. She married him and rode with him on his forays, although they were supposed to be living peacefully on a Kentucky farm.

George had been born on a farm near Independence in Jackson County, Missouri, on January 17, 1842. His taste for the military life came at an early age. He was only fifteen when he joined the troops of General Albert Sidney Johnston when operations were brought against the Mormons in Utah. He returned to Missouri in 1859 to operate the family farm with his brothers John, James, and William.

When the Civil War broke out it was natural for George to join the Confederate volunteers, for his family, like many other Missourians, had come from Virginia. He saw action at the Battle of Wilson's Creek where he first met young Frank James, who was captured in that fight but given a field parole. Shepherd also saw action at Pea Ridge, Arkansas, where Confederate General McCulloch was killed by a Union sharpshooter said to have been "Wild Bill" Hickok. When General Price and his men were ordered east of the Mississippi River Shepherd returned to Jackson County and joined Quantrill's guerrillas.

He was present at Independence, Missouri, on January 3, 1862, when Quantrill's band inflicted terrible loss on the Union garrison commanded by Colonel Burris. He and Cole Younger had both been prominent during the fight at the home of John Flannery.

The Maddox brothers were as equally furious fighters as George Shepherd and his brother Oliver (called "Ol"). All were present at the Tate house when Federal militiamen surrounded it and demanded their surrender. George had been guarding one of the doors of the house when a young Union officer knocked on it and called for them to come out, hands up. Quantrill fired through the wooden door, and the shot caught the officer smack in the chest, killing him instantly.

Quantrill, then devising an escape, deployed his men throughout the house. Cole Younger and six other men, including the fierce Dick Maddox, defended the upstairs, while Shepherd commanded the guerrillas who occupied the first floor. The Federals fired the house, at the same time keeping up an unceasing fire of rifle and revolver shots into the building.

There was only one thing for Quantrill to do — make a desperate sortie from the house. He led the charge, followed by

George Shepherd, Cole Younger, the Maddox brothers, and other members of the band. Their shotguns cut a bloody gap through which they escaped. Every one of the seventeen men succeeded in gaining the safety of the brush.

In the spring of 1862 George Shepherd, Cole Younger, and "Ol" Shepherd were surrounded while in the home of George's brother in Jackson County. They were outnumbered ten to one. Cole Younger was about to lead an attack against the Federals when several other members of Quantrill's band appeared and attacked the Union men from the rear. This diversion enabled the besieged men to escape from the house.

In the fall of 1862 Captain George Todd, one of Quantrill's finest, commanding about fifty men, prepared an ambush on the road leading from Kansas City to Harrisonville. Although the place was strategically selected and the utmost caution was taken, it came near to being the slaughter pen of the guerrillas who lay patiently in their rifle pits, awaiting the approach of some unsuspecting troops. George Shepherd was down the road, south of the ambush location, acting as sentry. It was near midnight, and nothing broke the somber stillness but a rustling of the leaves by the slight breeze in the trees.

Suddenly Shepherd was conscious of a tall form near him. A cautious glance told him there were many crouching forms all about him, all heavily armed.

At the command, "Surrender!" George shot the dismounted trooper in the chest and dashed away to arouse his comrades in the rifle pits. The Federal forces, under command of Major Hubbard, Sixth Missouri Cavalry, had dismounted, prepared to spring a surprise attack upon the guerrillas, but Shepherd's nerve and presence of mind saved his comrades from complete disaster.

In August of 1863 Quantrill began to rally around his standard all the small, detached bands in western Missouri in an expedition against Lawrence, Kansas. Colonel Holt of the regular Confederate Army, on a recruiting mission in Missouri, offered the help of his own hundred soldiers. Quantrill warned his men that they would have soldiers on all sides during their march to the defenseless town of Lawrence.

As will be detailed shortly, that was destined to be a black mark on the history of the country. George Shepherd was there, as were the Maddox brothers, and they shared prominently in the terrors and tragedies of that dreadful day. Even today people still visit Lawrence to view the monument to the brave men and boys who died in the senseless raid. They still talk about the horrors of that fateful day in August.

Quantrill and his men were more or less inactive during the following winter which they spent in the vicinity of Sherman, Texas. Returning to Missouri in the summer of 1864 they engaged Federal troops at Pink Hill in Johnson County and at Pleasant Hill. Shepherd was active in both skirmishes, shooting soldiers right and left. In September he was active during the removal of the doomed soldiers from a hospital train at Centralia, Missouri.

After Centralia, Captain "Bloody Bill" Anderson joined the main command under Captains George Todd and Tom Todd (no relation) to await the forces of Major A.E.V. Johnson, who was en route from Sturgeon to Centralia with 185 men to repel the guerrillas. When the Federal troops came into view Thrailkill saw 160 men riding two abreast, armed with what appeared to be Enfield muskets. To set a trap, George Todd rode to a rise above the guerrilla positions and dismounted. At his back eighty men of his own force were hidden in the timber, waiting. At his left, Tom Todd sat ready with fifty men. At his right, Anderson sat with sixty-five men.

Some three miles from Centralia, Johnson ordered three fourths of his troopers to dismount, each fourth man in charge of four horses, a cavalry custom. Ahead Thrailkill and his ten men dismounted, tightening the cinches on their horses. This move apparently threw Johnson off, since he obviously thought the guerrillas planned an attack on foot.

Johnson, riding in front of his foot soldiers, came forward about half a mile. Todd waited until the dismounted men were well away from their horses. Then he raised and lowered his hat three times.

At that signal the guerrillas attacked, streaming in from the woods on both sides of Johnson's line, teeth clenched on their reins and Dragoon pistols in each hand. Each of them carried several cylinders loaded and tied to his saddle horn so that he could toss out the used cylinders and reload his pistol at top speed. With Rebel yells bursting through their clenched teeth, they charged Johnson's dismounted cavalry. Of course Johnson's men immediately opened fire, but it was ineffective.

The guerrillas raced on, sixty yards, fifty yards, forty yards, until suddenly the entire frontline of charging guerrillas blazed at once. The first burst cut down fifty-seven of Johnson's men before the rest turned and ran in confusion. The guerrillas followed in, blazing at the already fallen soldiers, then reloading and blasting the retreating men. Jesse James, having singled out Major Johnson, riddled him almost at the moment the attack began. Only eighteen men escaped death that day.

By the following spring and summer Lee had surrendered and the Confederacy was no more. Those guerrillas in Missouri who were so inclined were permitted to surrender, and George Shepherd returned to Kentucky, where he married the widow Maddox.

We know that his wife remained with him until March 20, 1868, the date of the daring robbery of the Russelville, Kentucky Southern Bank, also known as the Long and Norton Bank. On that occasion the finger of guilt could not be pointed at any one man or group of men. Some said five of those present were Thomas Coleman (alias Coburn, right name Cole Younger), Robert Boggs (right name "Ol" Shepherd); John Wood (right name Jack Shepherd), John Dawson (right name John Jarrette), G.W. Smith (right name George Shepherd). A great grandson of Nimrod Long, president of the bank at the time of the robbery, stated that eight men had participated in the raid and that two of them were Jesse and Frank James. Frank himself later implicated those named, but the name of the eighth man was never learned, if in fact, there was an eighth man.

Shortly after that Russellville robbery "Ol" Shepherd was tracked to Missouri by Louisville, Kentucky officers, Detectives D. T. "Yankee" Bligh and Gallagher who had sent a message to Missouri authorities to be on the alert for the return of Frank and Jesse James and "Ol" Shepherd. Shepherd returned to his old home near Lee's Summit, Missouri, unaware that he was a prime suspect in the recent bank robbery. But "Ol" was an ex-guerrilla. When called upon to surrender he fought it out with the posse and was killed, seven bullets having penetrated his already battle-scarred body.

This is the generally accepted story of Ol Shepherd's death, but his grandniece, Margaret Shepherd, claims it happened as follows:

Only Uncle George could have been at Russellville, Kentucky on March 20, 1868. My grandpa was a strict and firm Catholic and refused to take part in any wrong-doing. Uncle Oliver and Aunt Etta moved in with grandma and grandpa until the new baby arrived. Uncle Frank lived nearby and got fresh milk from grandpa's cows. On the evening of March 17, 1868, grandpa and my dad and his brother were milking cows. The kids were taking care of the calves so there would be milk left for the kids. Uncle Frank was out helping them. Grandpa was sitting on a milk-stool milking a cow when someone from ambush shot grandpa in the back, in the right lung. The screams of the kids brought Uncle Oliver and grandma out. They all carried grandpa into the front room of the house. Everyone knew then that Uncle Oliver was there. The family figured whoever shot grandpa thought he was shooting Uncle Oliver. Grandma removed the bullet from grandpa's lung and delivered Aunt Etta's baby that night of March 17, 1868, in Jackson County Missouri.

On April 4, 1868, the lawmen came to grandpa's and called for Uncle Oliver to throw out his guns and come out with his hands up and there would be no shooting. He showed no resistance on account of his family and went out with his hands over his head. He was shot down like an animal and had twenty bullet holes in him instead of just seven as reported. My dad said he saw it happen and saw my grandma and an old doctor count the bullet holes. He said grandma checked Uncle Oliver's guns to see if they were loaded and put on Uncle Oliver's gun belt and guns. Aunt Etta was younger than grandma and never got along very well after Oliver got killed. From then on grandma had her own kids and Aunt Etta's kids to care for. Every kid that was old enough went to school. Grandma took help from her brothers-in-law and from the James boys. My mother told me how grandma at one time hid Jesse James under a kitchen work table and got away with it.

George Shepherd of Nelson County, Kentucky, was another prime suspect in that bank robbery. Yankee Bligh and his men supposedly surrounded his home and arrested him, but Shepherd claimed that he had left Kentucky after the robbery, and that after a chase of several hundred miles he was overpowered and arrested in a little drug store in Tennessee.

At any rate, George was taken back to Russellville and jailed. Later he was transferred to Louisville for safe-keeping until the trial should take place. Showing her old pluck, his wife Martha went to work among her friends in Missouri and Kentucky, raising $15,000, the amount of his bond. No doubt she intended to free him and let him skip the country. Somehow the authorities got wind of her intentions and prepared several other indictments, so that they could re-arrest George as soon as he was out of jail. It is claimed that she sought to help him escape from the train while it was enroute from Louisville to Russellville, where the trial was to be held. To avoid suspicion she arrived in Louisville to accompany her husband, and, on entering the car where he was seated, found that the officers had taken the precaution of filling the car with an armed escort. She coolly left the train at the first station and wired her accomplices at Bardstown not to make an attack upon the train.

At the trial George Shepherd was represented in counsel by Wm. R. Kinney of Louisville, John W. Caldwell of Russellville, and W. L. Dulaney of Bowling Green. The Grand Jury indictment charged Shepherd with aiding and abetting the robbers, for horses they used had been taken from his farm. He was tried, found guilty, and sentenced to three years in the state penitentiary at Frankfort. He managed to escape once, getting thirty miles from the prison before he was captured and returned to his cell.

During the time Shepherd was in prison his wife tired of living alone, married a well-to-do neighbor of her father, Alexander McMakin, a most respected gentleman of the community.

After his release from prison Shepherd returned to Logan County, only to find his wife had remarried. It is said that this broke him up badly, especially since Martha chose to remain with McMakin. Soon afterward, perhaps at the instigation of Shepherd, she was arrested on a charge of bigamy. She obtained a pardon from the Governor and secured a divorce before the case could come up in court. When it did, it was dismissed. George then returned to Missouri, finding employment with the Jesse Noland drygoods store in Kansas City.

Steady employment must have been tiresome for the thrill-seeking and adventurous George Shepherd, though nothing occurred for some years that placed him in the public limelight. But on October 7th, 1879, the famous Glendale Train Robbery took place. Shepherd told Major Liggett, marshal of Kansas City, that he could find the clues necessary to implicate Jesse James, and that he was willing to take on that chore. Liggett recalled that Shepherd had been a guerrilla as well as a one-time bandit, and also that he wanted a chance to get back at Jesse James for the death of a cousin years earlier. Besides, the reward money looked good, so he secured a false newspaper clipping stating that Shepherd was suspected of participation in the Glendale robbery, so that this would strengthen his position when he talked with Jesse James.

Shepherd went from Kansas City to Clay County, where he visited at the home of Mrs. Samuel, Jesse's mother. He complained of the persecution he was having to endure because of the suspicions cast upon him. He told her that he was anxious to join the gang. Therefore he was blindfolded and led away. When he was relieved of his eye bandages he found himself in the midst of the old gang, confronted by Jesse James. The reception was not pleasant, according to Shepherd, since he had viciously denounced these former comrades after the bank robbery at Russelville for their not coming to his aid. Yet he was evidently able to convince the outlaws that he was sincere.

"Now that this is over," Shepherd told Jesse, "I'll have to return to Kansas City for a little while to get outfitted and make arrangements."

Liggett was informed by Shepherd that Jesse James and his men would leave Clay County at a certain time; that they would cross near Sibley. Marshal Liggett went to the designated spot and at the given hour he saw a body of armed men, among whom was George Shepherd. The robbers camped at Rogue's Island in the River Marais des Cygnes, near Fort Scott, Kansas. They planned to rob the bank of Street & McArthur at Short Creek, Kansas.

The bandits next camped on Shoal Creek, nine miles southeast of Short Creek. The morning before the date planned for the robbery, November 2, 1879, at three o'clock, Jesse James rode into Short Creek on an inspection trip. There, to his amazement, he saw guards posted all around the bank building. He then realized that somehow the authorities must be aware of the impending attack upon the bank. His band broke camp earlier than Shepherd had anticipated, thereby frustrating an ambush that had been prepared. Evidently Mike and Tom Cleary were prepared to waylay the band as they passed the trail on a certain date and time.

Shepherd stated that now he had to act alone. As they were riding through the woods he was riding a little to the rear of Jesse James. Suddenly he drew his pistol and shot the famous outlaw just behind the left ear. Jesse James fell heavily to the ground.

Then Ed Miller rushed to the aid of Jesse, while Jim Cummins went in hot pursuit of the fleeing Shepherd. After a pursuit of several miles Cummins was able to hit Shepherd in the left leg. Then Shepherd wheeled his horse and fired a shot into Cummins' side. Shepherd then rode into Short Creek to have his own wound attended to.

How true was this story of Shepherd's? If true, how long would he have lived after the incident? No doubt Jesse James would have made every effort to kill him. If Jesse had been killed by Shepherd's shot, then the outlaw's friends would have arranged for a quick demise of that gentleman. It is true that Jesse's mother said he had been seriously wounded: that was why no one heard from him for over a year after the Short Creek affair. Was Jim Cummins really wounded? The doctor who treated him said he had a fractured sixth rib and a wound in the intercostal artery, but there is no information as to the cause.

In any event, Jesse James lived until April, 1882, when Bob Ford shot him at his home in St. Joseph, Missouri. And other train robberies occurred between 1879 and 1882, all attributed to the handiwork of the James gang.

Another startling sideline is the story that George Shepherd, basking in the fame of his own making, told in 1882 and which appeared in the Kansas City newspapers, prior to the death of Jesse James:

> Kansas City, March 6, 1882 — A sensation was created here among the police and county officials by the fact that George Shepherd, the ex-guerrilla and bank robber, who claimed to have shot Jesse James, the notorious outlaw, near Joplin, Missouri, just after the Glendale train robbery in 1879, had proved a traitor through that trouble. He now admits that his wound in the leg and the account of the killing was all a put-up job with the James brothers for the purpose of procuring the reward offered. The plan to get the reward having failed after long perseverance and much sweating, he now says that he would no more shoot Jesse James than he would his own brother.

Considering the nature of George Shepherd, it is easy to accept the story as truth. The wound was an old one, convenient to strengthen his story of murder. However, considering the nature of Jesse James, it is more than easy to accept the whole story as a farce, since Shepherd was still alive years after the supposed occurrence.

CHAPTER 9

A Unique Experience

WITH THE COMING OF SPRING, when he could move about without being trailed, Cole Younger made ready to inflict full and terrible punishment upon his enemies for their winter crimes. As a necessary preliminary he took his forty men to have their horses shod. Reconnoitering until they found a safe place, they came to John Hopkins' blacksmith shop in Jasper County, near the Blue Springs. Dismounting his men, Cole set out pickets in all directions.

Most of the horses had been shod by the time the lookouts reported that a troop of soldiers, eighty strong, under the command of Captain George Johnson, was approaching. Commanding them to mount, Cole led his men into the brush where he formed them in lines, with orders not to shoot until the soldiers were directly opposite them.

Soon the Federals appeared, their captain several yards in advance. One of the guerrillas, overly anxious, raised his rifle and fired.

"Don't shoot!" cried Johnson, thinking the hidden men were Union soldiers. "We are Federal cavalrymen."

More shots were the answer, although none struck home. Surprised, Captain Johnson reined up. In a flash it dawned upon him that the men were guerillas. Turning his horse, he dashed back to his troops. In less time than it takes to tell it, the Federals wheeled and in a body disappeared.

The death of his father and the humiliation of his sisters in the filthy Kansas City jail made Cole Younger determined to shoot down the murderers. He had the names of six of those who had slain his father. On Christmas Day, 1862, he, together with Abe Cunningham, Fletcher Taylor, Jack Traber, George Todd, and George Clayton, dressed in uniforms of the Federal cavalry, found the six men in a saloon and shot all of them without ceremony.

Since his betrayal by the Federal spy, Cole had kept his men in Todd's camp while he himself made frequent trips about the countryside alone. On one of these occasions during January, 1863, he was surprised. He was preparing to spend the night at the home of a friend, an old farmer who was Southern in his sympathies and who had crossed his fingers while taking the oath required by Federals from all who desired to be free from their raids and depredations. Cole tied his horse in the woods and walked toward the barn in a trail left by the farmer's cattle. He then went to the house, where he was welcomed and fed.

About nine o'clock the dogs began to bark furiously. Cole and his friend heard the grating of the gate as it opened.

"Dammit!" muttered Cole. "I thought it was too cold for the Feds to be out tonight."

With that he dashed out the back door of the kitchen, not lingering to put on his coat and boots. His host quickly hid those items of apparel. No sooner had he done so than there was a loud rapping on the door. The door was opened and the Federals, with pistols raised, rushed into the room.

"Where is that damned Younger?"

"I don't know. I haven't seen him for months, although he was here this morning and forced my wife to feed him."

"Why didn't you report this?"

"I was going to in the morning," lied the old farmer.

Fortunately his story coincided with what the officer had learned from a spy in the neighborhood: that Cole was seen near the farm during the day. After the soldiers had thoroughly searched the house, the farmer suggested that they search the barn also.

"We've done that, and he is not there."

"Then he's probably holed up in a warm cornstack somewhere," suggested the farmer, smiling inwardly.

"Then he can stay there. We're not going to look any more tonight. It's too damned cold."

While this was going on Cole managed to run through the orchard to a pasture trail which was well trampled by cattle hoofs. Along this he ran until he came to the home of another friend. When he beat on the door he was challenged, and when he replied the man inside recognized his voice and hastily admitted the cold and tired young guerrilla.

"Damn, you must be frozen, Cole."

"Not quite. I'm getting used to this sort of thing. But I can use some clothing and boots. How about a horse, too?"

"Clothing I can give you gladly, but no horse."

"Why?"

"Because the Feds would burn down my house on learning of it."

"Well, saddle one for me. In the morning go to headquarters and report it stolen. I'll get the blame and you will be safe."

Thus reassured the man did as Cole requested, and when the sun rose, Cole was safe in Lafayette County.

On another cold and windy evening he was visiting in another section of that country when two of the women of the family offered to stay on the watch outside, in order to notify him of the approach of any of his enemies. However, as darkness fell, cold and bleak, he called them in, declaring that he would rather take the chance of being surprised than compel those two women to keep watch on such a cold night. Then the troops arrived and the commotion was heard by those inside the house. There was a loud knock on the door.

Mammy Suse, with great presence of mind, seized a large bed quilt from the foot of Mrs. Younger's bed and threw it over her head, whispering to Cole to slip under it. Stopping only to blow out the light, Cole obeyed and was completely hidden by the ample folds of the blanket. Suse then went to the door and opened it. In rushed ten men, guns raised.

"Where's Cole Younger?" demanded Captain Davidson.

"I dunno," replied Mammy Suse. "Don't shoot me. Ise on'y de po' ole niggah servant."

"We know he's here. We saw him come in."

"Ah tells yo' I don't know. You all gotta look for yuhselfs I reckon."

"We're not interested in you. Get out of the way."

Outside it was very dark, and when they had gone a short distance from the house Younger jumped from beneath the quilt and ran for the cover of the brush. Mammy Suse, unable to restrain herself, yelled out, "Run, Massa Cole, fo' gawd's sake run."

The Federals heard her and knew they had been duped. Yet, although ignorant of the direction in which Cole had fled, they discharged several volleys, after which they entered the house and reported to Captain Davidson that they had killed Cole. Davidson's exultation gave way to chagrin when they were unable to find Cole's body. Not one of the many shots had struck him, and he had made his way to the brush where he lay concealed. Cole at length decided that the Federals intended to remain until morning. When they renewed their search he made his way through the wooded area to his camp.

Tired of waiting in the cold weather the Federals decided to burn the house. Then, if Cole were really inside he would be forced to flee. In the light from the flames he would prove an easy mark.

While some of the men went to the barn to get hay which they piled about the house, others went inside. There they found Mrs. Younger in her sick bed, her terrified children huddled around her. The sight of the woman suggested a diabolical idea to the Jayhawkers. With harsh words they compelled her to rise from her bed and they led her into an outer room.

"What do you want with me?" she sobbed.

"You'll find out soon enough," laughed several of the men.

"Just do what we tell you."

In mortal fear the shocked woman was taken from the house, followed by her weeping children. Halting near a pile of hay, a soldier thrust a torch into Mrs. Younger's hand.

"Light that stuff," he cried.

Mrs. H.W. Younger

As she hesitated he added, "Lively!" and raised his pistol.

With a shriek Mrs. Younger jammed the flaming brand into the hay, thus being forced to set fire with her own hands to her own house. The Jayhawkers remained until the flames had gained such headway that they could not be extinguished. Then they rode off while the children and Mammy Suse carried Mrs. Younger as best they could to the home of a neighbor. From there she was later moved to a shanty near Waverly, in Lafayette County, Missouri, where it was thought the family would be free from further persecution.

In February the commandant at Harrisonville, Captain J. Davidson, sent out an orderly to the Younger plantation with the request that Cole's mother come to his headquarters. Unable to go because of illness, Mrs. Younger asked the captain to call at her home if the matter was important. Without delay Captain Davidson did so.

He told her that if she would persuade Cole to go south with her and the rest of the family, he would give them all a pass and guarantee them safe conduct. Eagerly the bereaved woman accepted the offer, for she believed that it was made in good faith. To herself she pictured a happy home once again, with all her sons and daughters about her, in a place far from the scenes of terrible memories.

However, the proposition was merely bait held up by the Federal officer to lure Cole back home, upon which Davidson immediately set a constant watch.

True to her part of the agreement Mrs. Younger sent word to her son of the offer, and with all speed he started for the plantation to learn more about it and to discuss its acceptance with her. Upon his arrival word was sent by the hidden watcher to Davidson, and that night the officer, with a hundred men, surrounded the house, bent on capturing Cole dead or alive.

Prior to the arrival of the troops Cole had placed one of his sisters and a loyal Negro mammy (Suse mentioned earlier) to watch the road for the appearance of the enemy.

Just as Cole had expected, very soon some Union troops appeared at the shanty where Mrs. Younger was living. However, it turned out that Captain Johnson was the only one who had the presence of mind to discharge his pistol as he retreated from the surprise Cole had prepared for him. His shots were the only ones fired by the eighty Union troops. For a mile and a half Cole and his men chased them through the timber, rushing them into a ravine which led to a creek. With no other way of escape open for them, the Federals jumped their horses into the water and, as they tried to swim to the opposite shore, the guerrillas killed more than half of them.

Cole then led his men back to the scene of the one-sided fight, picking up such of the plunder discarded by the Union men in their flight as the men desired. Suddenly a man dressed in black emerged from the woods.

"Surrender!" cried Cole.

The man wheeled his horse and dashed away. Cole and "Ol" Shepherd both fired and the man fell, dead, his neck broken by one shot and his head pierced by the other, as they discovered upon examination of the body. The search revealed a Bible and a hymn book.

"Damn! We've killed a parson," said Cole.

It was later learned, however, that the man was a Union spy, disguised as a parson preying upon the local residents and obtaining information valuable to the raiding Jayhawkers.

"Good riddance, then," was Cole's only later comment.

As might be expected, the outrages committed against the Younger family, so wanton and brutal, aroused the Younger boys at home with a zealous desire for revenge. John and Robert were too young to join their big brother Cole and the other guerrillas. But the crimes against the family made indelible impressions upon their childish minds. They vowed that when they grew up they would avenge each tear shed by their mother and their sisters who were left to them.

Jim Younger was fourteen, and after the murder of his father he was the comfort and mainstay of his grief stricken mother. But in January of 1861 Jim rode away to join his brother, Cole, driven to the deed as others had been, by the treatment of his family at the hands of the Jayhawkers and Federal soldiers. Endowed with spirit and daring, Jim had not the military genius of Cole, but he courageously took part in many raids.

It was with mingled feelings that Cole received his young brother to membership in his own company. He believed that the boy should have remained at home to protect their mother and sisters and brothers, yet he could not resist the boy's pleas to be allowed to help avenge their wrongs.

Young Jim Younger did not figure prominently in the war as Cole and others had done, but some interesting papers were found among his personal belongings after his suicide. One such incident mentioned therein occurred while Jim and several other guerrillas were visiting Kansas City.

Cleverly they dodged the pickets and were soon inside the city limits, when they rode into a dark alley and tied their horses. For several hours they enjoyed themselves until the police learned their identity and endeavored to arrest them.

The young guerrillas started in the direction of the river. They realized they could not recover their horses, so they trusted to luck to find a boat in which to cross to the other shore. So close were the patrolmen that Jim was forced to dodge into an alley, leaving his comrades to care for themselves as best they could.

Arriving at the bank of the Missouri River, Jim was searching for a boat when he again caught sight of the officers. He leaped into the river without stopping to take off his clothes and struck out for a sandbar which he had often noticed while passing and knew to be about 300 yards from shore.

As he swam, the policemen on the shore heard the splash of his motions and sent bullets after him, but none struck the boy. He reached the strip of sand on which he found a lot of driftwood. After taking a short rest he had just begun to take off his clothes so that he might be less hampered in his long swim to the other bank, when he saw a flat-bottomed steamboat coming up the river.

Stretching out flat on his stomach, the youth tried to hide behind some of the driftwood. Finding none large enough he piled it hurriedly on top of himself. On came the boat within a stone's throw of the sandbar, the lights streaming over the narrow island so brightly that Jim feared he had been discovered. But the steamboat passed by, and he was safe.

Quickly he stripped and plunged into the water. The distance was far, and he was thoroughly exhausted when he gained the bank. His lack of clothes did not cause him to delay. To ascertain if his companions had been equally successful in crossing the river Jim hooted like an owl, a signal often used by the guerrillas. Four answering hoots greeted him in quick succession, and soon the little band was reunited.

Jim's friends laughed at his predicament, and his appearance caused them to punctuate the accounts of their own escape from discovery with peels of laughter. The boys were then in Clay County, not far from the town called Liberty, where there was a Federal camp.

"Say, fellows, this is no joke. I've got to get some clothes," said Jim.

"There are plenty of clothes in Liberty."

"But you are not dressed to travel," one of them said with a laugh.

"Let's go to the Union camp and grab some clothes," said Jim.

Accordingly they made their way to the road and proceeded along it until they saw houses of the town of Liberty looming in the darkness. Turning to the left they entered the town from the rear of those houses and quietly went toward the camp. Suddenly Jim caught sight of the figure of a giant between him and a smoldering fire. Halting his comrades he went ahead. He found one man stationed on the opposite side of the town.

Rejoining his friends, Jim led them to a ditch he had discovered. Crouching low, they followed it, passing the guard until they came to an alley which led them into the Federal camp. Jim quickly grabbed some clothes, fearful all the while that the sleeping soldiers might awaken.

Quickly donning the stolen clothing, Jim led the way until they came to where the horses were corraled. It was but a matter of a few minutes to select the horses they needed, then saddle and bridle them. The young guerrillas were at the point of riding away, when Jim remembered that he was unarmed.

"I've got to get some guns," he said in a whisper.

With the stealth of a cat he crawled inside a tent and grabbed two revolvers. He and his friends then followed the same general course by which they had entered, and in due time they gained the bank of the river at a ford below Independence.

Just as the sun was rising in the east, the jubilant young men rejoined Cole.

CHAPTER 10

The Sack of Lawrence

IN THE AUTUMN OF 1854 a few families from New England had come to the Kansas Territory and named their new home Lawrence in honor of Amos Lawrence, their leader. The population increased due to the continuous arrival of northern settlers. It was not long before the crude log cabins were replaced by brick and frame and stone dwellings. The town's prosperity aroused the envy of the pro-slavery elements in the Territory and became the center of attack in what is known as the Wakarusa War.

The citizens of Lawrence fortified the town by building seven-foot-high earthworks around it, connected with long lines of entrenchments and rifle pits. Here the men drilled daily under Charles Robinson (first governor of Kansas) who also set up an around-the-clock guard until December of 1855. Even after that most men there still carried weapons, already prepared for danger, because there were rumors that Missourians were planning to invade Kansas for the sole purpose of destroying Lawrence.

In the spring of 1855 mobs of ruffians arrived. Alabama sent a band of fighters under Colonel Buford. Colonel Titus and his men came from Florida. South Carolina sent Colonel Wilkes with several companies to assist in the fight of winning Kansas Territory for slavery. The President of the United States placed Federal troops at the command of Territorial Governor Wilson Shannon and Chief Justice Samuel D. LeCompte of Douglas

County, Kansas. These two men declared openly that all those who resisted the law would be found guilty of treason.

That infamous character, Sheriff Samuel J. Jones, now came into the picture. He was called the "bogus" sheriff of Douglas County because he had been appointed by the bogus Shawnee Legislature on October 23, 1855. This constitution was smothered in the United States Senate after having passed the House, and the officers never took their seats. Nevertheless, the movement served as a bond among the free-state men, and it was their rallying point for two years.

Jones arrested all those he pleased and saw to it that the grand jury declared as nuisances the Free State Hotel and the two newspapers, *Herald of Freedom* and the *Kansas Free-State*. Free-staters were molested and killed on the roads and highways, or publicly robbed, with not a soul daring to correct the outrages. At this time a large army of the pro-slavery element was daily increasing in numbers and strength to the right and left of Lawrence, all of them loudly boasting that they had been sent by Providence to destroy the traitorous city and its abolitionist inhabitants.

The night of May 20, 1856, Colonel Buford's troops were encamped a few miles southeast of the doomed town. To the west, about ten miles, were the armed companies of Colonel Wilkes and Titus. The latter was reinforced by General David R. Atchison with his famous riflemen and two pieces of heavy artillery. Later that night more reinforcements arrived in the form of companies headed by Captain Dunn and General Clark and those of General B. F. Stringfellow. Buford's forces formed the lower division of the invading army; the others formed the upper division.

These forces actually were not under the leadership of any military official but under the direct orders of United States Marshal I. B. Donelson, who considered the entire force a means to "assist him in the execution of his official duties." His deputy, Mr. H. Fain, entered Lawrence during the early morning hours of May 21st and tried to provoke incidents that would give him an excuse for arresting the citizens. However, they acted wisely and cooperated with the deputy marshal in his making of several token arrests. The marshal then saw that his plan to attack the town was unnecessary. So he dismissed his troops, stating that he had no further need of them. On second thought, he turned the men over to Sheriff Jones, who seemed to have some business to attend to in Lawrence.

That same afternoon Jones, with twenty-five men, rode up to the Free-State Hotel and demanded that General Samuel C. Pomeroy surrender all weapons. He declared that if his order was not complied with within five minutes the troops would shell the town. Pomeroy had only a few small arms and one howitzer which was not private property, and this was turned over to Sheriff Jones. Jones then advised the people that he would have to carry out the orders of the Douglas County District Court to destroy the newspapers that had been named as nuisances. The presses of these papers were demolished and the pieces thrown into the Kaw River. The soldiers carried out all the furniture and other contents of the buildings and dumped them into the street where they were burned.

By this time four cannon had been brought up in front of the Eldridge House by General Atchison, and he ordered his men to fire away at the hotel. Their aim was so devastating that the building burst into flames and was quickly burned to the ground.

At the first roar of the cannons the women and children of Lawrence began to flee the town. Their plight was pitiful, for they didn't know where to go nor which way to turn. Their men stood by, offering no resistance to such an overwhelming force, helplessly watching their homes and places of business looted and destroyed. All afternoon this plundering and destruction went on but, strange to say, there was no killing. Not one human life was lost, even though those reckless men of pro-slavery sentiments were crazed with drink and wild with lust for plunder.

The Free-State men acted wisely in submitting while they were so helpless, and they refrained from later violence against their enemies. But after it was all over, driven to desperation, they organized bands of roving guerrillas in an effort to prevent another such disaster. Perhaps the town of Lawrence was under an evil sign, as some people supposed, for there was even worse suffering in store for its peaceable citizens. The never-to-be-forgotten sacking took place on August 21, 1863.

On the black night of August 19, 1863, a band of rough and desperate-looking men gathered near the Blackwater River a few miles from Columbia in Johnson County, Missouri. The cunning guerrilla chief, William Clarke Quantrill, had assembled his men at the Pardee home earlier in the evening, and from there they had ridden over to Lone Jack in Jackson County. Quantrill divulged that he had planned a raid on the town of Lawrence, the home of his arch-enemy General (Senator) James Lane. He had planted a spy in Lawrence some weeks earlier and soon there was a report of what had been learned.

"All right, Fletch Taylor," said Quantrill, nodding to one of his guerrillas. "Give it to us now."

Taylor told how he had gone late into Lawrence disguised as a horse trader with plenty of money. It had been easy for him to get all the information he wanted, for he had stayed at the Eldridge House, had sat at the same table and eaten his meals with the hated General Lane. Taylor said the town was weakly garrisoned and the Union camp just across the river was meager. Now was the perfect time to strike because the thought of Quantrill and his raiders was far from the people's minds. They felt secure because the Union troops were near.

Lawrence had been rebuilt since its earlier catastrophes, and it was a beautiful town, known to be the most sightly in the State of Kansas. Having been founded by Amos Lawrence in 1854, it had wide and clean streets lined with trees, many fine stores, neat and comfortable homes. Its population of 1200 was prosperous and happy. It was a bustling recruiting center for the Union army and therefore it was easy for Quantrill and his gang of outlaws to come riding into town with Stars and Stripes flying at the head of the column to avert suspicion.

At the secret rendezvous on the bank of the Blackwater River that hot night in August, 1863, Quantrill listened to the report and said, "Men, you have heard what Fletcher Taylor says. But remember, all of you, taking Lawrence is a big venture, one of the biggest we've ever tackled. It will not be any child's play. We will be harrassed all the way, there and back. We must decide while knowing all this."

Quantrill's keen snake-like eyes turned to "Bloody Bill" Anderson as he said, "What do you say?"

"I say let's sack the damn town and kill every male thing there," was Anderson's firm reply.

"Todd?"

"Lawrence it is, regardless of the cost."

"Gregg?"

"Lawrence is the home of Jim Lane — isn't that enough? That's enough for me. I say 'Lawrence or death'!"

"Shepherd?"

"I say it's about time we wiped that town off the map."

"Jarrette?"

"Burn Lawrence to the ground, just like Lane did Osceola."

"Maddox?"

"Sack Lawrence. Destruction and death to everyone there."

"Yeager?"

"Lawrence or Hell. Let's be quick about it, too."

It was unanimous. The men Quantrill had asked were those who had sworn revenge against anything Federal for the rest of their lives. Such men did most of the killing. They worked methodically, not spasmodically as some of the others did.

Quantrill supplied them all with maps of Lawrence, with all the objectionable houses marked for destruction.

It was agreed that they would attack Lawrence the following day, August 20th, but as it turned out the raid actually did not occur until August 21st. In some mysterious way the rumor had gotten out many weeks earlier that it was Quantrill's intention to raid Lawrence and slaughter the citizens and burn the town. So guards had been stationed at all roads leading into the town. When nothing happened for about three months, the people laughed at their own fears. Therefore, when Quantrill struck he found no guards and the town asleep to its danger.

The band rode forth from Lone Jack toward the Kansas border. There were three hundred of them — 150 of Quantrill's own men and the same number under Confederate Colonel Holt who had been detailed there by General Sterling Price. Possibly Price did not know Quantrill's intention, although some people later claimed that Holt had chosen to ride along especially because he owed General Lane a debt of long standing.

At five o'clock in the evening the raiders crossed over the border into Kansas in plain sight of a Federal command under Captain J. A. Pike whose force was much too small to invite a clash. Of course Captain Pike hastened into the town of Aubrey and sent word to Kansas City about the guerrilla movement. Why he did not warn the citizens of Lawrence remains a mystery.

At eleven that night the guerrillas passed Gardner, Kansas, on the old Santa Fe Trail. There they burned a few houses and killed several men. Even after this, word failed to reach Lawrence of Quantrill's advance.

At three in the morning Quantrill passed through Hesper, and here he forced a young lad to lead the band to Lawrence because the night was pitch-black and the raiders were not familiar with the lay of the land. Quantrill kept the boy with him throughout the raid, then released him and sent him home. Near Captain's Creek one daring Kansan made a desperate effort to give the alarm in Lawrence, but his fast-galloping horse fell and was killed. The name of this Kansas Paul Revere should have been preserved, but was not recorded.

In the first faint light of dawn Quantrill and his band entered Franklin, four miles east of Lawrence. A few persons who were up at that hour saw the men ride through but never dreamed they were any but Federal soldiers. When they were two miles from their destination the guerrillas passed the farm of the Reverend Snyder. They rode into the minister's yard and killed him. His name was on the hate list because he was a Union officer of colored troops.

One mile out of the doomed town they came upon Hoffman Collamore, the young son of Lawrence's Mayor Collamore. The boy was out hunting game, and he supposed the body of horse-men were Federal troops on the march. When he was asked where he was going by one of the mounted men, Hoffman told them he was out early hunting. Without any warning some of the guerrillas began firing at him. He turned and ran into a field but was brought down by a volley of gunfire. He had the presence of mind to lie perfectly still on the ground, to make the murderous raiders think he was dead. After they had ridden on he crawled to the nearest house where he was given help for his severe thigh wound.

The weak eyes of another man, Joe Savage, saved his life that early August morning. Two of the guerrillas knocked on his door, meaning to kill anyone inside. Unable to find his eyeglasses Savage did not open the door right away. When he did finally open it his visitors were gone. He too figured they were Union soldiers.

So quiet and unsuspecting was Lawrence that Quantrill was able to send two scouts into the town to look things over. They rode down the main street and were seen by a few citizens who were up and about, but no slightest suspicion was excited. The two men went back to the waiting guerrillas to report that all was well and that the attack should commence at once.

Across the Kansas River there were about four hundred Union soldiers, but on the Lawrence side there were no more than seventy. Quantrill's men guarded the river front and took possession of the ferry, thus making sure that the troops could not cross the river. The soldiers on the Lawrence side were slaughtered as they slept, probably never knowing what struck them.

However, this diversion did not check the speed of the general advance. A few of the guerrillas turned aside in pursuit of some fleeing soldiers, but the main body swept on down Rhode Island Street.

Suddenly Quantrill yelled, "On to the hotel! Quick!"

Along Massachusetts Street tore the raiders, on toward the Eldridge House. Each horse and rider seemed to be one as the guerrillas went racing by, firing at every moving thing and into every house as they went. Men who came out to see what was happening were shot down, left wounded or dying on the wooden sidewalks. Women ran screaming in shock and terror. Those hardened murderers were not avenging Osceola — they were slaughtering Kansans merely because Quantrill wanted it that way. It was his personal revenge he sought in that particular town — because once he had been driven out of it.

Not even among those who ordered the Slaughter of the Innocents or the barbarian warriors of Attila the Hun, or those under Ghengis Khan had there been more merciless and vicious killers than those who spread destruction and desolation that day in Lawrence, Kansas. With demoniacal yells the raiders dragged husbands and fathers from their homes and shot them down in the presence of loved ones. Entreaties fell on deaf ears and stony hearts as the death-dealing maniacs ravaged the town. The glare of the rising sun blended horribly with the glare of flames from burning houses along the main street that had been marked on the maps. All the stores and business houses were burned except one.

In front of the hotel known as the Eldridge House Quantrill reined his horse. The building was silent. The grim guerrilla chieftain hesitated, fearing that the silence was a trap. Suddenly Captain A. R. Banks, Provost Marshal of Kansas, opened a window and displayed a white sheet, signifying surrender. He called out to Quantrill that he would turn the hotel over to him and asked that the people inside it be spared and treated as prisoners of war. Quantrill accepted the surrender. He marched the occupants of the hotel to the corner of Winthrop Street and told them to take refuge in the City Hotel, where they would be safe.

"I once stayed at the City Hotel, and the Stone family were kind to me," he announced. "Nothing will happen to them or their property while I'm in town."

The torch was then applied to the Eldridge Hotel, and the raiders left it in flames as they rode on, intent on pillage and murder. They spread out in groups of six or eight, taking over each street methodically, house by house. They recognized no code. They were utterly devoid of pity as they killed and destroyed and plundered. The military men and others who knew Quantrill's past record fled in panic toward wherever they could find a refuge. Later there were rumors that Jesse James was present at the Lawrence massacre, but that was not true. However, his brother Frank and Cole Younger were there. Jesse at that time was only a new recruit and Quantrill had refused to let him ride on the dangerous raid. Cole Younger had so far never seen Jesse James.

Hiram James George

Henry Clements

It is impossible to narrate all the horrors that were perpetrated in Lawrence on that never-to-be-forgotten morning, and the few incidents mentioned here were only a small percentage of the outrages committed. Many people were killed, while many others were hiding in houses or barns at the outskirts of the town with no way of knowing what was happening to friends and neighbors. They could, however, see the high-shooting flames and hear the agonized screams.

After the raiders had fired the Eldridge House they went galloping to the Johnson House. There the male occupants were marched across the street and shot without formality. One of them, a man named Hampton, fell to the ground and feigned death. After the raiders rode on he crawled to safety although badly wounded. The three Dix brothers were wounded, and they tried to escape by crawling through a rear window. They were discovered in the effort, and two of them were killed, while the third climbed through a window and hid.

The Mayor of Lawrence, George W. Collamore, lived in the western part of town, and there the guerrillas dashed, thinking he might try to organize resistance. Collamore saw them coming and realized there was no safe place to hide in the house. Quickly he thought of a trick that he hoped might work. He and a friend, Pat Keefe, slipped down into the well. The raiders, failing to find him, burned his home to the ground. After the flames had died down and the outlaws had ridden on to continue their work of destruction, Mrs. Collamore went to the well and called to her husband. There was no response. Captain J. G. Lowe then lowered himself down into the well to see what had happened to the Mayor and Pat Keefe. In Captain Lowe's haste he slipped and fell to his death. The Mayor and Keefe were already dead, suffocated by the dense smoke from the burning building. Mrs. Collamore did not yet know that her young son had already been wounded early that morning on his innocent hunting trip.

Close to the home of the Mayor lived Mr. Griswold with State Senator S. M. Thorpe, Josiah Trask, editor of the *State Journal*, and Harlow Baker, with their wives. The bloodthirsty guerrillas attacked the house, demanding that the occupants surrender. The men inside were armed and were determined not to give up their

Ted Sanders

lives without a fight. More of the citizens of Lawrence might have been armed for protection that black day had it not been for the Mayor's decree that all guns and ammunition should be kept in a central arsenal — and that arsenal had fallen into the hands of Quantrill at the first onslaught.

The leader of one of the raiding bands shouted to those inside Mr. Griswold's residence, "Come out, men! We don't mean to harm you. We mean to burn the town, not to kill its people."

Incredibly the four men inside the doctor's house believed this lie. They walked out and were taken prisoner. About 100 feet from the house they were deliberately shot while their four wives were looking on in horror. The screaming, weeping women were not allowed to go near the bodies of their husbands.

After this shooting the killers returned to the house, plundered it of all the valuables they could carry, then burned the building. Half an hour later others of the raiding party rode by, saw the bodies lying on the ground, and shot them again. The women had no way of knowing whether their husbands were still alive until the raiders had left. Then it was found that Dr. Griswold and Mr. Trask were dead. Thorpe died the following day, and Harlow Baker, though wounded, lived to tell of this horrible experience.

One small gang raided the home of Judge Louis Carpenter whose kind and genial disposition surprised the outlaws and so impressed them that they left without harming him or destroying his home. A later detachment, however, was less inclined to appreciate him. One rider dismounted and chased the Judge into his home, firing at him as he ran. Badly wounded, he ran to the cellar and, later, when he went out into his yard he fell mortally wounded. His bride threw herself over him to protect him from the waiting outlaw who had shot him. The brute walked around her, pistol in his hand, seeking a way to finish the wounded judge. He finally jerked up the girl's arm, thrust the revolver under it, and fired into the head of the helpless man, splashing his brain's into her face. The raider then set fire to the Carpenter house, but the judge's sister-in-law managed to put out the flames.

At the Fitch home, when Mr. Fitch came to the door to inquire about the loud knocking, he was shot point blank and fell dead in the doorway while his murderer kept firing bullets into his dead body. His wife, shrieking hysterically, was forced out of the burning house without being allowed to take her husband's picture from the wall. Even with shooting and killing going on all around him, the heartless killer noticed the new boots his victim was wearing and knelt down to remove them, then put them on his own feet. While the house was burning the outbuildings caught fire, and several of the ruffians spied a small United States flag tacked on the wall of a child's playhouse. The sight of the flag seemed to evoke a burst of bitter hatred, for they cursed.

They next entered the country store where James Eldridge and Jim Perine were working as clerks. The intruders demanded the key to the store's iron safe, promising the two men safety if they complied. Given the key they plundered the safe of all the money, then turned on the two clerks and shot them dead. Men were killed right and left in cold blood. No pity was shown except in very rare cases. Cole Younger, sickened by the carnage, maneuvered to save a few lives that day, and this was remembered in his favor many years afterward.

A man named Burt was slain as he handed all his money to one of the raiders. A Mr. Murphy was shot through the head, while another victim drank some water he had brought him. Ellis, a blacksmith, grabbed up his child and hid in a nearby cornfield, and they might have escaped had not the baby begun to cry. When their hiding place was found the father was killed, the baby left in his arms still crying. One house that was set aflame was the home of a very sick man. He was carried from his bed and put down in the yard at what seemed a safe distance from the burning house. One of the raiders came up to the sick man and shot and killed him in the presence of his wife and children.

Each horrible deed was surpassed by another as the day of terror dragged on.

Just south of the business district a Mr. Palmer had a gun repair shop. His building was apart from the others, and a customer was chatting with him. Suddenly the two men became aware that the place was surrounded by guerrillas who opened fire. Both men were wounded. The building was set afire. While the flames leaped up, the brutes tied the hands of the two wounded men together and threw them both into the fire. Several times the victims made desperate efforts to escape, but each time they were pushed back into the fire.

J. W. Thornton went running out of his house, but he was shot three times — in the hip, through the shoulder, and through the cheek. His would-be-murderer cursed: "Damn you, I can kill you another way!" With that he beat the injured man over the head with his revolver. Mrs. Thornton came rushing to her husband's defense, and the guerrilla laughed at her as he walked away. Strangely enough, Thornton lived for many years after that, but he was crippled. He did not like to talk of his horrible experience, which he called "a bloody massacre."

No male citizens — not the young, nor the middle-aged, nor the old — were spared. Even some of the small children were killed. Otis Lonley, a man past sixty, lived a short distance from Lawrence. Two pickets stationed to watch for soldiers paid him a visit and shot him while his poor wife wept and begged them to spare him.

"He has not committed any crime," she cried. "He never took part in anything political!"

"He's a damn Kansas Jayhawker, and that's enough crime," they replied.

It took a number of shots to kill that old man.

It is true that sometimes the pleadings of the women did save some property, though seldom the life of a male citizen. George Sargent was slain while his frenzied wife clung to him. The bullet came close to killing her, too, so the rest of her life she carried a scar on her neck.

Former governor of Kansas Charles Robinson saw the entire carnage from beginning to end. He stayed hidden in a large stone barn on his farm overlooking the town. The raiders went to his farm dwelling and, when they were told that the governor was not at home they eyed the stout-looking stone barn but kept a healthy distance from it. Perhaps they remembered other stone and brick buildings and wanted no part of Governor Robinson's big rock barn.

It was later said that if the people of Lawrence had received a little warning before the raid and had had time to entrench themselves in some of the stone buildings with guns and ammunition or even without them, the raid would not have cost so many lives. But such warning had not come. The town had been caught entirely unaware.

It was easy to identify the raiders, for they all wore clothing of a butternut hue. At the butternut-garbed horsemen the soldiers across the river did fire Mini balls as soon as they came in range. For that reason a number of buildings within the range of the soldiers' rifles were saved from destruction. The guerrillas had come to Lawrence to shoot and kill — not to be shot at.

Those men of Lawrence who were not killed had escaped by fleeing into the cornfields and hiding among the tall stalks and weeds. One of the most effective refuges was the large cyclone cellar in the center of the town. It had an entrance almost totally hidden from view, and near it a brave young woman took her stand and directed men and boys who were being chased by guerrillas. The raiders questioned her, but she insisted she had no knowledge of the missing men. Some were killed before they could reach the storm shelter. One man was saved because when he was shot in the arm he fell in such a position that the body of another victim almost covered him. The pursuing raiders thought both those fallen men were dead and ran past.

District Attorney Samuel A. Riggs had a remarkable escape. Set upon by one of the vilest of the gang, he struck the ruffian's pistol from his hand before he could shoot him. Then he ran for his life while his wife grabbed the bridle rein of the guerrilla's horse and clung to it. The horseman rode after Riggs, all the time with Mrs. Riggs clinging to the reins. She held on, while she was dragged around the yard, over a woodpile, and back into the street. When the guerrilla was about to fire another shot Mrs. Riggs jerked violently and spoiled his aim. By the time he got control of his plunging, frightened horse, the brave lady was safely away. Lucky for her that Quantrill had ordered his men not to shoot any women.

The Reverend R. D. Fisher also had a remarkable escape. The preacher was particularly wanted by the Quantrillians because they knew he served as chaplain of a Kansas regiment doing war service in Missouri. Fisher realized that flight was out of the question, so he hid in the cellar. It was partly excavated, and he climbed onto a bank under the floor of the house and hid in a drain by the farthest wall. The raiders came down into the cellar searching for him or anyone else who might be hiding there.

Fisher heard one of the searchers say, "Damn that Yankee preacher!"

Another growled, "Yes, damn him. He's got to be somewhere around here. He didn't have time to get away."

"Set the dirty place on fire! Kansas wood burns fast."

"Yes. That oughta flush him out."

Mrs. Fisher kept putting out the fires the guerrillas set until they became too many. She quickly went through the motions of pouring water here and there, while she aimed so that the water went through the floor and fell upon her hiding husband. When she finally had to flee the burning house Fisher crawled out of a window near the rear door. His clever and loyal wife was there to cover him with a large carpet, and she rolled him up inside it. A neighbor helped Mrs. Fisher drag the rolled carpet out through the back yard and into some weeds and tall shrubbery. All sorts of household furniture and utensils were then piled around the edges of the carpet, and so the Reverend Fisher was protected from the wrath of the raiders.

Young William Speer, 15, hid under a sidewalk, but the heat from the burning buildings set the walk on fire, and he was forced into the open street. Surrounded by the guerrillas he gave his name as Billy Smith, and all unknowing he saved his life by doing so. One of the ruffians had friends named Smith and therefore that name was not on the hate list.

William had a 17-year-old brother named Robert, who had been sleeping in the office of the *Tribune*, his father's newspaper, when the raid began. The family thought he must have been burned to death. After the raiders left the pitiful old father was seen raking the ashes in search of the bones of his boy, but no sign of Robert was ever found. Though William Speer had been spared, one of his brothers had been shot before the Bullene home, so old John Speer, Sr., sustained a double loss that day.

Another strange escape was that of a man named Winchell. When chased by the raiders he ran into the home of Dr. Charles Reynolds, first minister of the Lawrence Episcopal Church. The doctor was away, but there were three women in the house. Winchell was not killed by the implacable raiders, thanks to some quick thinking on the part of the women. One of them quickly shaved off his whiskers, another found a lady's bonnet to put on his head, and they hustled him into a wheel chair beside a table covered with medicine bottles and spoons. In reply to the questions of the outlaws the women said this was an ill aunt of Dr. Reynolds, come to Lawrence for treatment. The raiders stomped through the house, unable to find Mr. Winchell. Now and then one of them eyed the quilt-covered old "woman" in the wheel chair, but they made no attempt to investigate further. Sighs of relief came from the four persons in the house when the cursing guerrillas went away to continue their bloody mission at other homes.

Mr. Bullene, whose residence was on New Hampshire Street, was away from his home at the time of the sacking. Only his wife and children were present. Being situated in the center of Lawrence, this house was used as a meeting place for the marauders. Captain George Todd ate breakfast there, and he promised Mrs. Bullene that her home would be spared from the flames. And so it was, although several times that day groups of the ruffians tried to set it afire and stopped when Mrs. Bullene told them that Captain Todd did not want it destroyed. One of the Bullene children, William, watched in horror while his young friend, the Speer lad, was shot. The boy fell to the ground and was still breathing when another outlaw rode up, reined in his plunging horse, and fired two more shots into the wounded boy's head — being sure then that he lay still and lifeless. The murderer then spied William Bullene and took aim, but Mrs. Bullene rushed out and grabbed the horse's bridle while she explained again that Captain Todd had promised to protect them.

The mounted soldiers shot at a young man in the next block, and he fell headlong into the gutter. His wife screamed and wept so violently that his would-be killers thought he was dead and galloped on. The young wife was relieved when her husband whispered, "Don't cry, darling. I don't think any of their bullets hit me." And so it proved. He had not been scratched.

Another such instance occurred when the Sargent home was burned. The young printer living there was fired at as he ran from the doomed house. When he fell close to the flaming building and lay there, the raiders supposed he was dead and raced on. After they were gone rescuers found that he had not been hit. But he had been burned severely. Lying motionless close to the flames had taken severe discipline, but it had saved his life.

There were not many wounded who lived to tell about it. The outlaw raiders nearly always returned to those they had shot and kept firing to make sure they were dead. Sometimes they fired into a pile of lifeless bodies lest one or more of them still had a spark of life left. And their mistreatment of the wounded was incredibly heartless. They were so filled with hate and with a lust for killing that they seemed to enjoy killing a man by slow degrees. First a bullet in the shoulder, or arm, then another here and still another there, until the luckless victim was finally a corpse.

The thing that almost drove Quantrill mad was that the main object of his raid on Lawrence had escaped. General Lane had miraculously gotten away, for he well knew what would happen to him if he should fall into Quantrill's hands. At the first sign of the attack Lane fled from his house and dashed into a cornfield behind it. From there he made his way through the large field and rode to safety on a fleet-footed horse. To Mrs. Lane Quantrill remarked, "Give your husband my compliments, Madam, and tell him I should be most happy to meet him."

"That I will do, sir," she replied. "I am sorry that it was not convenient for him to meet you this morning."

Gritting his teeth in rage, Quantrill stamped out of the Lane parlor, set fire to the house, and then rode back to the center of Lawrence. Todd, Gregg, Colonel Holt, "Bloody Bill" Anderson, and others of his top men were assembled there, and they advised him that it was time to leave. They pointed out that Federal Cavalry were on the move from Kansas City, since someone had at last got word of the raid to the commandant there.

Quantrill agreed: "All right, men. Four hours of this is all any man can stand. Formation! Mount! We all ride for Missouri in a body!"

He knew it would be safer for them to stick together, at least for this one time.

Quantrill was about right in his estimation of the time consumed in ravaging Lawrence. From all accounts by survivors, the attack began at about five o'clock and the raiders left at approximately nine. It had been four hours of ruthless brutality, pillage, and murder. The business district had been burned first; all male citizens in sight had been killed. Then the invaders had left the center of town and headed south, systematically killing and burning. When they finally left a smoking and ruined Lawrence, wild-eyed men and boys began to come out of hiding — but it was not all over yet.

Up to this time not one of Quantrill's men had been killed. While they were riding on, headed back to Missouri, Larkin Skaggs, a former "hard shell" preacher who had turned bandit and who was now disgruntled because he felt he had not gotten his rightful share of the booty, wheeled his horse around and rode back to the City House.

The occupants of that spared building, thinking they were safe, were all standing out in front of the hotel, gazing in dismay at the ruin around them, when the lone rider came galloping back. He dashed up before the hotel, firing his revolver. He turned and started to ride away when a son of John Speer, whose little brother and an elder brother had been murdered, picked up a rifle and fired at Skaggs. The shot brought Skaggs to the ground wounded. White Turkey, a Delaware Indian, shot Skaggs through the heart. (He never would have made it back to Missouri alive, anyhow, if on the return trip Quantrill had learned that his last volley killed Mr. Stone, Quantrill's friend at the City House). Skaggs' body was dragged through the littered street, then thrown into a ravine. No one offered to touch it or bury it.

Not all the guerrillas reached Missouri safely. Four wounded were captured and killed by soldiers under Lieutenant Cyrus Leland, Jr., on the Fletcher farm where the Fort Scott Road Crossed East Ottawa Creek.

Back in Lawrence it was almost impossible to get exact figures concerning the dead or the amount of property damage. A close accounting showed 154 of the best buildings in the business and residential districts destroyed, with a property loss of $1,500,000, an appalling sum for those days. It was found that 185 men had died.

The story of the sufferings and the heroism of these people of Lawrence will be told for generations to come.

Quantrill and his guerrillas struck out directly south, crossing the Wakarusa River at Blanton's Bridge. Then they went on through Prairie City, on their way to a retreat in the Sni Hills of Missouri. They made their escape to the headwaters of the Little Blue River.

It seems incredible that 300 armed killers were able to travel over forty miles of Kansas territory by night and pounce at daybreak upon a town like Lawrence with no warning being given. It seems still more incredible that these same men were able to accomplish their horrible purpose uninterrupted, especially when Federal Forces were close at hand. But such was the case.

CHAPTER 11

Baxter Springs
Massacre

THE FUROR OVER THE NEWS of the Lawrence affair brought the entire nation screaming for retaliatory measures against the invaders from Missouri. No doubt it would have been easy for thousands of the Kansas Jayhawkers and Redlegs to pounce upon small Missouri towns and destroy them and their inhabitants. However, cooler heads prevailed to bring the situation under control.

A few interesting messages following Quantrill's raid are produced here for the interest of the reader:

Kansas City, Mo., August 26, 1863

Maj. Gen. John M. Schofield
St. Louis, Mo.

I shall not permit any unauthorized expedition into Missouri. No citizens are in now, and none went except my troops. I do not much apprehend any attempt of the kind except, perhaps, secret efforts of incendiaries to destroy Independence, Westport, or Kansas City, although the people of Kansas are mortified and exasperated, and those on the border considerably alarmed. I will have to clear out a good many rebels in Independence, Westport, and Kansas City. I need Lieutenant-Colonel Van Horn,

Order #11 issued by General Ewing

Twenty-fifth Missouri, to command this post. Please detail him, if you can. He is now in St. Louis.

THOMAS EWING, Jr.
Brigadier-General

Maj.-Gen. John M. Schofield
Commanding Department of the Missouri, St. Louis, Mo.

My troops are still in pursuit. Quantrill's men are scattered, the worst having gone out of the border counties. At last reports we have killed from 50 to 60. I have ordered all families out of the border counties of Missouri in fifteen days, allowing Union men to remain at or come to military stations, or go to the interior of Kansas, and compelling all the rest to leave the district. I will destroy or take to stations all forage and subsistence left in those counties after date fixed for removal. I have written you the reason for issuing this order. I am sure you would approve it here.

(This was Ewing's infamous order No. 11.)

This raid has made it impossible to save any families in those counties away from the stations, for they are all practically the servants and supporters of the guerrillas. I anticipate the collection on the border of a large number of guerrillas of southwestern Missouri to resist or revenge the execution of this measure. If you can send me more troops, please do so. I can use the Twenty-fifth Missouri or the Tenth Kansas to good advantage garrisoning the posts. There has been no failure to exert every possible effort to catch Quantrill, except at Paola, Friday night, when a great occasion was lost. I will see that the censure for that falls where it belongs. The charges set afloat from Leavenworth are false and malignant, so far as they apply to me and Major Plumb, and are instigated and paid for by political Quantrills.

Thomas Ewing, Jr.
Brigadier-General

Little Santa Fe, Mo.
September 4, 1863

Brigadier-General Ewing
Commanding District of the Border, Kansas City

Sir: Since I came to camp I have received information that the rebels, under Quantrill, will start south tomorrow, or between now and the next two days, and from what I can learn they do not intend any raid into Kansas. I would suggest that, if there is any cavalry at Lexington, Mo., they be ordered out after them. I will start, with all my available force, for Pleasant Hill this evening. I hear today that Star was killed yesterday by one of Todd's men.

Respectfully, Your obedient servant,

C. F. Coleman
Captain, Commanding

Hdqrs. Detachment of the Eleventh
Cavalry, Warrensburg, Mo., Sept. 4,
1863

Brigadier-General Ewing
Commanding District:

General: I have the honor to respectfully represent that, in obedience of your orders, I divided my command at Dresden, Mo., and sent two companies, under command of Major Ross, with orders to scout Lafayette County in search of guerrillas; afterward to report at Little Santa Fe, and await my arrival.

I arrived at this point on the 30th ultimo, with four companies. I have vigilantly scoured this county in search of Quantrill's men and guerrillas from that time up to the present. My scouts have captured and killed a number of guerrillas, one of whom was the notorious Captain Dobson.

The state of affairs in this county is truly lamentable. Union men solemnly declare that they have not nor cannot get protection from the military powers which have been stationed here. I deeply regret to say to you that the representations of the unconditionally loyal men of this county lead me to fully believe such are the facts, and I respectfully state to you that, in my opinion, the well-being of this county demands a change of commanders as well as policy. Union men from every part of the county are here as refugees, and have not been to their homes for twelve months. I can see no excuse for this, save the base negligence of the military stationed here, and the utter repudiation of their claims and interests. There are, and have been, soldiers enough here to hold every part of Johnson County free from guerrillas, so as to allow business, at least, to assume its wonted phase.

I leave, with my command, for Sibley, Mo., tomorrow, in the morning. After my arrival I will hasten to report to you in person.

I have the honor to be, your obedient servant

L. C. Pace,
Major, Comdg., Detachment of Eleventh Regt.
Missouri Vol. Cav.

Lexington, September 8, 1863

General Ewing: No sign of Quantrill yet. I advised Colonel Neill not to break up camp yet, as we were able to take care of Lexington. I will try and find out today if Quantrill is anywhere in the country. There is a report here that Quantrill crossed the river last night. No truth in the report, I think. If he is on the river, we can corner and capture him by letting him have a day or two to settle.

B. F. Lazear
Lieutenant-Colonel

Four days after the Lawrence raid, General Thomas Ewing, Jr., issued his celebrated General Order No. 11. This order required all persons living in Jackson, Cass, and Bates Counties, and in that part of Vernon included in that district, except those living one mile of the limits of Independence, Hickman Mills, Pleasant Hill, and Harrisonville; and except in that part of Kaw Township, Jackson County, north of Brush Creek and west of Big Blue, to remove from their homes within fifteen days of the order, August 25, 1863, issued at Headquarters District of the Border, Kansas City, Missouri.

The torch was then set to those designated areas. It was the depopulation of western Missouri; any citizen not within the limits of a military post after September 9th was regarded as an outlaw.

After the guerrillas had left Lawrence, a courier was dispatched to General Ewing's headquarters at Kansas City. Arriving at his destination close to noon, the courier handed the dispatch to Major Preston H. Plumb, chief-of-staff, since General Ewing was at Leavenworth, where he couldn't be reached.

Major Plumb mustered some thirty men, and just before one o'clock he rode west along the Old Santa Fe trail in search of the raiders. Plumb did not follow the roads, but struck out across the prairie, meeting Captain Coleman at Blue Jacket Crossing, in the Wakarusa River.

While Major Plumb was trying to outflank Quantrill, General James H. Lane rode out from Lawrence with a small body of men, mounted on old mares and plow horses. Near Brooklyn the general ordered Lieut. John K. Rankin to hang on the left flank of Quantrill, south of the Fort Scott Road until he reached Prairie City. Shortly thereafter, a farmer named George Wood advised Lane that Major Plumb was nearby with several hundred cavalry-men.

When Quantrill was forced to flee from Brooklyn at the sight of Lane's men, he retreated on the Fort Scott Road. Major Plumb kept on the east side of East Ottawa Creek, where he was to attack Quantrill as the guerrillas tried to ford the stream. At that point Captain Charles Coleman attacked Quantrill from the rear. Quantrill, not knowing that Plumb was to the front of him, turned and counter-attacked the Federal soldiers.

Major Plumb, hearing the firing, thought a general battle was going on. Coleman was driven back, to find Plumb at his rear, waiting to join in the battle. He had abandoned his post at the ford by coming to the aid of a fellow officer, thus allowing that avenue of escape open to Quantrill and his men.

Other skirmishes occurred along the way. At Paola some heavy fighting occurred between Quantrill and Lieut. Cyrus Leland, Jr., with the latter trying to hold his own until the arrival of Major Plumb's forces, to no avail. The main body of the guerrillas was only four miles from the Missouri line, near the Grand River. It was not long before the guerrillas had found safety in their retreat in the Sni Hills of Missouri. They had made their escape to the headwaters of the Little Blue River.

At the time of the issuance of Order No. 11 Quantrill informed his men that the enforcement of it left them nothing on which they could live, so he decided that his men should travel into Texas for a period of time. He sent runners to inform his men and those of Confederate Colonels Holt and Robinson to meet at the Pardee farm in Johnson County, at an appointed time.

On October 2, 1863, the guerrilla command left their rendez-vous and marched to the Grand River, camping there for the night. It was their intention to head for Texas on the old trail leading through Seneca country, passing north and south through what is now Baxter Springs, Kansas. Some claimed that Quantrill intended to strike Fort Baxter, but most writers agree that Quantrill was unaware of a fortification there.

The garrison consisted of one company of the Second Kansas Colored Infantry, commanded by Lieut. R. E. Cook, and Company D., Third Wisconsin Cavalry, under the command of Lieut. John Crites. On October 4th Lieut. James Pond arrived from Fort Scott with part of his command and took over the command of the post. The so-called fort consisted of some log cabins covering about a hundred feet of frontage on Spring River. To the rear of these structures there were earthen breastworks about four feet high. Pond's tent was several hundred feet west of the fort, and his men were extending the embankments to enclose that area.

Sixty soldiers left the fort on October 6th for foraging pur-poses, thus cutting the strength at the compound to twenty-five white soldiers and seventy black troopers. The foraging party never did return to the fort, for when they heard of the disaster they rushed to Fort Scott and other points of safety.

Dave Pool, in command of Quantrill's advance, captured a Federal supply wagon-train at the Spring River ford. From them he learned there was an encampment of soldiers at Baxter Springs. However, they did not inform him of the fort. Quantrill, on learning of this matter, quickly ordered his men to arrange for an attack. Pool, carrying an American flag, rode to the front of the column, and this evidently confused the Federals somewhat. Captains Gregg and Pool formed the right of the attack, while Quantrill led the main body of his men.

At noon the guerrillas charged the fort. Pool cut off the soldiers who were eating dinner at the kitchen section of the area, while west of the camp Lieutenant Pond was also cut off from the fort. He ordered his men into camp and, then running at full speed he broke the guerrilla line, reaching the fort in safety. Here he hurriedly fired a small howitzer he had brought with him from Fort Scott, encouraging his men to such an extent that they rallied and put up a stiff fight against the guerrillas. The real outcome of the fight at the fort could never be determined, since the guerrillas rode off toward the Fort Gibson Road, where they accidentally ran into the forces of General James G. Blunt. This officer, in total ignorance of Quantrill's presence, was riding straight toward him at Baxter Springs. Apparently his vanity saved his life, for he had stopped on the prairie to arrange for his entry into the fort amid flying colors and to the music of his military band.

West of the road the Federals faced the guerrillas, while Quantrill had placed a line of reserves in the tall timbers to the rear. Major H. Z. Curtis, of Blunt's command, forced several soldiers back into position when they tried to flee. Even then, more soldiers decided to attempt the same thing. It was the opportune moment for Quantrill, who ordered an immediate charge. The guerrillas pounced upon the enemy like cats on a mouse. Twenty-four troopers fell dead at the first volley, a dozen more writhed in the tall grass wounded. Major Henning raced to the fort to give Lieutenant Pond his appraisal of the situation.

The guerrillas chased many soldiers into a deep ravine, where they were slaughtered. General Blunt and Major Curtis also were in a bad fix.

"Major!" cried Blunt, "Let's try for the breaks in the line now."

Both men raced ahead, Curtis for the break in the guerrilla line near the ravine, Blunt for the break at a shorter distance, separating the banks of the ravine. Major Curtis did not make it. His horse was shot and fell, the next volley carrying a bullet through the major's head. General Blunt's mount, racing at full speed, was able to clear the distance between the sides of the steep ravine. He managed to escape after suffering the worst defeat in his military career. Not many of his command escaped. The prairie was strewn with the dead and dying.

During the fighting, Blunt's military band, fourteen in number, tried to escape by driving their wagon from the scene. A guerrilla named Bledsoe called for them to surrender and was shot and killed. Captains William Gregg and George Todd gave immediate chase, caught up with the wagon, and killed every man in it. The bodies were then thrown under the wagon, which was set on fire, consuming the bodies of their victims.

It was a great day for Quantrill. He strutted around his men and cried out, "By damn, neither Jo Shelby nor Marmaduke could whip Blunt, but I whipped him proper!"

John Fry, known as "Pony Johnny," one of the famous Pony Express riders, was among the eighty or so Federal soldiers killed at Baxter Springs. At one time during the fight Cole Younger and Captain Jarrette pursued twenty Federal soldiers, killing all but four of them. Captains George Todd and "Bloody Bill" Anderson wanted to attack the fort after the Blunt massacre, but Quantrill would not consent to it, now knowing it was a stronghold. To capture it would have cost too many of his men. Besides, he did not like the idea of going up against a howitzer.

In the fall of 1863 Cole Younger joined up with General Henry E. McCulloch, brother of General Benjamin McCulloch who had been killed at the Battle of Pea Ridge, Arkansas. General Henry McCulloch was in command of Northern Texas, stationed at Bonham, and Cole did scouting work for him, receiving the commission of captain in the Confederate States of America Army.

In November of the same year General McCulloch sent Cole to report to General E. Kirby Smith at Shreveport, Louisiana, the headquarters for the Trans-Mississippi Department. There he met two of Quantrill's captains, John Jarrette and Dave Pool, and they were ordered to campaign against the cotton thieves and speculators who infested the Mississippi River bottoms. Cole Younger was placed in command of one company, Captain Pool in command of the other, both captains under the direct orders of Captain Jarrette.

Near Tester's Ferry on Bayou Macon they met a cotton train under the protection of fifty Federal cavalrymen. The convoy escaped with ten survivors, while every driver was shot and four cotton buyers were hanged from the rafters of a nearby cotton gin. At Bayou Monticello they decided to cross the river and attack a cotton train across the bayou.

Captain Younger plunged into the cold water, surprised to find that the depth of it was beyond his expectation. While he floundered in the water, his soldiers raced toward a bridge which spanned the river. When Cole landed on the other side of the river he found himself alone. His men finally rescued him, but it was not before they had killed fifty-two Federal officers.

In February of 1864 General John Sappington Marmaduke sent a message to General Jo Shelby asking for an officer and forty of the best mounted and best armed men he had. It was but natural that Captain Younger and his men should be sent. They were well mounted and well armed, each with a pair of Navy Dragoon pistols and a Sharps rifle, much better armament than most confederate soldiers carried.

On his arrival at Warren, Arkansas, Captain Younger reported to General Marmaduke's headquarters. The general looked at the beardless boy, only twenty years old, but finally he advised Cole his intentions without commenting on his personal appearance. The General wanted to learn if General Frederick Steele at Little Rock was preparing to move against Sterling Price at Camden, and a check should be made at Pine Bluff and Little Rock while he was to return by way of the western output at Hot Springs, Arkansas.

Between Pine Bluff and Little Rock Cole and his men encountered a train of wagons, followed by an ambulance carrying several women and accompanied by mounted Federal soldiers.

Gen. Joseph Orvill Shelby

General Marmaduke

Cole and his men captured the wagons and the ambulance but released them because nothing of importance was involved in that capture. The soldiers fled toward the Pine Bluff at the sight of the Confederates.

Cole and his riders were able to scout the territory as outlined, bringing back a satisfactory report of their findings to General Marmaduke.

On May 20, 1864, Quantrill's men announced their return to Missouri by attacking the town of Lamar. A small Union garrison, entrenched in a solid brick house, refused to surrender and offered a stiff fight. The guerrillas abandoned the attack after a number of their men had been killed. At this point Bates, Jackson, and Cass Counties were made part of the Central District of Missouri, under command of General Brown. It was through that district that the guerrillas rode during May and June, usually under the command of George Todd and Bloody Bill Anderson. Supply trains were destroyed, Federal troops were ambushed and slain; even the steamboats on the Missouri River were attacked by the raiders.

It was also in May of 1864 that Captain Cole Younger, C.S.A., joined with Colonel George S. Jackson and a force of 300 men, traveling to Colorado to intercept Union wagon trains and to destroy what communication lines they could. What real effect these raids had never were seriously evaluated, even though they did put fear into the hearts of the Union authorities.

With the Battle of Westport looming on the horizon, General Price called for all available manpower to hasten to Missouri in an effort to dislodge the Union forces from that area. Colonel Jackson and Cole Younger answered this call, as did thousands of other scattered Confederate soldiers. Price told them as he moved across Saline County that Kansas City was his first goal; if successful there, Fort Leavenworth would be his second objective.

Between Price and his goal stood General Samuel B. Curtis, newly appointed commander of the Department of Kansas, which replaced General Ewing's Department of the Border. Curtis had placed his defenses from the Little Blue River, eight miles east of Independence, to the Kansas border. Heavier concentrations of Union troops had been placed between Kansas City and

Independence along the banks of the Big Blue River, while troops under General Alfred Pleasanton and General A. J. Smith picked away at the rear of Price's troops.

Cole Younger and Colonel Jackson were performing good fighting by helping to protect Price's flanks and rear, with the aid of General Marmaduke's men. On October 21, 1864, General Marmaduke's troops reached the Little Blue. Facing him was General James Blunt, who had instructions to withdraw to the defenses of the Big Blue when the pressure became too great for him to bear. After hard fighting, Price captured Independence, while Blunt fell back to the Big Blue. Heavy fighting occurred between Pleasanton and Marmaduke along the Little Blue and in Independence itself.

The Confederate troops under General Jo Shelby had out-flanked the Union troops on the south, forcing Curtis to with-draw to the strong fortifications around Kansas City and Westport, north of Brush Creek. General Jo Shelby and James Fagan's divisions camped that night west of the Big Blue.

On October 23rd, 1864, heavy fighting broke out. The Battle of Westport began at sunrise, with heavy fighting going on for hours with neither side gaining a foothold. About noon the Union troops moved south of Brush Creek, but the forces of Shelby and Fagan held their positions.

It was also on that day, near Independence, that the gallant Captain George Todd was shot and killed by members of Captain H. Wagner's Second Colorado Cavalry. It had been Captains Todd and Anderson who destroyed the forces of Major A.E.V. Johnson at the Battle of Centralia on September 27, 1864, and it had been Anderson who massacred the Union soldiers taken from the train at the Centralia depot on that same day. Anderson met his death on October 27, 1864, when he rode into a Union ambush near Orrick, Ray County, Missouri. The Union troops that day had been commanded by Captain Cox.

About two o'clock that afternoon General Pleasanton's troops routed Marmaduke's division, exposing Price's rear and right flank. The Confederates attempted to reform their lines, to no avail. The Battle of Westport was won by the Union.

Bloody Bill Anderson and Gen. Jo Shelby

Bloody Bill Anderson, dead

The guerrillas left the scene of death by the Fort Gibson Road, taking with them General Blunt's barber, whom they used for their own purposes. Near the crossing of the Arkansas River they captured twelve Indian soldiers, whom they shot and killed in cold blood after they had surrendered.

CHAPTER 12

The End of Quantrill

AFTER LEAVING KANSAS Quantrill and his own men retreated into Texas. He stopped at the camp of General D. G. Cooper six miles south of the Canadian river, from which point he sent a report of the Baxter Springs affair to General Sterling Price in Missouri. He also stated that he would submit a full report of his summer operations at a later date, however, he never did. He later went on to Colbert's Ferry on the Red River, where he crossed and established his camp at Mineral Springs, near Sheridan, Texas.

It was there that dissension arose and the disintegration of the command began. Quantrill never ruled the guerrillas again. He got into trouble with Confederate General Henry McCulloch, Commander of the Northern Sub-District of Texas at Bonham, regarding the arrest of some Federal guerrillas who were supposedly operating in Texas. Against the orders of General McCulloch Quantrill managed to kill more of the men than he arrested. That was the beginning of the end.

Quantrill had hardly left Missouri before General Jo Shelby, on orders from General Sterling Price, swept through Missouri from Arkansas with several thousand Confederate troops. They raced north through Neosho, Sarcoxie, Humansville, Warsaw, Cole Camp, and Tipton, reaching Boonville on October 11, 1863. Near Marshall, Shelby encountered Federal troops under General Egbert B. Brown. After five or six hours of heavy fighting, the Confederate forces managed to escape. The pursuit by General

Brown was so close and so intense that the Confederates had to abandon their cannon and wagons, the latter filled with loot taken during their raid.

After Shelby's cyclone raid through Missouri, the State was quiet for a long while, since Quantrill's forces had gone to Texas. General Ewing, acting upon the suggestion of General John W. Schofield, softened some of the conditions of his horrible Order No. 11. Although some people were permitted to return to the scorched areas, few were willing to do so because there was nothing left for them to protect or use.

After General Price's defeat at Westport he, with other Missouri Confederate officers, decided that because of Union feeling building up in Missouri against the Confederacy and those who fought for it, there would be no peace for returning Confederate servicemen to the state at the war's end, which the general thought was not far away.

With president Jefferson Davis' approval, General Price, accompanied by Cole Younger and his close friend Ike Settle, a former Morgan's raider officer, and several other Missouri Southern sympathizers, left for Mexico City late in 1864. It was Price's intention to enlist the aid of the Mexican Government's Emperor Maximilian in securing a Mexican land grant.

Maximilian had been emperor of Mexico only a few months, influenced by his brother, Emperor Franz Joseph of Austria. At the urging of the Mexican Conservatives, Napoleon III had given the aid of a large French army to establish a Mexican empire.

General Price outlined his plan to the Emperor and his desire to establish and organize a colony for all Confederate servicemen and others who wished to settle in Mexico. The Emperor and his government without hesitation declared the grant would be legally drawn up with the boundaries to extend from twenty-five miles south of El Paso del Norte to Chihuahua, west of the Rio Yaqui, then north.

General Price, as a military man, soon realized the smoldering unrest among loyal liberal Mexicans, under the leadership of Benito Juarez, whose headquarters were at El Paso del Norte. After a careful inspection of a portion of the land covered by the grant and its location in reference to El Paso del Norte, Price reached the unhappy and disappointing conclusion that a colony such as he and his friends wanted in that part of Mexico was not wise or expedient.

Should France be compelled to withdraw her troops, and unless the Americans could be on friendly terms with both Maximilian and Juarez by refraining from taking part on either side of their cause, the colony would have no gainful purpose. Occupying as it would land directly between the liberals in the North and the conservatives in the South, it would be a difficult situation to cope with, entailing, as it might, distrust of the Americans emanating from both factions, making neutrality impossible to maintain.

General Price discussed all this freely with the entire party, and all agreed that under prevailing circumstances they would be no better off settling in Mexico than in one of the United States or territories. There being no other location offered, and with all this in mind, General Price, with most of his party, returned to Texas to await further military orders.

Of that little known historical event Cole Younger had this to say:

"This was my first and last visit to Mexico and, to say the least, it left me highly enlightened yet with a great disappointment. We all knew General Price made the right decision.

"It was a strange country. The inhabitants were not at all friendly, especially toward the military. The Alamo and San Jacinto in 1836, the occupation of Mexico City by General Scott and the Battle of Buena Vista were still very vivid in the minds of many. They drew no distinction between the United States troops in blue, those who took part in the Mexican-United States War, and the peaceful mission of the Confederates in gray in those later years.

"I do not claim to be overly blest with sagacity, but even I could see it would be many years before conditions in Mexico would change for the betterment of the people, or its would-be investors. The colonization plan was never further negotiated. The grant was never signed. It may never have been really written."

Captain Younger's next and final service to the Confederacy was a secret assignment to travel to California to raise recruits and to take command of two vessels of the Alabama type, built in British waters. They were to be delivered to Victoria, British Columbia, for the Confederate States of America.

In company with James Kennedy, a Confederate secret service officer, and Captain Jarrette, with an escort of twenty men, Cole Younger began his trek to the Pacific coast. From El Paso they went down through Chihuahua and Sonora to Guymas, where the party split up. Captain Jarrette went to the mainland, while Kennedy and Younger, disguised as Mexican miners, boarded a ship to San Francisco. From that point they traveled by stage-coach to Puget Sound. Then they sailed for Victoria. On their arrival there they learned that General Lee had surrendered at the McLean House at Appomattox, and the great war was over at last.

In Missouri many of the guerrillas had fled to Texas when the last stages of the war began to unfold, Jesse James among them. However, Jim Younger and Frank James accompanied Quantrill and some of his men into Kentucky.

On May 10, 1865, Quantrill and his men were forced to seek shelter from a heavy storm. They rode into the barn of the Wakefield Farm, near Smiley, where they were surprised by Captain Edward Terrell of the Kentucky Union troops. Quantrill was mortally wounded and died in a Catholic hospital in Louisville, Kentucky, on June 6th.

Before he died Quantrill had earnestly requested that his men surrender. This they did, on July 26, 1865, to Captain C. Young of the United States Regulars at Samuel's Depot, Nelson County, Kentucky. Jim Younger was sent to the military prison at Alton, Illinois, but he was released in the latter part of 1865.

On June 6, 1865, at 3:45 P.M., a man was dying on a cot in the Catholic Hospital at Louisville, Kentucky. At 4:00 P.M. he gasped several times and then went limp. William Clarke Quantrill, the notorious and vicious guerrilla leader during the Civil War in Missouri, was dead.

At first taken to the Wakefield home, Quantrill was later hauled in an army wagon to the military hospital at Louisville. Shortly before his death he was taken to the Catholic Hospital, where a priest baptized him into the Roman Catholic faith. It is

Wakefield barn: Smiley, Ky. where Quantrill was captured

GUERRILLA QUANTRILL

William Quantrill, alias Captain Clarke, 4th Mo. Cav., taken here May 10, 1865 ending four months Central Kentucky guerrilla raids. Surrounded in Wakefield's barn by Captain Terrill's 30 Kentuckians. Quantrill tried escape, mortally wounded and moved to Louisville Military Prison Hospital. He died June 6th, ending career as outlaw, anti-guerrilla for Southern cause.

Guerilla Quantrill plaque

said that Quantrill gave the priest a thousand dollars in gold for that service. Another such amount, the last he had, Quantrill gave to Kate King Quantrill, his wife. She later went to St. Louis where, it is reported, she opened a flourishing bawdy house.

At the time the guerrilla chief died nobody was present except the priest, a Catholic sister, and Kate. No records indicate that Kate showed any grief. It is known that she never visited his secret grave in St. John's cemetery (now Portland Cemetery), nor did she participate in the removal of some of his bones when his boyhood school chum, W. W. Scott, and his mother, Caroline Clarke Quantrill, moved them to his home town at Dover, Ohio, for burial there.

How many bones were actually buried in that cemetery in his home town is not known. A small box was buried — no one knows exactly where at this late date. It is known for certain that W. W. Scott kept Quantrill's skull at his home for many years in the second-floor room above Scott's newspaper plant at the rear of his home at 308 South Wooster Avenue, Canal Dover. The city fathers refused to allow the remains of the bushwhacker to be buried in Dover's cemetery on East Fourth Street. Several weeks later it was agreed that they could be buried there but only in a secret grave. A few people attended the service, among them his mother and W. W. Scott.

Scott tried in vain to sell Quantrill's skull to the Kansas State Historical Society; he had already given them a shinbone of the skeleton.

After Scott's death in 1902 his son, Walter, managed to hide the skull long enough to put it to good use. It was used for years in the initiation ceremonies of the Alpha Phi Fraternity, Zeta chapter. Apparently it was used in these ceremonies until 1941, when it was purchased from the chapter by Nelson D. Macmillan and deposited in the vault of the Macmillan home until its owner, then a Trustee of the Dover Historical Society, presented it to Sam Ream, historian for the Society, where it rests today.

The full story of Kate King Quantrill has escaped researchers until now. It was a warm spring day in 1861 when she first saw Quantrill near Blue Springs, Missouri. She was only thirteen years of age and not too concerned with the livid tales of John

Kate King Quantrill

Brown's raids and those of the Kansas Jayhawkers into Missouri. She had heard the name of Quantrill now and then when her parents spoke of the Kansas outlaw, but surely it did not impress her.

As she skipped along the dusty road from the country school-house young Kate King saw a horseman riding toward her. She was impressed by his handsome features, his smooth-textured skin, his poise of confidence, and the grace of his six-foot body in the saddle. How did this same girl, at the age of seventeen, feel as she sat at the bedside of the dying guerrilla leader?

The unknown Quantrill had turned his winning smile upon the schoolgirl and she, of course, returned the courtesy. As the days passed those two met secretly at a spring not far from the modest home of her parents, Robert and Melinda King, both God-fearing people who wanted the best for their children.

When Robert King learned of secret riding trips over the countryside by his daughter with William Quantrill, he was furious. Her parents forbade her to see him again. Yet she slipped out at night to meet her lover secretly. Things were fine while Quantrill and his raiders were riding against the Federalists in Missouri, but as soon as he had to return to Jackson County he encouraged her to join him in his camp.

In 1863 she was only fifteen years old. Some writers appear anxious to throw a dash of extra romance and mystery into this story, saying that Quantrill kidnaped her. Probably her father made such a claim rather than admit publicly that his daughter had eloped. Apparently Kate and her parents never were reconciled — that is the version that has been claimed by some writers. Four or five years after the close of the Civil War she returned to her parents' home in Jackson County and even built a new home for them because their original home was burned to the ground by Federal soldiers. She kept house for her brother and her nephew in the same dwelling from 1912 to 1920.

Charles Taylor, a prominent member of the Quantrillians, later stated that his chief took Kate to a preacher six miles from their camp and officially married her. Taylor further stated that he loaned his horse to Kate for that trip. Therefore it is easy to assume that Kate King went willingly with Quantrill. Their honeymoon was spent in an abandoned log cabin, as Kate later explained.

Most of her time with Quantrill was spent in a tent near his men during the summers and in places farther south during the cold Missouri winters. Hardly anyone knew she was not a member of the band. She assumed the name of Kate Clarke as a safeguard in case she was ever captured by Federal authorities. By using Quantrill's mother's maiden name (his own middle name as well) it would have saved her embarrassment had she been questioned.

It has been said that, when Quantrill was laid up in Jackson County with a bullet wound in his face, Kate asked him, "Why did you attack the peaceful town of Lawrence?"

The claim is that he replied, "To capture and kill that damned Jayhawker, General Lane, the worst of the lot. I would have burned him at the stake if I'd have caught him, even though my men would have preferred to publicly hang him in Jackson County."

Quantrill's retreat into Texas after the Lawrence raid caused dissension in the ranks of the guerrillas, inasmuch as the others, such as George Todd and Bill Anderson, wanted to take the lead. Upon losing command Quantrill returned to Missouri a broken man. With the deaths of those two guerrillas during the raid of General Price on Westport and Kansas City, Quantrill again wanted to save the Confederacy in Missouri. He therefore returned to Jackson County and met with some of his former followers at the home of the Widow Dupree, in Lafayette County. Some of the guerrillas had gone to Texas, but others rode with Quantrill into Kentucky.

By nature Quantrill was mean and vicious, and he was also a superstitious fatalist. Even his horse seemed to have absorbed some of his mean nature, for no other man could handle that animal. It would kick, bite, and squeal if anyone beside Quantrill tended it. Several days before his death, one of the guerrillas was shoeing this animal, and it became hamstrung in its struggle. When Quantrill was told of this he recoiled as though a snake had bitten him.

Quantrill's band

"That means my work is done. Death is coming. The end is near."

The end did come shortly after that, during the fight near Smiley, Kentucky, at the Wakefield farm.

Kate King Quantrill spent many of the ensuing years in St. Louis and Jackson County, Missouri, and she married a man named Woods. In 1930 an 82-year-old woman died at the Jackson County Old Folks Home. Her name was Sarah Head at the time, for she had been married three times — to Quantrill, to Woods, and to Head. Only a few confidants knew that this was actually Kate King Quantrill, for she had kept her secret well, seemingly happy to sit and dream of days gone by. Although she was a friendly person she kept to herself for the most part. She was buried in the little cemetery at the Jackson County Old Folks Home.

CHAPTER 13

The Ordeal of
John Younger

THE DEFEATED STRAGGLED HOME. They walked, they rode gaunt
slatsided horses. They came by river boat. They stole rides on
cattle cars. They carried strange names in their heads: Spotsylva-
nia, Manassas, Shiloh, Cold Harbor, Antietam. They had left their
homes to fight against the merchants and mechanics of the
North, and they had lost.

To them the war was boredom and butchery. They were disillu-
sioned and bitter, and they were weary. They were beaten in body
and spirit, wanting the quietude of their homes. These were the
ones who had left Missouri to wear the gray.

For the guerrillas, however, it was a surprise to them that the
war was lost. They had not been up against the riders of Phil
Sheridan, had not faced the guns of Hooker or Meade, the brass
cannon of Hunt. They had been fighting the gun-shy State Enrolled Militia, and they had always been the victors. Now they put
down their arms, tired of the game, ready to go back to their
farms.

But a pestilence was upon the land. The blue-belly militia,
which had ever been ready to turn tail and run, was now the
conqueror determined to grind the "dirty rebels" under heel.
They did their best. They made it illegal for former Confederates
to own guns, thus making it impossible for them to hunt wild
game, a staple in that land. They requisitioned horses and mules
and unhitched them from the plows of former Confederates. If

the Southern sympathizers could not farm they could not meet their mortgages, and Yankee carpetbaggers were waiting to buy up land for little or nothing. Men who had kept their homes when the fighting was hot now rode out in bands to burn and kill. It was called "Reconstruction," and it was an outrage, a legal excuse for pillage and murder. It was a blot on the history of this nation. The men who had seen the big war suffered the indignation is silence. The fight was out of them. The guerrillas suffered as long as they could, and then they struck back.

More than any other, two families were the constant target for the militia in the western counties of Missouri — the Jameses and the Youngers. The boys in both families had ridden with Quantrill. They were not related, but they were friends, Frank and Jesse James, Cole and Jim Younger. The Federal militia forced these men into the same mold, hoping to goad them into violence and then hang them. But the collusion had the effect of combining nitrogen with glycerine and beating it with a sledge.

The sledge was the Drake Constitution Amendment, the most vicious implement thrust at the Southern sympathizers, former Confederate soldiers, and guerrillas.

Charles D. Drake of St. Louis was a member of the Radical Party and of the 1865 Constitutional Convention. In his zeal to have the proposed constitution ratified despite clauses that aroused objections in many quarteres, he was determined to kill the opposition among his fellow Radicals as well as among the Conservatives. Realizing that the convention's adoption of the emancipation ordinance of January 11, 1865, might split the Radicals, he clouded the issue by bolstering the desire for the Radicals to "punish" the Secessionists. With this argument he was able to persuade the convention to pass an ordinance disenfranchising any voters who could not pass the test of loyalty by signing the so-called ironclad oath. This oath was written in language that would make any Southern sympathizer who signed it liable for prosecution. One the other hand, unless a man signed this oath he was not allowed to vote, to hold public office, or even to be deacon in a church or enjoy any other privilege as a citizen. As a result, many Missourians were barred by law from holding public office, and the State was overrun with carpetbag officeholders who during the war had been bushwhackers up and down the Kansas border.

Cole Younger did not return home right away. Instead, he first visited his Uncle Thomas Younger in California. In the fall of 1865 he returned to his home in Jackson County, where his mother had moved from her shanty home in Lafayette County. A week or so later Jim followed, having been released from the Federal prison at Alton, Illinois. It was a happy reunion, with the boys willing and ready to fix up the plantation, confident that the peace of Appomattox had wiped out their war record.

When Captain Neugent and his followers from the Enrolled Missouri Militia heard that Cole and Jim Younger had returned to Missouri, they vowed to take the lives of these ex-Quantrillians. Under the guise of enforcing the Reconstruction policy these men intimidated anyone friendly to the Younger family. No doubt this persecution was instrumental in their choice of activities.

There are many black pages in the history of the border counties of Kansas and Missouri, but none are blacker than those which record the inhuman persecution of the Younger family by men who started in by being jealous of their social position and wealth and ended by fearing them because of their crimes during the war.

Because Cole Younger had hunted down and killed all but one of the men who had so wantonly murdered his father in the heat and stress of those awful days, should he be denied the right to live in quiet after peace had been declared, especially when the hands of the men who persecuted him were steeped in the blood of murdered innocents, girls, women, and children? Cole went to Lee's Summit for a time, though in constant danger of assassination. Then he went to Louisiana and remained at the home of Captain J. C. Lea, Tensas Parish, until the fall of 1867. He then returned home, hoping that the feeling against him might have died down. But it had not.

Learning of Cole's arrival, Captain R. S. Judy, who had been appointed Sheriff of Cass County, Missouri, rode out to serve a warrant on Cole for his alleged murder of the sheriff's young son during the war. It was general knowledge that Quantrill himself had killed John J. Judy at Olathe, Kansas.

Passing through Pleasant Hill toward Lee's Summit, where they terrorized the people, the sheriff and his posse then proceeded to the home of Widow Wigginton. There they induced George Wigginton, her son and a former guerrilla, to act as a decoy for Cole.

When they arrived at the Younger farm that night they broke in doors and windows and sprang inside, revolvers in hand. But they found only Mrs. Younger, very ill from consumption, and her children. Angered because Cole was not there, they ordered Mammy Suse to prepare supper for them.

The officers later took John Younger and led him to the barn, determined to make him disclose the whereabouts of his brothers. The brave lad, only fifteen years old at that time, showed no fear in the presence of this vigilante committee (as he called them). This angered the men. They got a piece of rope, put a noose around the boy's neck, and threw the end over a beam, declaring that unless he told them where his brothers were they would hang him. John refused to utter a word.

Three times the men hoisted the boy from the floor, holding him suspended until he was almost dead, then lowering and reviving him. Yet they gained no information. Furious, they raised him a fourth time and left him dangling until the rope had cut through the skin and sunk into the flesh. Limp and unconscious John lay still when they finally lowered him, and it was almost an hour before he opened his eyes. As before, the boy refused to speak.

Giving up hope of learning anything from him, the men raised him to his feet and forced him to accompany them some distance from the farm. Not until morning did the boy get back to his frenzied mother, whose death was no doubt hastened by the awful suspense of that night.

John Younger had learned to take care of himself even before that terrible ordeal. In January of 1866 he had gone to Independence to gather some supplies, when a man named Gillcress forced him into an argument concerning his brothers Cole and

John Younger

Lizzie Daniels

Jim. When Gillcress left during the heated argument, John figured the man had gone to secure a weapon, so he proceeded to his wagon to get a pistol which was under the seat.

Gillcress returned with a heavy slungshot fastened to his wrist, intent on using it on John. (A slungshot is a small heavy weight attached to a leather strap or thong and used as a weapon.) When the man again became abusive and threatened the boy with his weapon, John shot him dead. The coroner's jury agreed that the lad had acted in self-defense.

The torture of young John by the Judy group was the final wedge driven in between Cole Younger and the law. Not only that, but it brought to an end a beautiful love affair. Yes, Cole had a sweetheart, although this has never been common knowledge, nor has it been published before. Her name was Lizzie Daniels of Osceola, Missouri. Her brother Ed was to play, later, an important role in the attempted arrest of John and Jim Younger. Cole never talked to anyone about Lizzie in later years, and we are happy to be able to make this revelation at this point. In later years Lizzie married Thomas Monroe.

After the close of the war former Rebels were considered little better than dirt, and that was too much for the former guerrillas to swallow. Angry men oiled their guns which they had kept secret from the militia. The Jameses and the Youngers, with several neighbors, banded together to fight back in the only way open to them. But in the state election of 1870 the Drake oath for voters was abolished by constitutional amendment, and all citizens once again had the right to register their will at the polls.

During the summer of 1868 Cole and Jim were in Sedalia, Missouri, where they met a man named Consollas, a store proprietor in Brownington, Henry County, Missouri. While eating lunch at the Sedalia Hotel, Consollas approached them and asked if they would like to play some poker with him. They declined, but the man was insistent and Cole finally consented to play. Luck ran against Consollas.

Cole offered several times to stop the game, but Consollas said he wanted the opportunity to get some of his money back. At the end of three hours Cole had won $150 from the merchant, all the cash he had with him. In no uncertain words the poor loser claimed that Cole had cheated him.

"You know that is not true," said Cole.

"You did, damn you, you did!" cried Consollas.

"Luck was against you. I did not cheat, and you know it," replied Cole, restraining himself with difficulty. "If you lost all your ready cash in a fair game, I'll be pleased to stake you to enough to get home."

"Hell you will!" stormed the man. "You'd probably wind up cheating me out of that too."

Cole could restrain himself no longer. He stepped up to Consollas, slapped his face, and left the room.

Dropping the matter from his mind, Cole with his brother Jim continued on their way to Texas, where they had purchased a ranch with the intention of moving their whole family down there. They went by way of Lafayette County to complete the arrangements.

Many of their friends had already settled in Texas, and others were congregating near Monegaw Springs, St. Clair County. The Youngers had agreed to meet them there and accompany them part way. The route to the springs led through Brownington. Consollas chanced to see the Youngers and decided to get revenge for his loss during the poker game at Sedalia.

Consollas rode to his neighbors, telling them that a dapple gray horse had been stolen from his pasture and he thought the thieves were headed for Monegaw Springs. Of course horse thieves were most unpopular, so Consollas had no trouble in rounding up about fifteen men to pursue the Youngers. Cole and Jim had reached the springs before Consollas and his followers arrived.

"There's the two that stole my horse," Consollas cried, pointing a finger at the Youngers.

"That is ridiculous," said one of Cole's friends. "Pick out your horse."

"I don't see him. They have probably already sold him," lamented the merchant who had not expected anyone to speak in favor of the Youngers, not knowing they would be meeting friends in this area.

They failed to find the gray he was talking about, and many people there assured him that Cole and Jim were not horse thieves. Therefore the posse rode off. On their return to Brownington members of the posse found a dapple gray in Consollas' pasture. So incensed were they at the trick played upon them that they gave Consollas a thorough thrashing.

In the fall of 1868 Cole, Jim and Bob Younger went to Texas. Their mother's health had failed rapidly, partially as a result of her exposure at the time the militia forced her to burn her home. It was her sons' intention to move to a milder climate for her sake. Some time was spent there gathering and driving cattle, while one of Cole's sisters joined them to keep house for them near Scyene, Dallas County.

To the persecuted Younger brothers in June of 1870 there came a blow that cut the last tie to their desire to live decent lives.

Just as their mother was preparing to join them on the Texas ranch she died of consumption (called tuberculosis today) at the home of her cousin-in-law, Lycurgus A. Jonas. All of her sons were away at the time, but they hastened home, and on their return to Texas they took Mammy Suse and their only unmarried sister back with them.

In January of the following year John Younger was clerking in a store at Dallas, Texas. One night John and one of his friends were in a saloon, drinking and amusing themselves with a halfwitted fellow named Jim Russell who was the butt of many a drunken jest. John told him to stand still and he would show him how close he could come to shooting off his nose without hitting it. In terror the man protested, but John drew his revolver and fired several shots, each bullet missing the man's nose.

Immediately the loungers surrounded Jim Russell, telling them that John Younger had been trying to kill him and urged him to swear out a warrant for John's arrest.

John Younger had retired to his hotel, and there Sheriff C. W. Nichols, a former Confederate soldier and friend of the

Youngers, found him. Thomas McDaniels, a friend of John's was also present when the sheriff entered the hotel room accompanied by John McMahan. In an argument which followed a brother of Jim Russell walked in and shot John in the arm with a load of buckshot. McDaniels then shot the sheriff, and John had his wound treated. He and McDaniels then proceeded to the home of another friend on the Chalk Level Road in St. Clair County, Missouri, where they remained until June. John then when to California to visit his uncle Thomas C. Younger, who operated a general store there. Later he boarded a train for Missouri. About 200 miles west of Denver two detectives boarded the train, apparently in search of some wanted man.

John was occupying a seat with some other man, and the officers took a seat nearby. After gazing at Younger and his companion, one of the detectives drew a revolver, pointed it at them and demanded their surrender. Thinking they were after him, John whipped out his pistol, shot one of the officers, and then leaped from the window of the moving car. It was afterward learned that the officers were after the man who occupied the seat beside John.

John Younger was lost among the lofty peaks of the Rocky Mountains. As best he could he laid his course for Denver and finally arrived in that city, exhausted and footsore, at the home of a friend on Green River, seventy-five miles from Denver. Later he paid the friend $75 to drive him to a town nearby where he obtained passage on a wagon train headed for Kansas. From that point he made his way to the home of his uncle, Dr. L. W. Twyman, at Blue Mills, in Jackson County, Missouri.

Poor John. He returned to Missouri in time to be suspected of complicity in the train robbery at Gad's Hill, near Piedmont, Missouri, on January 31, 1874.

Of course he had not heard of that event. It was part of the carnival of crime in which Jesse James, his brother Frank, and the Youngers were supposed to have been involved.

Learning that Jim and John Younger were in St. Clair County at the time of the Gads Hill train robbery, the Pinkerton Detective Agency in Chicago dispatched two men to that part of Missouri to trace the movements of those boys.

One of the detectives was Captain Louis J. Lull, using the alias of W. J. Allen. The other man was James Wright, also considered a topnotch detective on the Pinkerton force. For some time Wright had been in Osceola, Missouri, and the surrounding country, ostensibly to purchase cattle, and in this research he became acquainted with Edwin B. Daniels, a brother of Lizzie Daniels, Cole's sweetheart.

Daniels had often acted as a deputy sheriff of St. Clair County. Gaining his confidence, Wright disclosed the nature of his real business and hoped that, by offering a good-sized share of the reward he could secure Daniels' promise to help catch the outlaws. It is not known what Daniels' feeling toward Cole Younger was or if he knew that his sister was in love with that young ex-guerrilla. On the other hand, he may have wanted a means to dispose of the Youngers and thus cut off this romance.

On the morning on March 16, 1874, the two men left Osceola, announcing that they were going to Roscoe twelve miles away, to inspect some cattle. Ed Daniels knew all the back roads and wooded areas up and down the Osage River. He could be a good guide in a quest to capture or kill the Youngers.

Along the road Captain Lull, calling himself Allen, joined them, and they proceeded to Roscoe where the three men passed the rest of the day and night. The next morning they started for the house of Theodrick Snuffer, a friend of the Younger family and the man who had induced their grandfather, Charles Lee Younger, to move from Jackson County to St. Clair County and to purchase a large tract of land near Osceola. The officers suspected they might find several of the Younger brothers, as it was known that they often stopped there when traveling through St. Clair County at Chalk Level.

On the way Wright called at the house of a former resident of Maryland, also his own home state, a man named L. H. Brown. Daniels and Allen continued on their way and rode by Snuffer's farm, carefully scrutinizing the house and grounds for any sign of their quarry. Seeing none, they doubled back on their tracks, determined to interview Snuffer.

Riding up to the front gate they hailed the old man and, after passing the time of day, asked the way to the home of the widow

Home of John and Hanna McFerrin

Sims. At the time, Jim and John Younger were in that house eating their dinner. As they caught sight of the two callers their suspicions were aroused, for they saw that they were strangers and, without disclosing their purpose, the two brothers watched the detectives closely.

When they noticed that the strangers did not follow the directions to the home of Colonel Sims, their suspicions seemed confirmed, and the brothers decided to follow them and learn what they were up to. Mounting their horses, the two Youngers, armed with shotguns and pistols, took a short cut which brought them out on the Chalk Level Road, about half a mile from the house.

Just around a turn in the road they came upon three men who apparently had just left the cabin of a Negro named John McFerren and his wife Hannah. Jim and John Younger had attended a dance on Tuesday, March 16, 1874, and had spent the night at the McFerren cabin. These Negroes were good friends of the Younger family. The McFerren son, John, and a daughter named Missouri, shared the two-story log cabin with their parents. That couple's married children lived in the area, and one of them had married a man named George "Speed" McDonald. Speed often served as look-out for the Youngers when they were hiding out in a cave overlooking the Osage River near Monegaw Springs. From the highest point of the bluff Speed could look for miles in all directions. This spot was named Younger Lookout and retains that name to this day.

Bidding the strangers the time of day, Jim and John reined in their horses. Across John's saddle rested his shotgun. Suddenly Allen (real name Lull), who had been watching for his opportunity, drew his revolver and shot John in the throat, severing his jugular vein.

Incredible as it may seem, while the life blood was spurting from his neck, John raised his gun, took careful aim, and discharged both barrels into Allen's chest and left arm. He then dropped the gun, drew his revolver and, following the two men who had rushed their horses into the woods, shot Daniels dead and continued to fire until he toppled from his saddle, apparently dead.

Almost at the same moment that Allen had fired at John, Daniels had fired at Jim. To escape being hit, Jim threw himself to the right side of his horse so quickly that he lost his stirrup and fell to the ground while the animal bolted and ran away.

At the first sign of the Youngers, Wright had turned and fled, while Jim sent a bullet in his direction, doing no more damage than to dislodge the man's hat. John, after shooting Daniels and Allen (really Lull), grabbed his saddle horn with both hands, trying to make it back to where the fight had begun. He reeled, after giving one last long look at his brother Jim, and fell dead into a hog pen directly across from the McFerren house.

When Jim reached his brother he saw that he was dead. He called to Speed to inform Snuffer what had happened and to take care of John's body. Jim then caught John's horse and rode west to the Chalk Level Road to see if he could find Detective Wright — to no avail. He then returned to the Snuffer home. Later he started out for Arkansas, where he would eventually meet up with Cole and Bob.

After notifying the Snuffer family of the tragedy Speed Mc-Donald raced back to stand guard over John's body, lest some of the hogs molest it. Another neighbor, "Ol" Davis, told his father when he heard the shooting. John Davis ran the short distance until he came upon the body of Ed Daniels. Blood was running from his nose and mouth. He was dead. John Younger lay about a hundred feet away, but it was easy to see that he too was dead. Walking down the road a short way Davis saw Allen (Captain Lull) who had crawled across the road and had managed to pull himself up to a sitting position against a tree.

Davis carried Captain Lull to the porch at Aunt Hannah McFerren's cabin, where his wounds were seared, and he was then carried into the room where John Younger's body lay. Later that evening the wounded man was taken to the Roscoe House, a hotel located on Main Street in Roscoe.

Detective Wright had ridden eastward to Osceola to report to Sheriff Johnson that Daniels and Lull had been caught by two men whom he believed to be the Youngers. He did not know if they were alive or dead. A posse was formed by some of Daniels' friends, while Cole's sweetheart, Lizzie, wept bitter tears in the

*Stone marker commemorating battle
between John Younger and detectives*

darkness of her room over the death of her brother and over the peril which Cole must face. The posse quickly reported to Sheriff Johnson that Daniels was dead, Captain Lull was at the Roscoe House badly wounded, and also that John Younger was dead.

A young man named David Crowder was asked to guard John's body, to prevent any of Daniels' friends from snatching it and hanging it up for everyone to see. Arming himself with a shotgun young Crowder entered the McFerren cabin and sat near the body. He placed his shotgun across his knees and settled in for the night.

The next morning John Younger was buried in a shallow grave under a large cedar tree near the Snuffer home. That evening it was decided to bury the body permanently in the old Yeater cemetery, a few miles southeast of the south side of the Chalk Level to Osceola Road. That night Speed McDonald and Snuffer loaded the body onto a wagon. The grave was dug at an angle and John was buried with his head to the northwest and his feet to the southeast. Today the grave remains the same, unmolested for over a hundred years.

On March 18th, the day following the battle, the coroner's jury rendered the following decision:

We, the jury, find that John Younger came to his death by a pistol shot, supposed to be in the hands of W.J. Allen (Captain Lull). We, the jury, also find that Edwin B. Daniels came to his death by a pistol shot, supposed to have been fired by the hand of James Younger.

> Signed: A. Ray, Foreman
> John Davis
> G. W. Cox
> W. Holmes
> R. C. Gill
> H. Greason

Captain Lull's condition made a turn for the worse. His wife, Marian Lull, and William Pinkerton came from Chicago to be with him at the last. Drs. A. C. Marquis and L. Lewis decided to

Roscoe House where Captain Lull supposedly died

call Dr. D. C. McNeill in on the case. McNeill was a veteran of the Civil War and the Mexican War. Apparently Lull's life could not be saved, for on March 23rd it was reported that he had died and that his body had been taken to Chicago for a Masonic Rites burial.

Some people claimed that Captain Lull did not die as stated. They said the report was a trick to throw off possible retaliation by friends of the Youngers. In any event, Charles F. Nesbit, whose father, Frank Nesbit, was a close friend of Dr. McNeill, stated that such was the case when he wrote the Nesbit family history in 1932.

One evening while I was at home playing, my father opened the door in response to a knock, and I saw Dr. McNeill with his long white beard. He was the big doctor of that section. He had been a surgeon in the Confederate Army and went all through the war. I knew of no one sick and could not understand his coming. He sat down and began to talk to my father. "Frank, what will happen to me if I say a man is dead who isn't?"

"Well," said my father, a lawyer, "doctors often make mistakes, but I didn't know they made them as bad as that."

"I am serious about this," said Dr. McNeill. "It is no laughing matter."

My father asked me to leave the room. I did go out of the room but I was very careful to leave a crack in the door and put my ear to it. The doctor then explained the situation. "You know that Pinkerton detective who was shot when John Younger was killed? Well, he is going to get well. But the Youngers and their friends have indicated that he will never leave the county alive. It is twenty-five miles to the nearest railroad, and I do not think he will ever get to it if he starts. Now, the Pinkerton Agency at Chicago has sent a detective down here, and they want me to say he is dead and ship him out in a coffin. It is the only way we will ever get him out, but I don't know what to do."

The doctor was an honest man, but he kept remembering his promise to save lives. This, no doubt, is the reason he considered such a move.

"Well," my father answered, "I don't think it will hurt. Doctors often make mistakes, and if you can stand making a mistake like saying a man is dead when he isn't, I don't see that anybody can do anything about it."

The next week the paper stated that the detective was low and much worse and that Dr. McNeill did not think he would get well. A few days later a notice appeared that he had died. He was put in a coffin and carried in a farm wagon to Clinton, Missouri. The casket was put in the baggage car and after the train started the Pinkerton detective got out and got away to Chicago.

It might also be noted that in later years Cora Lee McNeill, daughter of Dr. McNeill, authorized a book entitled *Mizzoura* in which she leaves no doubt that the Pinkerton detective did not die at that time. Besides, Cora Lee McNeill was Jim Younger's only true love. It was she who worked so long and diligently on behalf of Cole and Jim Younger after they had entered the Minnesota State Prison. More on this follows later in this work. Jim had even suggested the spelling *Mizzoura,* perhaps to carry the "izz" of Lizzie McDaniels, the only love of his brother Cole.

The above account of John Younger's death was given by Jim Younger to Mr. Snuffer a few moments after the meeting and was repeated to an intimate friend in the evening, just before Jim left Missouri. No doubt that "intimate friend" was Cora Lee McNeill.

However, in many particulars it differs from the story told by Captain Lull as he lay wounded and from the accounts which were given by witnesses before the coroner's jury. These are given at this point:

W. J. Allen, being duly sworn, testified as follows; this same text was published in the *Osceola Democrat* March 20, 1874, and it substantiates the authors' findings in the death of John Younger.

Yesterday, about half-past two o'clock, the 17th day of March, 1874, E. B. Daniels and myself were riding along the road from Roscoe to Chalk Level, which road runs past the house of one Theodrick Snuffer, and about three miles from the town of Roscoe, in St. Clair County, Missouri. Daniels and myself were riding side by side, and Wright a short distance ahead of us. Some noise attracted our attention, and we looked back and saw two men on horseback coming toward us. One was armed with a double-barreled shotgun, the other with revolvers. I don't know if the other had a shotgun or not. The one with the shotgun had it cocked, both barrels, and he ordered us to halt. Wright drew his pistol and put spurs to his horse and rode off; they ordered him to halt, and shot at him and shot off his hat; but he kept on riding. Daniels and myself stopped, standing across the road seated on our horses. They rode up to us and ordered us to take off our pistols and drop them in the road; the one with the shotgun covering me all the time with the gun. We dropped our pistols to the ground, and one of the men told the other to follow Wright and bring him back, but he refused to go, saying that he would stay with him. One of the men picked up the revolvers we had dropped, and looked at them, remarked they were "damn fine pistols," and that they must be made a present of them. One of the men asked me where I came from, and I said, "From Osceola." He then wanted to know what we were doing in this part of the country. I replied, "Rambling around." One of them said, "You were here yesterday," and I replied that we had been at the Springs, but had not been inquiring for them, that we did not know them; and they said detectives had been up here hunting for them all the time, and they were going to stop it.

Daniels then said, "I am no detective; I can show you who I am and where I belong." And one of them said, "What in hell are you riding around here with all them pistols for?" I said, "Good God! Isn't every man wearing them when traveling? And haven't we as much right to wear them as anyone else?" And the one who had the shotgun said, "Hold on, young man. We don't want any of that," and he lowered the cocked shotgun in a threatening manner. Then Daniels had some talk with him. One of them got off his horse and picked up the pistols; two of them were mine and one was Daniels'. The one on his horse had the gun drawn on me, and I concluded they intended to kill us. I reached my hand

behind me and drew a Number 2 Smith & Wesson pistol, cocked
it and fired at the one on horseback. My horse frightened at the
report of the pistol and turned to run. I heard two shots and my
left arm fell, and I had no control over my horse, and he jumped
in the brush and a small tree struck me and knocked me out of
the saddle. I got up and staggered across the road and lay down
until I was found. No one else was present.

Subscribed and sworn to, before me, this 18th day of March,
1874. James St. Clair. Justice-of-the-Peace.

W. J. Allen

It is most doubtful if Jim and John Younger would have
harmed the two men. Their main objective was to disarm them
just as they had disarmed Marshall Cobb of Appleton City some
time before at Monegaw Springs, and had forced the posse
members to have breakfast coffee with them at the old Monegaw
Hotel. Cole was present at that time and had said to Cobb, "That's
about it, you men. You can go home and tell your folks what devils
the Youngers are, and bear in mind this lesson we have taught
you. We Youngers forgive you and your murderous intentions.
Don't go around believing all you hear about us, for if half of it
were true you'd all be corpses now."

The following additional evidence was taken at the coroner's
inquest:

I heard a shot a couple of hundred yards from my house, and I
found out after the first shot that it was John and James Younger;
after the first shot they ceased firing for some time, and then
commenced again, but I had not seen any of the parties; but after
several shots had been fired, another man, who I did not know,
came down the road, and I think they were both shooting at one
another; I am certain that John Younger was shooting at the
other man; he continued to run down the road east of here; I
think Younger passed the man on the gray horse; about the time
John Younger passed him I saw him sink on his horse, as if going
to fall; don't know what became of him afterwards; then Younger
turned to come west and began to sink, and then fell off his

horse; then James Younger come down by here on foot, to where John Younger was lying, and the horse that John Younger was riding, and that was the last I saw of James Younger.

John McFerren

Subscribed and sworn to before me, this 18th day of March, 1874.

James St. Clair, J.P.

The testimony of John R. McFerren, a son, was corroborative of that of John McFerren, both of whom were present.
Other interesting testimony followed:

Two men came to my house and inquired the way to Mrs. Sims; the third man came along afterwards and overtook them; the two Youngers, John and James, after they had passed, followed them; I saw James Younger after the fight; he told me that John Younger was dead; that they had killed one of the men and that one other had been wounded, Allen; that Allen had a pistol secreted and fired the first shot.

Theodrick Snuffer

Subscribed and sworn to before me, this 18th day of March, 1874.

James St. Clair, J.P.

John Younger fell from his horse; James Younger came running up to where John had fallen and called me to him; he then turned him (John Younger) over and took some revolvers off of him and a watch and something else out of his pockets; I do not know what else; I saw John Younger and another man shooting at each other, when the firing first commenced; I think James Younger took four revolvers off of John Younger, his brother; he threw one over the fence and told me to keep it; he then told me to catch a horse and go down and tell Snuffer's folks.

G. W. McDonald

Sworn to and subscribed before me, this 18th day of March, 1874.

James St. Clair, J.P.

All we know concerning the death of the two men, being the same that the inquest is being held over, is that the one, John Younger, came to his death from the effects of a gunshot wound, which entered the right side of his neck, touching the clavical bone, and the upper side, and about two inches from the meridian, went nearly through the neck; the orifice is small, indicating that he was shot with a small ball. The other man, Edwin B. Daniels, came to his death from the effects of a gunshot wound, which entered the left side of the neck about one inch from the meridian line, and about midway of the neck, opposite the aesophagus, and as per examination, went nearly straight through the neck, striking the bone; the orifice was pretty large, indicating that the ball was of a pretty large size.

A. C. Marquis, M.D.
L. Lewis, M.D.

Subscribed and sworn to before me, this 18th day of March, 1874.

James St. Clair, J.P.

CHAPTER 14

A Carnival of Crime

ON FEBRUARY 13, 1866, AT 8:55 A.M., the Clay County Savings Association Bank at Liberty, Missouri, was robbed of over $50,000 by a daring band of men. This first great bank robbery was not effected in the same dashing manner as were others to follow, but many people expressed their belief that the Jameses and at least one of the Youngers, probably Cole, were guilty. Some citizens said they saw a sickly, gaunt rider in the group who rode out of town shooting in every direction. Could this have been Jesse James, still suffering from the effects of the 1865 lung wound he had received near the close of the war?

Various people suggested others as planners and executors of the daring robbery: "Ol" Shepherd, Bud Pence, Jim White, J.F. Edmundson, Bill Chiles, Arch Clements, and Dick Burns — all ex-guerrillas.

Whoever the outlaws were, they did not harm Greenup Bird or his son William, but a young man named George Wymore was killed as he walked to school. In all probability that shooting was an accident. Henry W. Haynes, on the way to William Jewell College with young Wymore, reported that he and Wymore had heard Mr. Bird yell that the bank was being robbed, calling to Wymore to give the alarm. As he did so the bandits began firing in savage fury. Haynes said that he himself quickly took shelter behind a tree, but the Wymore lad, not so fortunate, was struck by four bullets and killed.

167

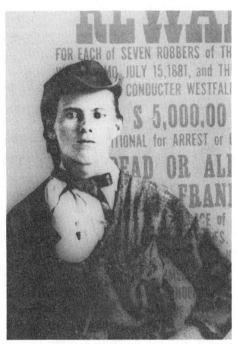

Jesse James during Civil War

James Homestead at Kearney, Mo.

The old bank building still stands, and several years ago it was dedicated as the site of a museum. At that opening were Allen Case and Chris Jones of the late TV show, "The Legend of Jesse James." This museum is still operating and is run by Jack Wymore. Tourists are invited to walk into the bank vault from which the money was taken during that first bank robbery.

Other robberies and holdups were reported on subsequent dates. Around one o'clock on October 30, 1866, the Mitchell Bank at Lexington, Missouri, was robbed of $2,011. No one was in the bank at the time except J.L. Thomas, the clerk. After the bandits had located the $2,000 in paper money and $11.50 in silver, they held guns to the head of Mr. Thomas, demanding the $100,000 they said must be in the bank. Thomas denied there was any such amount there, but he was searched for the vault key which he did not have. As they left they warned Thomas not to give the alarm under pain of death.

Soon a posse, which included Jesse Hamlet, David and John Pool, James Cather, and Hedge Reynolds, started after the bandits and spent two days in a fruitless search.

The Youngers were loud in their assertion that they had nothing to do with the robberies. Nevertheless, they were friends of the Jameses, or were supposed to be, and their names were linked with those of Frank and Jesse as accomplices in these and various crimes to follow.

One March 2, 1867, the private bank of Judge William McLain at Savannah, Missouri, was raided. It was high noon, and no one was in the bank except Judge McLain and his son. As the bandits rode up four of them dismounted, leaving their horses in charge of two others. As the four entered the bank with drawn pistols, the Judge looked earnestly over his spectacles, and he drew a heavy revolver from a desk drawer and began firing. His shots missed, however, and one of the bandits gunned him down. That robbery was a failure, and Judge McLain lived to die a natural death after the amputation of one of his arms due to the bullet wound. He was the local hero for a long time.

The Hughes and Wasson Bank at Richmond, Missouri, was open for business as usual on May 23, 1867, when a band of armed men entered and helped themselves to $4,000 in gold coins.

Mayor Shaw tried to intercept these raiders. He seized a re-volver and ran across the street, at the same time trying to arouse the citizenry. Three of the bandits rode him down and fired four bullets into his body. They then dashed toward the jail, appar-ently intent on releasing the prisoners. They failed, but in the attempt they killed both the jailer, B.G. Griffin, and his son Frank.

Early in March of 1868 a group of well-mounted horsemen entered the quiet little town of Russellville, Kentucky. Frank James later stated that this body of men consisted of himself and Jesse James, Cole Younger, Jim White, George and Oliver Shep-herd, John Jarrette, and Jim Younger. However, members of the Shepherd family said Oliver had been in Missouri at that time.

These strangers spent an entire week in that town buying up all the fast horses and guns in that small village of 2400 people and, evidently, studying the situation there. They claimed to be horse and cattle buyers but never did explain why they bought so many guns. On the first day of spring the citizens found out.

Nimrod Long, president of the Southern Deposit Bank, was at home eating when he heard the excited cry, "They are robbing the bank!" He dashed into the street and entered the bank at the side door. Jesse James met him in the hallway and fired, grazing his head in two places. The robbers escaped with $14,000, drop-ping a $100 bill during their getaway. This was picked up by Mrs. Grubbs and returned to Mr. Long. The robbers galloped out of Russellville along the Franklin Road, not knowing they had missed $50,000 in the bank vault.

That old bank building still stands, for a long time being used as a county library. A new building but a block away houses the present bank with the same name, Southern Deposit. Painted across an entire wall of the new bank is a mural depicting the raid by those Missouri bandits.

Jesse and his men were accustomed to outdistancing posses. But the Russellville banker had engaged the services of a Louis-ville detective named D.T. Bligh. "Yankee Bligh," as he was called, got closer to Jesse than any other lawman had ever done — so close that Jesse left Missouri for New York, boarded an ocean

Jesse James, age twenty-four

Fletch Taylor, Frank James, and Jesse James

Jesse James on "Stonewall"

liner and went to Panama. From there he crossed the Isthmus and went to Paso Robles, California, where he stayed for awhile with his uncle Drury Woodson James. The Youngers also managed to visit their Uncle Coleman in California when things got too hot for them in Missouri.

At noon on December 7, 1869, Cole Younger and Jesse James stepped up to the teller's cage of the Davies County Bank at Gallatin, Missouri.

"Got change for this $100 bill?" Cole asked.

"Yes — just a minute."

Before he could count out the change the teller was looking down the barrel of a heavy Navy Dragoon revolver. Jessie eyed the teller, then muttered something to Cole. Suddenly he shot the teller.

At that time a young boy named James McDowell saw what was going on and ran down the street, yelling that Captain Sheets had been killed. John Lewis, a seventeen-year-old brother-in-law of Captain John W. Sheets, veteran of the Union Army, ran into the bank and saw a man pulling Sheets' body from under the counter. This man then ran from the bank and tried to mount his horse. The animal became frightened and threw its rider to the ground, his left foot still in the stirrup. By the time anyone could arrive at the scene to interfere, another bandit rescued his partner from the ground while his horse went racing off.

"Jump up behind me!" yelled the mounted bandit.

Limping slightly, evidently because of an injured ankle, the fallen robber managed to leap onto the horse behind his comrade.

"Why all the shooting in the bank?" asked the rescuer.

"Oh, I just killed S.P. Cox, the fellow who killed Bloody Bill Anderson in the war," was the cool reply.

This was Jesse, all right, but he had made a mistake about the identity of that day's victim.

One June 3, 1871, the Corydon County treasurer's office at Corydon, Iowa, was visited by a group of armed men intent on relieving that county of its tax collection. The frightened clerk was unable to open the timelock safe. When he finally convinced the outlaws that he was telling the truth they walked down the street and robbed the Ocobock Brothers Bank of $46,000. The rumor was that this robbery caused the bank to close permanently.

Late in April of 1872, five strangers rode into Columbia, Kentucky. They said they were stockmen who wanted to acquaint themselves with cattle in the area. In reality they were getting the lay of the land for a quick getaway. On April 29th these same five men stopped in front of the Kentucky Deposit Bank. Three of them dismounted and entered the building. The other two, still mounted, drew heavy Colt's revolvers and began shooting and yelling at everyone to mind his own business. The surprised citizens ducked for cover.

Inside the bank R. A. C., Martin, the cashier, made a foolish move. He reached for a gun and it was his last act. A heavy slug tore through his head, and he dropped dead to the floor. With less than $14,000 in the faithful grain sack, the outlaws made their getaway. Some jewelry scooped up from the vault added to the loot.

A posse was formed, with Captain J. R. Hindman, later a lieutenant governor, in charge. However, the bandits had made a clean getaway. Mr. Alexander, president of the bank, offered a reward of $2500 for the arrest of the robbers, but the reward went unclaimed. Various descriptions identified the five strangers as Frank and Jesse James, and Cole, Jim, and Bob Younger.

Not to be outdone by the fanfare and excitement offered by the Kansas City Fair held during September of 1872, Jesse and Frank James staged a little show of their own. Some reports include Cole Younger also. On the 26th they dashed up to the main gate and demanded the cash while the Zeller band of Lexington played martial music. Nearly 20,000 people were attending the fair, and many of them saw the outlaws but thought it was nothing more than an added attration. It was just that, only not rehearsed. It cost the Fair Committee over $10,000. With the cash in the proverbial grain sack, the bandits disappeared as quickly as they had arrived.

Many people claimed that a whole gang of men had raided the fair grounds that day, but it was only Jesse and Frank. In later years Frank told the whole story to Colonel Venable. He even told how Jesse had been wearing the tight-fitting black suit he had taken from a school teacher when they robbed the stage-coach at Lexington, Missouri.

The winter of 1872-73 had been a severe one, and when the month of May rolled around the bandits who had been waiting for Jim Younger and Frank James to return from California became restless. Jesse James, Bob Younger, Clell Miller, Bill Chadwell (alias Bill Stiles), and Cole Younger decided to rob the bank at Ste. Genevieve, Missouri in the meantime. On May 1, 1873, the five outlaws left their hiding place in Jackson County and stopped at a country place a few miles south of Springfield. From there they went to Bismarck on the Iron Mountain Road, and the following day they rode through Ste. Genevieve County. On the morning of May 27, shortly after nine o'clock, they appeared again, three entering from the south and two from the north.

When three of them entered the Ste. Genevieve Savings Association building, only a cashier, O.D. Harris, and a son of State Senator Firman A. Rozier were inside. The robbers leveled their pistols and ordered one of them to open the safe. Rozier began to speak but was cut short.

The bandits were unhappily surprised, for the loot they had intended to carry off was already in a St. Louis bank. They had to be satisfied with about $4,000 in silver, all the money in the bank. A posse followed the trail of those bandits yet, as in many other cases, were induced to return home after the outlaws had fired a few volleys in their direction.

The first train robbery west of the Mississippi River was credited to the James-Younger band. Around 8:30 P.M. on July 21, 1873, the robbers pried loose a rail on a curve of the Chicago, Rock Island, & Pacific track just about a mile from the whistle stop of Adair, Iowa. When the engine hit the loose rail it toppled over on its side, and the cars came to a stop upright. John Rafferty, the engineer, was trapped in the engine and scalded to death. Dennis Foley, the fireman, was seriously burned in the wreckage of the locomotive.

The outlaws rifled the express car, no doubt expecting to find the $100,000 in gold they believed aboard because of secret

*Plaque erected at site of
Adair, Iowa train robbery*

Type of train robbed at Adair by James-Younger Gang

information they had received. However, they had stopped the wrong train, for the limited was to come by that same spot several hours later. Angry and disappointed, the bandits sauntered through the train, relieving the passengers of money, jewelry, and other valuables. When Conductor William A. Smith tried to interfere they chased him back into another car. Their loot, combined with money taken from the express car, amounted to around $26,000.

Elmer Johnson of Greenfield, Iowa, still owns one of the rings which the bandits discarded in an unfarmed area in the Nodaway River bottom. His father, John Johnson, had found a number of cheap rings in that area.

On January 15, 1874, bandits popularly supposed to be the James-Younger gang, waylaid a stagecoach between Malvern, Arkansas, and the fashionable Hot Springs. The robbers relieved the passengers of their money and other valuables to the amount of $4,000. So commonplace were such events that this stage robbery didn't even make the front pages of newspapers.

The year 1874 was a busy one for the bandits. The stagecoach plying between Austin and San Antonio was robbed on April 7th, 1874. One December 8th the train at Muncie, Kansas, was robbed of a fortune in gold dust. Very little or nothing was published concerning the robbery of the Tishomingo Savings Bank at Corinth, Mississippi which occured the day before the action at Muncie.

Another train robbery was planned for Wayne County, Missouri, near Gads Hill on the Iron Mountain Road at three-thirty in the afternoon of January 31, 1875. Seven men took charge of the railroad station at Gads Hill, placed the station master under guard, and set the semaphore signal at "Stop." At six o'clock the train came to a stop at the platform. Conductor Alford stepped off one of the cars and was immediately made to surrender. Several of the outlaws were posted to guard the train crew, while the others robbed the express car and the passengers of around $12,000.

On September 6, 1875, four well armed and well mounted men, dressed in long linen dusters, rode into Huntington, West Virginia, and stopped before the bank building. While two remained mounted, firing into the air and yelling to everyone to keep indoors, Frank James and Tom McDaniels entered the bank and ordered the lone occupant, Cashier Robert T. Oney, to open the safe or be killed on the spot. The two outlaws in the street were Cole Younger and Tom Webb. They all escaped with more than $20,000.

The pursuit by the enraged citizens, led by the sheriff, was a diligent one. Never before had the outlaws been so hard-pressed. Ten days later they were in southeastern Kentucky, near the Dillon home in Rockcastle County. By that time the exciting news had been spread far and wide, and the Dillon boys were on the alert when they saw four heavily armed strangers in the woods near their home.

The Dillons called on them to surrender, and their reply was a volley of shots. The Dillons returned the fire but did not know the results of the fight until the next morning. In the woods they found a mortally wounded man who said his name was Tom McDaniels. He was taken to the Dillon home and a doctor was called, but it was too late to save him.

After the stranger's death a photograph was found on his person, and Mr. Oney positively identified McDaniels as one of the Huntington bank robbers.

Tom Webb (alias Jack Keen) was later captured in Fentress County, Tennessee, and he was taken back to Huntington, where he admitted his part in the robbery. At his trial he was found guilty and sentenced to twelve years in the West Virginia State Penitentiary at Moundsville. He was received at the prison on December 8th, 1875 as Prisoner #457. Later the prison officials could find no record of his release, and some said he had died in prison. However, much later, through the efforts of the Research Committee of the Wheeling Area Historical Society and the work of Colonel Tom Foulk, Jr., James C. Dunklin, and Mr. Pyles, this record was found. The 1880 Census records showed Webb working in the wagon shop of the prison. Later it was learned that on February 8, 1885, West Virginia Governor Beeson Jackson wrote a pardon for Thomas J. Webb, releasing him so that he could return to his home in Pike County, Illinois.

Almost a year after the fantastic holdup of the Huntington Bank, the news in the local papers covered the Custer battle in far off Montana Territory. On the morning of July 8, 1876, the wires buzzed with news that stirred the nation into excited conversation. Word had come to Liberty, Missouri, that another train had been robbed by the James-Younger gang. The Missouri-Pacific Railroad train had left Kansas City at 4:45 P.M., as usual, with several coaches, two of the new Pullman sleeping cars, and a combination express and baggage car. At Sedalia it took on an M. K. & T. express car, locked and without any express messenger aboard. John D. Bushnell, in charge of two safes, occupied the Missouri-Pacific baggage car. Bushnell was a United States express messenger, in charge of the express company's only safe. The other safe belonged to the Adams Express Company. Also in the baggage car was the railroad's baggage master, Louis Peter Conklin of St. Louis.

Prior to the holdup the bandits, Frank and Jesse James, Cole and Bob Younger, Clell Miller, Charlie Pitts, Bill Chadwell, and Hobbs Kerry, had taken command of the watchman at the bridge over the Lamine River at Rocky Cut, near Otterville, Missouri. That old gentleman, a Swiss immigrant named Henry Chateau, was blindfolded and placed on the track. He was ordered to swing his red lantern for the train to stop. All but two of the gang went down to the tracks, leaving Miller and Kerry with the horses. One of the bandits said to the watchman, "Now you have three choices, old man: being run over, stopping the train, or stopping a bullet."

As the express steamed into Rocky Cut at ten or eleven o'clock on the night of July 7th, a red light swung frantically across the track. Chateau, to whom it was a matter of life or death, was doing his best to stop the train. Knowing that he was approaching the bridge, where signals were expected and having no reason to be suspicious, the engineer applied the brakes and brought his train to a halt.

The moment he did so the robbers piled up an obstruction behind the train so that it could not be backed away. It has been said that the robbers sent a man back to the bridge to halt an oncoming freight train, but no record can be found of this or of any freight train expected at that point at the time.

Pete Conklin, the baggage master, having nothing to do until the train reached the next station, had been sitting peacefully in a chair by the open side door of the baggage car, trying to cool off and watching the scenery flow past on that hot moonlit night. As the train slowed down his peaceful meditations were rudely interrupted. There was a shot. The bullet struck the door near where he was sitting. Three men with red bandannas over their faces climbed in through the open side door.

Bushnell, farther back in the car, realizing that something was wrong, instantly slipped through the rear door, ran through the train, and handed the key of his express safe to the brakeman. He then tried to lose himself among the passengers while the brakeman tucked the key into his shoe.

Conklin, who had no chance to get away, always believed that Jesse James and Cole Younger were two of the trio who invaded the baggage car, and he guessed that Frank James was just outside. He never knew the third man. Soon the engineer and fireman were brought to the baggage car, pushed in, and lined up against the wall with Conklin. As soon as they found that the key to the safe was missing, the bandits forced Conklin to go back through the coaches with them and point out Bushnell. Then Bushnell was forced to point out the brakeman who, in turn, was forced to give up the key. No one dared to offer resistance except a newsboy named Lou Bales who had a small firearm which made more noise than damage, much to the amusement of the robbers.

Contemporary accounts state that there were two other revolvers on the train, one in the hands of the brakeman, which Jesse James took over, and one in the hands of a Texas girl who threatened to shoot anyone who tried to rob her. She actually did no shooting, however.

The holdup was further enlivened by Clergyman J. S. Holmes of Bedford, Westchester County, New York. During the robbery he prayed aloud that all persons might be spared, yet if anyone should be killed that person might repent while there was still time. When the preacher had finished his prayers he sang hymns.

All this stirred no responsive chord in Jesse James, though in his early youth he had been a pious member of the local Baptist church at Kearney.

The bandits returned to the express cars where they easily opened one safe. They then discovered that there was no key to the Adams Express safe anywhere on the train. It was a through safe which had been put aboard locked and was not to be opened until it had reached its destination. Though made of only sheet iron, it resisted the bandits' efforts for some time. One man, probably Cole Younger, went to the locomotive and brought back the coal pick. They banged at the hinges of the safe with the pick without result.

Cole Younger finally got on top of the safe, took a piece of chalk and drew a circle on the safe. Then with the sharp pick he was able to batter a series of small holes in the sheet iron. A small circle of the metal fell away. However, the opening was too small for the big man's hand. Conklin later said it was "a fist like a ham." Another of the robbers, a small man wearing skin-tight silk gloves, managed to get his hand inside, but the leather money bag was too large to pull through the opening. He then seized a knife, cut open the bag, and removed the currency in small handfuls. No doubt this man was Jesse James, for he was noted for his finely formed and delicate hands, always wearing a No. 7 glove.

Not content with the express car haul, the robbers went through the passenger cars which were filled to capacity. One man held open the grain sack, and the passengers were ordered to drop into the sack whatever money and valuables they were carrying. With pistols drawn and ready, Jesse James walked behind the bagman, ready to emphasize the commands of his partner. Once aware that the holdup was in progress, some passengers managed to hide valuables here and there about the car. One man reached through the ventilator and laid his money and jewelry on the roof of the coach. He did not try to recover them until the train started again. When he did he found that the wind had swept his possessions from the roof of the car.

After an hour the train was allowed to proceed. When it reached Tipton, Missouri, Conductor Tibbetts wired the news to

St. Louis, Sedalia, and Kansas City. Posses rushed to central Missouri, but the robbers had already split the loot and scattered. A total of $17,000 had been taken from the two safes. The amount taken from the passengers was never ascertained.

Some weeks after the robbery Detective Sergeant Morgan Boland of the St. Louis Police Department asked Chief James McDonough if he might do some quiet investigating in southwestern Missouri. He went to Granby, Missouri, where he learned that Hobbs Kerry had been "living high on the hog." Sergeant Boland made friends with this stupid, boastful fellow, who soon told him of his own importance in the James gang. He foolishly boasted of his own part in the Rocky Cut affair.

When he was arrested he said his share of the loot had been $1200. He was taken to Boonville, Cooper county, where he made a full confession, telling the whole story and naming the participants as far as he knew them. For thus turning state's evidence Kerry got off with a ten-year sentence in the state prison at Jefferson City.

Again Jesse James was careful about public relations. A few days after Kerry's arrest, a stranger wrote to a *Kansas City Times* reporter a letter, dated August 14, 1876, Oak Grove, Kansas.

Of course the letter denied the presence of the Jameses and the Youngers at the robbery scene, even telling with whom they were that day. One part read: "Kerry knows that the Jameses and Youngers cannot be taken alive, and that is why he has put it on us. I cannot give the address of the people I was with because those cut-throat detectives would find out. My opinion is that Bacon Montgomery, the scoundrel who murdered Captain A. J. Clements (ex-Guerrilla) in 1866, is the instigator of all this Missouri-Pacific affair. I believe he planned the robbery and got part of the money."

The sheer impudence of all this was amusing to the public. But law enforcement officers and the railroads took a somewhat different view, especially when the James-Younger gang went right ahead with their criminal operations.

CHAPTER 15

Omnibus Holdups

At 6:45 P.M. On The Night of Sunday, August 30, 1874, the celebrated James boys played another of their tricks at North Lexington, Missouri. People had seen them in and about the city all through that day but apparently nobody seemed interested in making an attempt to apprehend the noted outlaws. Besides, this was more or less friendly ground for them.

Some time during the afternoon Henry Turner saw two of them down on the river bank near the soap factory. They had hitched their horses nearby and were peacefully resting upon the ground. About the same time a stranger, heavily armed, halted above town at the Smith and Hamlet Slaughterhouse and remained there half and hour or more.

The passenger omnibus crossed the river about 5:30 P.M. each evening. These three armed men rode on the ferry several times before the omnibus was due. The omnibus was driven to the depot in North Lexington, where it awaited the coming of the train. In the meantime several citizens noticed the armed men and spoke with them for a time.

The train pulled into the depot, and nine passengers alighted from the coaches and then got into the omnibus for the trip to the city. When almost in front of one of the larger houses at the outskirts of town, the three strangers rode out, handkerchiefs over their faces and menacing pistols in their hands. They called out to Jim Gibson, the driver, to stop, and he did so immediately.

The leader of the bandit trio ordered the passengers to alight from the omnibus and hold up their hands. He also ordered one of his men to ride down toward the ferry and pick up the stragglers. This man found George B. Nance and Miss Mattie Hamlet and half a dozen others leisurely strolling along. He ordered them to return to the omnibus.

Miss Mollie Newbold was one of the party. Declaring that she would not return she started on the run toward the ferryboat. The robber called out that he would shoot her if she did not stop. Nevertheless she ran on toward the boat and gave the alarm. The boat immediately steamed toward the opposite shore. The alarm spread over the city like a prairie fire, and before the robbers were half through relieving the omnibus passengers of their valuables, nearly a thousand people appeared on the bluff to witness the operation.

Miss Mattie Hamlet immediately recognized the robbers as the James boys whom she knew well. Her brother Jessie Hamlet (or Hamlett) had served with Jesse and Frank under Quantrill during the Civil War.

"Well, I know who you are in spite of that dirty cloth over your face," said Mattie.

The bandit laughed. "Well, who am I then?"

"You are one of the Younger brothers. You ought to be ashamed of yourself.

"You certainly are the same sandy girl you were a few years back," replied the rider.

By this time the bandit and the stragglers had reached the bus. Just as one of the robbers pulled a watch and chain from the pocket of W. T. Singleton, railroad agent at North Lexington, Miss Hamlet stepped up and placed her hand on the outlaw's arm.

"Why, Frank James, I'm astonished to see you have come down to such small work. I thought you never did anything except on a big scale."

He shook hands with her cordially and said, "Well, I'm a little ashamed of it myself. It is the first time we ever stooped to such small game. But you needn't call names out so loud here."

Miss Hamlet then asked Frank to give Singleton his watch back.

"Why? Is this man anything to you?"

She answered that he was, and Frank handed back his watch, but he kept the chain which was a very handsome and expensive one.

"No!" exclaimed Miss Hamlet. "Give him back the chain too. I won't have part of it if I can't get all."

After some discussion the outlaw returned the chain and watch to Singleton and also returned a watch he had taken from John C. Young prior to the appearance of Miss Hamlet on the scene, at her request.

Among the passengers was a handsome young professor from Lexington, Kentucky, who was planning to open a male academy at Lexington, Missouri. He was Professor J. L. Allen, from whom Frank James took $50 and a fine old watch which had belonged to the victim's grandfather. He then started to rip off Allen's fine coat and vest, when Miss Hamlet again interfered.

"Oh, Frank! Don't take that poor man's clothes. Your mother would be grieved to death if she knew how you are doing. I nursed you when you were wounded during the war. Now I believe I ought to have left you to die."

"It's a pity you didn't," said Frank sadly, still proceeding to remove Allen's clothing.

"I need some clothes myself," he said. "Mine will do him until he gets to town."

In the meantime Mr. Nance, seeing an opportunity, secretly handed his wallet to Miss Hamlet for safe keeping. The male passengers were lined in a squad and ordered to raise their hands. For a second time up went their hands in midair. After all the men had been searched Frank ordered the women to alight from the omnibus and line up with the others who had been walking. The women numbered only three.

"Frank, you wouldn't disturb a lady, would you?" asked Miss Hamlet.

"Miss Mattie, we have never done that and will not do it now," and Frank politely bowed to one of the women, Mrs. Graham of Bowling Green, Kentucky, whose uncle was Colonel Lewis Green of Lafayette County, Missouri. The outlaws were keenly disappointed with the results of their task, having netted only about $300 in money and jewelry.

When all the pockets had been rifled the outlaws turned their attention to the baggage. They opened and looked through the contents of all the carpetbags, taking such articles as they wanted and leaving the remaining contents strewn all over the ground.

The victims of the robbery were R. J. Holmes of the firm of Campbell & Holmes of Kansas City; W. T. Singleton, railroad agent at North Lexington; John C. Young, proprietor of the omnibus line; Captain L. Bergau, Swamp Land State Agent; Professor J. L. Allen; William Brown, a black man and an employee of the St. L. K. C. & N. Railroad, whose name is unknown.

This robbery was probably the smallest one in which the noted outlaws ever participated. Had it not been for Miss Hamlet, who knew the boys personally, most people would have discounted the report that the James boys had pulled it off. However, there was another side to the coin. Apparently the robbers had expected one Parson Jennings of Mayview to be on the omnibus. It was later learned that Jennings had been at St. Louis where he had collected $5,000 for the sale of a large number of hogs. He was supposed to be on the bus that day, but he had arrived home the evening before. Several passengers recalled the look of disappointment on the faces of the robbers as they looked over the crowd. One remembered that one of them said, "Dammit! He isn't here."

As the robbers left the scene, one of them looked back and called out to Miss Hamlet, "Goodbye, Mattie. You'll never see your old sweetheart again."

Many Missouri citizens were quick to criticize the people of North Lexington and Lexington because nothing was done to stop the robbery while it was in progress. The bandits had taken their good old time during the robbery, knowing that nobody would disturb them. It should be explained that North Lexington was on the north side of the Missouri River, immediately opposite Lexington. Besides the railroad buildings there were three or four houses in the village, only one of which was occupied. These houses were built upon the river bank, at the edge of the woods, and there were no fences or other improvements. The timber was very thick and extended to the river bank. The road from the depot skirted along the timber westward for about two hundred yards, and then turned northward across the open sandbar to the ferry landing. The robbers appeared at the turn of the road when they stopped the omnibus.

Every foot of the road from the depot to the ferry, and all the houses in North Lexington, were plainly visible from the bluff on the other side. The consequence was that the last half of the robbers' proceedings were seen by a large number of people. The robbers were in no hurry but did their work deliberately and well. The ferry boat was a slow affair and, after leaving the other shore, if floundered along in the middle of the river, where it was when the robbers had finished their work. It was then returned to the northern shore for the omnibus and the passengers.

There were several amusing incidents connected with the affair, one of them being the embarrassment of Professor Allen when he was forced to disrobe down to his underwear when Frank took his clothing. He quickly donned Frank's dirty and worn linen duster to hide himself. He also expressed the probable sentiments of all the passengers.

"Well," he said, "if we had to be robbed I am exceedingly glad that it was by first-class artists in the trade, nationally known by reputation."

Another passenger had this to say: "Taken altogether, it was an exploit which, in cool audacity, was worthy of its distinguished perpetrators, the James boys and one of the immortal Youngers. Rob Roy and Claude Duval must hide their distinguished heads in shame. Missouri is ahead in her banditti, as she is in her soil, minerals, beautiful women, her everything."

In his speech at Wellington, Governor Woodson said he did not have the James boys arrested because no one could make the proper affidavits charging them with any crime.

On the very heels of this robbery there occurred another such incident. The hack that left Waverly Monday at 2:00 P.M. to make connection with trains on the St. Louis, K.C., and N. Railroad at Carrollton, was halted by three masked men in a very thick woods five miles from Carrollton. There were four passengers in the hack, two men and two women. They took money and watches from all four.

One of the male passengers was a preacher. They took all his loose change but returned his watch. He tried to prevail upon them to return his money also, but they refused, stating, "This preacher business is getting too damned thin. I guess you heard that we also robbed the bus at Lexington, didn't you? Well, it's true, and we didn't get much more there than we did here."

The booty realized in the robbery that Monday amounted to $184 in cash and three watches.

The citizens of Missouri could hardly believe their ears when they learned that another such robbery occurred — or, at least, that an attempt was made on Sunday, September 3, 1874, along the road between Brownsville and Marshall, Missouri. The Lexington band had been at the Marshall Fair the entire previous week and had taken the $500 premium awarded to the best band. At midnight on Saturday they started to the depot at Brownsville, riding on the omnibus of J. W. Johnson of Brownsville, planning to take the Sunday morning train for Lexington.

While at Marshall they had heard all about the recent robberies at North Lexington and near Carrollton. Knowing the fact of their having money was quite public, they put their money in checks. Most of the band members also bought revolvers in the event an attempt might be made to rob them. They had reached within eight miles of Brownsville when suddenly Johnson saw three men in the road about twenty yards ahead, afoot, each with a horse. One of them remarked, "That's the band wagon now."

Johnson immediately stopped the bus and called to the men inside, "There they are now, boys!"

All twelve young men were immediately out of the vehicle, standing their ground beside it, their new revolvers glistening in the dawning day.

The robbers seemed for a moment irresolute, but they rode forward on the right side of the bus, with drawn revolvers beside their horses' heads. As they rode by not a word was spoken. After riding some fifty yards they reined in, turned around, and seemed determined to try the robbery anyhow. But they did not.

On this occasion each of the three bandits wore a brand-new chip straw hat. They were about twenty-three to twenty-six years of age. One had dark whiskers, one a sandy beard, and the youngest none at all. One rode a brown horse, another a sorrel, and the youngest a white pony. Obviously they had all three been in Brownsville the previous afternoon, and they had left there at about 2:00 P.M. and had been seen to be inquiring the way to Marshall. They never arrived there.

Were these boys the ubiquitous Jameses? Some of the band members claimed to have known the robbers, stating that they were not the James boys or the Youngers. At any rate these were not the three who had committed the same type of crimes at Lexington and Carrollton.

CHAPTER 16

Beginning of the End

In 1874 When John Younger was killed Cole and Bob Younger were in Florida, hoping to enroll young Bob in a school there, far from the troubles in Missouri. From Florida they visited friends in Carroll Parish, Louisiana, where they learned of John's death. Several days after the burial of John, Cole traveled to Osceola to pay his last respects to his brother by attending a small, private funeral service at the local Baptist church.

He then went on to Boone County, Arkansas, where he found Jim and Bob waiting for him. The boys talked over many things, including the planned double wedding of Cole and Lizzie Daniels and Jim and Cora Lee McNeill — a wedding which never took place. Cora Lee's father suggested that the Youngers import a number of Eastern Morgan trotters that could be trained to ride with wild horses in Texas. The result would be a goodly number of fine animals to sell to the United States government. They planned to pool their resources, and they asked their Uncle Thomas in California for a sizable loan which he had previously suggested. Had the Osceola wedding taken place, that might have been the last the world would have heard of any outlaw activities by the Youngers.

Jim traveled to California in order to effect the loan from their uncle, while Cole returned to Louisiana where Bob was happily working with friends. It was planned that they would all meet at Monegaw Springs for the wedding.

Jim's uncle advanced the thousand dollars needed for the initial expenses and agreed to send more whenever needed. He suggested it was time they got married and settled down. He also suggested that Jim return to Missouri by way of Dallas, Texas, where he would have an opportunity to investigate the land at Gainesville, the spot where they all planned the settle. Several days before Jim left California he received a letter from Cole postmarked Osceola much to his suprise, for he had thought that Cole and Bob were still in Louisiana.

This letter puzzled Jim, for it urged him to return to Missouri as quickly as possible, although no reason for haste was given.

Jim consulted with his Uncle Thomas who said, "You hightail it back to Missouri and let me know what has happened."

When Jim arrived in Monegaw Springs he could see that Cole was greatly troubled. The two of them were alone when Cole began to explain.

"Jim," he said, "John's death has affected Bob more deeply than we realize. He wanted to come to Missouri, saying he was homesick for the folks, so I came to Monegaw immediately."

"What's wrong with Bob?" inquired Jim.

"Well, Jim, I left him in Kansas City and came on to the Springs. He had met Jesse James on the street and they went to a hotel room to have a chat with Frank James. Of course they wanted Bob to join them in some caper. I am surprised that Bob did this, for he knows how I feel about Jesse. I've been trying to avoid that fellow as much as I can."

"I know that," said Jim. "We better get with Bob and see what this is all about."

Until September, 1876, the three Youngers were hunted from piller to post but, despite the enormous rewards offered for their capture, they found opportunity to shoot up towns and commit holdups and robberies. In the following letter, written from Harrisonville, Missouri, under date of November 15, 1874, and published on November 26th, Cole Younger attempted a vindication of his brother and himself. The letter was addressed to his brother-in-law, Lycurgus A. Jones:

Cass County, November 15, 1874

Dear Curg:

You may use this letter in your own way. I will give you this outline and sketch of my whereabouts at the time of certain robberies with which I am charged. At the time of the Gallatin bank robbery I was gathering cattle in Ellis County, Texas, cattle that I brought from Pleas Taylor and Rector. This can be proved by both of them, also by Sheriff Barkley and fifty other respectable men of that county. I bought the cattle to Kansas that fall and remained in St. Clair County until February. I then went to Arkansas and returned to St. Clair County about the first of May. I went to Kansas, where the cattle were, in Woodson County, at Col. Ridge's. During the summer I was either in St. Clair, Jackson, or Kansas, but as there was no robbery committed it makes no difference where I was.

(Cole was in error as there was a robbery committed on April 29, 1872, at Columbia, Kentucky.)

The gate at the fair ground was robbed that fall. I was in Jackson County at the time. I left R.P. Rose's that morning, went down the Independence Road, stopped at Dr. Noland's and got some pills. Brother John was with me. I went through Independence and from there to Ace Webb's. There I took dinner and then went to Dr. L. W. Twyman's. Stayed there until after supper, then went to Silas Hudspeth's and stayed all night. This was the day the gate was robbed at Kansas City. Next day John and I went to Kansas City. We crossed the river at Blue Mills and went up on the other side. Our business there was to see E.P. West. He was not at home, but the family will remember that we were there. We crossed the bridge, stayed in the city all night, and the next morning we rode up through the city. I met several of my friends. Among them was Bob Hudspeth. We then returned to the Six-Mile country by way of Independence. At Big Blue we met James Chiles and had a long talk with him. I saw several friends that were standing at or near the gate, and they all said that they didn't know any of the party that did the robbing. Neither John nor myself was accused of the crime until several days later. My name would never have been used in connection with the affair had not Jesse W. James, for some cause best known to himself, published in the Kansas City *Times* a letter stating that John, he, and myself were accused of the robbery. Where he got this authority I do not know, but one thing I do know, he had none from me. We were not on good terms at the time, nor have we been for several years.*

From that time on mine and John's names have been connected with the James brothers. John hadn't seen either of them for eighteen months before his death. And as for A.C. McCoy, John never saw him in his life. I knew A.C. McCoy during the war, but have never seen him since, notwithstanding the Appleton City paper says he has been with us in that county for two years. Now if any respectable man in that county will say he ever saw A.C. McCoy with me or John I will say no more; or if any reliable man will say that he ever saw any one of us who suited the description of A.C. McCoy, who is 48 or 49 years old, six feet and more in height, dark hair and blue eyes, and low forehead, then I will be silent and never more plead innocence.

Poor John, he has been hunted down and shot like a wild beast, and never was a boy more innocent. But there is a day coming when the secrets of all hearts will be laid open before the All-seeing Eye, and every act of our lives will be scrutinized; then will his skirts be white as the driven snow, while those of his accusers will be doubly dark.

I will come now to the Ste. Genevieve bank robbery. At that time I was in St. Clair County. I do not remember the date, but Mr. Murphy, one of our neighbors, was sick about that time, and I sat up with him regularly, where I met with some of his neighbors every day. Dr. L. Lewis was his physician.

As to the Iowa train robbery, I have forgotten the date, I was also in St. Clair Co., Mo., at that time, and had the pleasure of

---

*(It was Frank and Jesse who robbed the gate at that Fair.)

attending preaching the evening previous to the robbery at Monegaw Springs. There were fifty or a hundred persons there who will testify in any court that John and I were there. I will give you the names of some of them: Simeon C. Bruce, John S. Wilson, James Van Allen, Rev. Mr. Smith and lady. Helvin Fickle and wife of Greenton Valley were attending the springs at that time, and either of them will testify to the above, for John and I sat in front of Mr. Smith while he was preaching and was in his company for a few minutes, together with his wife and Mr. and Mrs. Fickle, after services. They live in Greenton Valley, Lafayette County, Mo. and their evidence would be taken in a court of heaven. As there was no other robbery committed until January I will come to that time. About the last of December, 1873, I arrived in Carrol Parish, Louisiana. I stayed there until the 8th of February, 1874. Brother and I stayed at Wm. Dickerson's, near Floyd. During the time the Shreveport stage and the Hot Springs stage were robbed; also the Gads Hill robbery.

You can appeal to the Governor in your own language, and if he will send men to investigate the above, and if not satisfied of my innocence, then he can offer the reward for Thomas Coleman Younger, and if he finds me innocent, he can make a statement to that effect. I will write this hurriedly, and I suppose I have given outlines enough. I want you to take pains and write a long letter for me and sign my name in full.

Thomas Coleman Younger

The following affidavits seem to bear out Cole's claims. The author checked with the Masonic Order at New Orleans and at Baton Rouge, and was informed of the authenticity of the Lodge at Floyd. Also, other statements were checked and verified. The following documents speak for themselves.

I have to state that on the 5th day of December, A.D., 1873, the Younger Brothers arrived at my home in Carroll Parish, La., and remained there until the 8th day of February, A.D., 1874, during which time Cole Younger was engaged in writing the history of

Quantrill and his own life. While at my house I asked Cole if he was a Mason, to which he replied in the negative.

Relative to the charges for this information, I will say that it is worth nothing unless it be a copy of the work you are now preparing to publish, which would be thankfully received.

Wm. Dickerson, Grand Master
Masonic Lodge, Floyd, La.

We, the undersigned citizens of Carroll Parish, Louisiana, and neighbors of Mr. William Dickerson, know and believe the statement of his written above regarding the Younger Brothers, to be true and correct.

R.G. Glenn	T.D. McCaudless
W.A. Chapman	W.A. Hendrick
A.L. Alley	Chas. H. Webb
I.L. Cheatham	C. Herrington
I.S. Herring	R.I. London

Floyd, La., August 7th, 1875.

Several other documents have been located in the family papers which seem to further substantiate the claims made by Cole.

I hereby certify that I attended Mr. Murphy, of St. Clair County, Missouri, during his sickness in November, 1872, and that on the day of the Ste. Genevieve, Missouri, Bank was said to have been robbed, I saw at the house of Mr. Murphy, in the County of St. Clair, Thomas Coleman Younger, generally called Cole Younger, and that he could not possibly have had any hand in said bank robbery, as he was sitting up and nursing Murphy during his sickness.

L. Lewis, M.D.
Treasurer and Collector of St. Clair County, Mo.

We, whose names are hereto subscribed, certify that we saw Thomas Coleman Younger at Monegaw Springs, St. Clair County, Missouri, on Sunday, July 20th, 1873, the day previous to the Iowa Train Robbery, which occurred on Monday morning, July 21, 1873, and that said Thomas Coleman Younger could not possibly have had any hand in said robbery.

Simeon E. Bruce
James Van Allen
Parson Smith
Robert White

Of course, many citizens believed all these affidavits and documents were smoke screens prepared by friends of the Youngers. Yet, the quality and high stature of those involved lend some credance to the statements.

That many Missourians felt that justice had not been done to the Younger Brothers, or to the James Boys, after peace had been declared, is evidenced by the resolutions offered in the Missouri Legislature by General Jefferson Jones, a prominent Callaway County attorney, in March, 1875, which received the approval of the Attorney-General of Missouri. Although this bit of curious legislation never did become law, it nevertheless, is essential to the history of the Youngers. Some of the most important sections are herewith used:

Whereas, By the 4th section of the 11th Article of the Constitution of the State of Missouri, all persons in the military service of the United States, or who acted under the authority thereof in this state, are relieved of all civil liability and all criminal punishment for all acts done by them since the first day of January, A.D., 1861; and,

Whereas, By the 12th section of the said 11th Article of said Constitution, provision is made by which, under certain circumstances, may be seized, transported to, indicted, tried and punished in distant counties, and confederate under the ban of despotic displeasure, thereby contravening the Constitution of the United States, and every principle of enlightened humanity; and,

Whereas, Such discrimination evinces a want of manly generosity and statesmanship on the part of the party imposing, and of courage and manhood on the part of the party submitting tamely thereto; and,

Whereas, Under the outlawry pronounced against Jesse W. James, Frank James, Coleman Younger, Robert Younger and others, who gallantly periled their lives and their all in defense of their principles, they are of necessity made desperate, driven as they are from the fields of honest industry, from their friends, their families, their homes and their country, they can know no law but the law of self-preservation, nor can have respect for, or feel allegiance to a government which forces them to the very acts it professes to deprecate, and then offers a bounty for their apprehension, and arms foreign mercenaries with power to capture and kill them; and,

Whereas, Believing these men too brave to be mean, too generous to be revengeful, and too gallant and honorable to betray a friend or break a promise; and believing further that most if not all the offenses with which they are charged have been committed by others, and perhaps by those pretending to hunt them, or by their confederates; that their names are and have been used to divert suspicion from and thereby relieve the actual perpetrators; that the return of these men to their homes and friends would have the effect of greatly lessening crime in our state by turning public attention to the real criminals, and that common justice, sound policy and true statesmanship alike demand that amnesty should be extended to all alike of both parties for all acts done or charged to have been done during the war; therefore, be it

Resolved by the House of Representatives, the Senate concurring therein:

That the Governor of the State be, and he is hereby requested to issue his proclamation notifying the said Jesse W. James, Frank James, Coleman Younger, Robert Younger and James Younger, and others, that full and complete amnesty and pardon will be granted them for all acts charged or committed by them during the late Civil War, and inviting them peaceably to return to their respective homes in this state and there quietly remain, submitting themselves to such proceedings as may be instigated against them by the courts for all offenses charged to have been committed since said war, promising and guaranteeing to them and each of them full protection shall be given them from the time of their entrance into the state, and his notice thereof under said proclamation and invitation.

General Jones made an earnest speech in advocacy of the Resolution at the close of the session of the 28th General Assembly. However, one member of the Legislature simply read a message which Governor Woodson had read to the 27th General Assembly, denouncing these very men as outlaws of the worst sort, and the resolution was defeated. Of course, the cold-blooded murder of Daniel H. Askew, a neighbor of Mrs. Zerelda James Samuel, mother of the outlaw brothers, on April 12, 1875, had a lot to do with changing the minds of many of the legislators with respect to the Resolution. Many persons openly claimed that Jesse and Frank James had killed Askew because they thought he had assisted the detectives on the night the home of their mother was attacked by the Pinkertons. Others stated that Jesse had killed Askew because of a property line dispute with Askew. One source stated that Jesse remarked, "No one is going to insult my mother and get away with it."

Northfield Square

CHAPTER 17

Disaster at Northfield

SOME TIME AFTER BOB YOUNGER'S MEETING with Jesse and Frank James in Kansas City, Cole and Jim were able to confront him with a direct question as to what they had discussed.

"Well, Jesse seems to have a plan where we can get $75,000 with little or no trouble. He intends to rob the bank at Northfield, Minnesota, when the vaults are bulging with grain money. Benjamin Butler and his son-in-law, General Adelbert Ames, are both big stockholders in that bank. You remember how those two Union generals beat into the ground the Southern people of Louisiana during the Reconstruction days."

"Who else is involved?" asked Cole.

"Well, Jesse said that he and Frank would be there, me and Charlie Pitts, Clell Miller, and Bill Stiles. I don't know any of them, but maybe you do. Jesse said he'd be known as Mr. Howard and they'd be calling Frank Mr. Woods."

"What did Frank have to say to all this?" Cole wanted to know.

"Frank never said a word, just let Jesse do all the talking." He told me not to tell you anything about it because he said you don't like him though he doesn't know why."

Cole tried to reason with Bob, but the young man was determined to go on the raid.

He did promise, "I won't give Jesse a definite answer until you and Jim have talked it out."

Cole wanted to visit Kansas City to have a showdown with Jesse James, even though he knew it wouldn't solve anything. Besides, he had always been on friendly terms with Frank.

"Bud, have you lost your reason, to even let Bob think of taking part in such a plot?" Jim demanded. "Hasn't Jesse James done enough to you in the past, implicating you in his robberies? I know Jesse figures you'll go along to protect Bob. That's just what he wants."

Cole did not reply. Jim then talked it over with his brother Bob.

"Robbery is not your way of life, Bob. Most of the false implications have been instigated by Jesse James. He is using you only to drag Cole into his scheme. He knows you wouldn't go without telling Cole."

Bob was not to be diverted. He was not interested in horses or a horse ranch in Texas and it seemed a good idea to get a lot of money without working for it.

"I'm twenty-three years old now," he said, "and I can take care of myself. The James idea looks good to me. After that I can go to Canada and live well."

Then Bob stormed out of the room.

Cole and Jim discussed the matter at length. Against their better judgment they decided to go with Bob and somehow change his mind if at all possible. When Cole informed Jesse James of his intention to ride along with Bob on their unsavory mission, James became furious. This brought on a mild attack of epilepsy to which he was subject after his long illness from previously suffered wounds.

He cried out, "You just want a greater share of the money — you'd be three Youngers against two Jameses."

Again Jesse went into one of his well-known tantrums, and Cole threatened to use force to prevent his young brother Bob from taking part unless he and Jim could ride along. Jesse seemed about to draw his gun on Cole, but Frank intervened knowing what the outcome would be. Cole already had his pistol out and was tapping Jesse on the chest with its barrel.

"Stay healthy, boy. Leave it as it is," Frank cautioned Jesse.

After that they made plans. Jesse insisted that the three Youngers must understand that the deal was his idea, although later it was given out as having been Cole's idea first. Jesse insisted he himself would issue orders, and Cole agreed to that for himself and his two brothers.

Later Jim explained to Cora Lee McNeill that he had to go north. Cole made the same announcement to Lizzie Daniels. They both said they hoped to return by mid-October. Jim carried a small picture of Cora Lee all through the journey and on to prison.

The gang was to meet in July of 1876 at the Samuel home near Kearney, Missouri. Jim Younger left Kansas City on the Lexington Road, where he waited for Cole and Bob. Three other men joined them, and this comprised the entire band of eight. Frank suggested that Cole, Charlie Pitts, and Bob should ride north together, leaving Miller, Stiles (the alias used by Bill Chadwell), Jesse James, and Jim Younger to take another route.

Near Parkville the band had to row across the Missouri River, and the man rowing them was Charlie Turner, a brother-in-law of Sam Wells (the alias used by Charlie Pitts). In order to avoid suspicion one man at a time was rowed across, the horse of each one swimming alongside the boat. Then the whole party of eight rode across Missouri and Iowa into Southern Minnesota. When they reached Albert Lea, Minnesota, Miller and Jesse stabled their horses, telling the liveryman, "Jim Younger is looking for fresh mounts, and whatever he does with these two animals is all right with us."

Posing as cattlemen Jim Younger and Stiles purchased four sturdy animals, turning in their own four as part payment. Jesse took a big-chested buckskin, an animal of speed and endurance. Jim chose a long-legged, friendly black, a dependable animal.

After a final meeting in the woods near Owatonna, the group split up as follows: Bob Younger and Sam Wells were to travel to St. Paul via the train, while Cole and Bill Stiles would ride there on horseback. Frank and Jesse James, Clell Miller, and Jim Younger, the rest of the contingent, rode their own horses to St. Paul but by a different route.

On August 20th Sam and Bob visited the livery stable of Hall and McKinney and looked over the best long-range animals available. They finally went on to the William Judd Stables, where they bought a black and a bay.

Bob Younger and Sam Wells visited Cole and Bill Stiles at the Merchants Hotel on Third Street and Jackson Avenue in Minneapolis, from which point they visited the gambling houses in the city.

Jesse and Frank James, Clell Miller, and Jim Younger arrived in St. Paul a short while after the others had, but they decided to visit the bawdy house of Mollie Ellsworth rather than try their luck at the gaming tables. From the Twin Cities Cole and Sam took a train to St. Peter. Bob and Bill followed on another train, while the remaining four later took the train to Red Wing. Under assumed names these four registered at the National Hotel in Red Wing.

The time they had scheduled for the bank robbery was near. The outlaws had kept only one of the original horses ridden to Minnesota from Missouri. This was the splendid buckskin which they had stolen from the Stewart stables in Kansas City. In Red Wing Cole registered at the hotel as J. C. King, and Bill Chadwell signed the register as J. Ward, cattle buyer. At Madelia Cole signed in at the Flanders Hotel as J. C. King and Bill Chadwell signed as Jack Ladd. At that hotel they became friendly with Colonel Thomas L. Vought, a man whom Cole would meet again under different circumstances.

The final meeting place of the outlaws was the secluded farm of Joe Brown. There they used their time in training their animals not to be gun shy.

They separated after leaving the Brown farm and met on September 2, 1876, near the town of Mankato, Minnesota. Together they rode into town, visiting the saloons and playing poker. Two of them later stopped at the Gates Hotel, two at the Washington Hotel, while the other two on Sunday night stayed at the home of George Capps at Kasota, five miles south of Mankato.

Apparently their plan was to attack the Bank at Mankato first, but the presence of a large group of citizens standing near that bank building discouraged that part of the mission. Perhaps in some manner the alarm had been given? Actually those people were a group of "sidewalk superintendents" watching construction work progressing on a building next to the bank.

At noon on Monday the bandits rode past the First National Bank, then out of Mankato by way of Main Street and Fifth Street. They approached their destination at Northfield in two groups, Bob Younger with three of the men on the southern route, Jim and Cole Younger and the other two men from the north. On September 6th Cole's group stayed at Janesville, while the rest of the band stayed at Faribault.

Early on the morning of September 7th they all rode toward Northfield, assembling in a wooded area near the town of Southfield. At ten o'clock Frank, Jesse, and two others rode into town and had breakfast at Jeff's Restaurant. Weatherwise it was a dreary day, and it suddenly turned cooler with dark clouds building up, indicating a possible rain. Frank James and Bob Younger ate breakfast on the west side of the Cannon River which separated the town. They also stopped at the saloon of John Tosney, where they purchased a quart of whiskey. The fact that Frank James and Bob Younger were drunk at the time of the raid is attested to by remarks made by Cole Younger: "Frank admitted he had a quart of whiskey which he and Pitts and Bob drank before going into the bank, and Frank thought they could get the cash and be ready to ride out by the time Cole and Miller should arrive."

Early in the afternoon the gang rode several miles toward Janesville to consult and arrange their plans. Frank drew a diagram of the main street of Northfield looking south of the bridge. They then separated to circle the town, Frank's party going west, Jim's going east. The plan was that Frank, Charlie Pitts, and Bob Younger, the three who were to enter the bank, were to ride slowly into town. They then were to stop at the hitch rail rack near the outside stairway of the bank building, but they were not supposed to enter the bank until Cole Younger and Clell Miller reached their own position, about two blocks behind them.

Jesse James, Jim Younger, and Bill Chadwell were to remain at the bridge. Should trouble arise Cole was to fire one shot, a signal for them to ride in. If the raid proved successful Jesse, Jim, and

Northfield Bank as it was in 1876

Bill were to ride south, then east to Rochester, where the eight would meet. From that point it would be easy to reach Iowa and escape to Missouri.

A bridge in the center of Northfield connected the east and west parts of the town and led into Bridge Square on the east side. At the corner of Division Street and Bridge Square there was a two-story building called the Scriver Block. The First National Bank stood at the south end of the block, near an alley which ran back of two hardware stores operated by J. S. Allen and A. R. Manning respectively. Opposite the Scriver Block was a group of three stores and a hotel called the Dampier House. There young Henry M. Wheeler, home on vacation from the medical college at Ann Arbor, Michigan, was passing the time of day with a friend.

From the start the timing was poor. Bob Younger was a bit fuzzy from the whiskey-drinking. Frank James also had been drinking, but he could hold his liquor better than Bob, although he was inclined to be a bit trigger-happy when in his cups. Bill Chadwell, who had once lived in Rice County, Minnesota, was elected to lead the bandits out of that state after the robbery.

Following their original plan Frank James, Charlie Pitts, and Bob Younger dismounted in front of the bank and tossed their bridle reins over some hitching posts beside the street. They then walked to the corner and lounged upon some wooden boxes in front of the Lee & Hitchcock Store, assuming the attitude of loafers. When they saw that Cole Younger and Clell Miller had started toward the bank down Division Street, they walked closer to the bank. They were supposed to wait until the two riders joined them to complete the party which was to go inside the bank, but instead they entered at once.

When Cole and Miller saw this they hurried to the bank, following in the wake of the trio already inside. However, they did not enter the building, but Cole dismounted and pretended to tighten the saddle girth on his horse. Miller went to the bank entrance and looked inside. He then closed the door and walked back and forth before it.

These actions aroused the suspicion of J. S. Allen, one of the hardware store proprietors. Allen started for the bank to see what was going on. When Miller ordered him away from the

Building of Jesse James' last raid

Sketch of Northfield

Colt Frontier 1875 .45 calibre model was used by Cole Younger in daring Northfield, Minnesota, bank robbery attempt. Badly wounded, Cole was caught, sent to prison, then pardoned in 1901.

Colt Frontier 1875 .45 calibre model used by Cole Younger

Dr. Henry Wheeler

building Allen left, but as he fled around the corner he shouted, "Get your guns, boys! They're robbing the bank!" He then proceeded to give the alarm as best he could.

A young medical student named H. M. Wheeler, at home on vacation from the University of Michigan Medical School at Ann Arbor, was standing on the east side of Division Street, and he quickly assisted in giving the alarm by yelling, "Robbery! Robbery!"

At that time Cole called to Wheeler to get inside. He also fired a shot into the air, the prearranged signal for the three outlaws at the bridge to know they had been discovered. Those three rode forward with such a roar of sound that it was thought a detachment was approaching at a gallop. At the same time a shot sounded inside the bank. Outside Chadwell, Jim Younger, and Jesse James fired their pistols and yelled at the people to stay away. One Swedish pedestrian named Gustavson did not understand English. Bewildered, he stood where he was, and he was shot down and died in a few days.

To the inhabitants of Northfield the minutemen defense of the town against the group of bandits recalled vividly Indian warfare when they grimly took up their rifles and shotguns. One citizen, Elias Stacy, fired a shotgun blast at Clell Miller as that bandit was mounting his horse. Birdshot peppered Miller's face, but he got away. Another townsman, A. R. Manning, shot at Charlie Pitts with a breech-loading rifle and succeeded only in killing the bandit's horse.

Cole Younger was ready to call off the robbery. He yelled to his fellow-robbers in the bank to come out for a getaway. His commands were interrupted by a blast from Mr. Manning's breech-loader which wounded him in the thigh. Manning backed away to reload and saw Bill Chadwell waiting beside his horse about eighty yards away. He took a shot at him, and Chadwell fell to the ground dead, a bullet through his heart. The horse ran to a livery stable around the corner.

After young Wheeler had aroused the town he hastened to the drug store where he usually kept a gun. However, remembering that he had left it at home today, he raced through the store to get a weapon he had seen at the hotel. When he found the weapon it was an empty army carbine. The owner of the hotel, Mr. Dampier, luckily located three cartridges in another room, and in quick order Wheeler was stationed at a second-story window of the hotel in time to join the gun battle.

Jim Younger was riding by at that instant, and Wheeler took a quick shot at him. His aim was too high, however, and the bullet missed. In vain Jim looked around for the sharpshooter who by then had picked another target, Clell Miller. The bullet passed through Miller's body, severing the great artery and killing him almost instantly. Wheeler's third cartridge fell to the floor, breaking the paper from which it was partly made and rendering it useless. But Dampier reached him with a fresh supply of ammunition, and another shot by the young man hit Bob Younger in the right elbow as he ran out of the bank. Bob quickly executed the "border shift" by throwing his revolver into his left hand, ready for use.

There ensued a brief lull in the fighting, as each side waited for the other to show itself. Taking advantage of the lull, Bob Younger raced up Division Street, where he mounted behind Cole. Then the remainder of the band of outlaws fled.

The battle had been as decisive as it had been brief. Six robbers were in flight, two of them wounded. In front of the bank lay the dead horse, and the body of Clell Miller a half block away on the other side of the street. The defenders rushed to the bank to see what had happened inside.

They learned that the three robbers had entered and quickly placed under their guns the teller, A. E. Bunker, the assistant bookkeeper F. J. Wilcox, and the head bookkeeper, Joseph L. Heywood, who was acting as cashier at that particular time (since the cashier, G. M. Phillips, was out of town).

It turned out that Heywood had told the bandits that the safe had a time-lock and could not be opened. An ironic twist was that, though the safe door was closed and the bolts thrown, the combination dial had not been twirled. All the bandits would have had to do to open it was to turn the handle! No money was taken from the bank.

Seeing a chance to escape, A. E. Bunker, the teller, had dashed behind the vault toward an exit door. Charlie Pitts took several shots at him, the second shot entering his shoulder. Frank James, last to leave the building, deliberately shot and killed Heywood for no reason but excitement.

Frank Wilcox, the bank clerk, said in part, "The door of the vault itself was open but not that of the safe inside. Mr. Heywood was ordered to open the safe. As one of the robbers entered the vault Heywood sprang forward and closed the door to the vault, shutting the robber in. Another man seized Heywood by the collar and dragged him away, releasing his partner. Almost immediately those two robbers took alarm and somehow jumped over the counter, making their exit. The taller man was the last to go. He mounted a desk at the front and, as he turned to leave, he fired and shot at Heywood, a shot that seemed to miss. Heywood dodged behind his desk and sank into the chair, but one of the robbers leaned over the desk and placed the revolver at Heywood's head and fired, shooting him dead."

For some reason Cole Younger always protected Frank James in the matter of Heywood's murder. He said that the killer was not Jesse James as was many times claimed. But he refused to name the real murderer except to say that he was the man who rode the dun horse at Northfield.

Jim Younger said, "Frank James was the last of those who entered the bank to come out. I heard the two shots in the bank after Pitts and Bob ran out. Frank admitted he fired at the man we later learned was Joseph Heywood because that man was aiming a small pistol at him. I was not in the bank at any time, nor was Cole. The man who rode the buckskin out of town was the man who killed Heywood, and that man was Frank James."

Usual accounts report that the six outlaws raced out of Northfield on the Dundas Road. According to Jim Younger, Jesse and Frank left town a few minutes before the remaining outlaws did by way of the Faribault Road. This is what Jim said:

It was perhaps a half mile out of town that we joined Jesse and Frank. A few miles farther on we met a farmer leading a broken down work animal which Cole paid the man thirty dollars for.

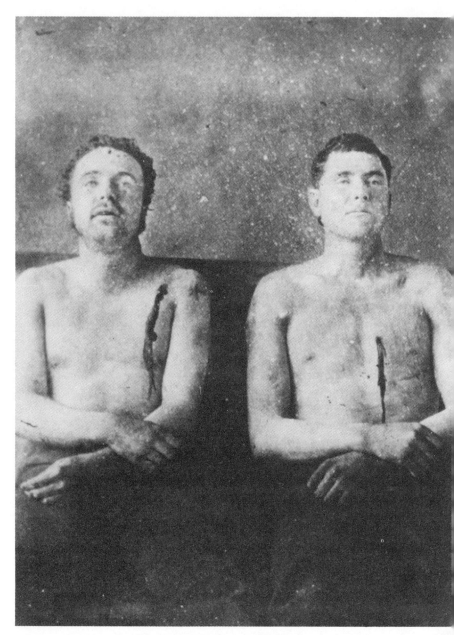

Bandits Clell Miller and Bill Chadwell

Pitts was to ride this animal, with Jesse and Frank offering no help toward the purchase of the animal; Pitts claimed he had no money. He seemed grateful, saying it was better than walking.

We rode along with Jesse and Frank in the lead. Frank called out, asking where Chadwell was. At our first report of news we learned that he and Miller were killed in the street at Northfield. When we stopped we learned Cole had been shot in the hip, while at the bank door, urging the boys to come out. Neither Jesse, Frank or Pitts had been hit during the shooting.

Cole questioned Frank as to why he and the two boys did not wait until he (Cole) and Miller arrived, as planned, before they entered the bank.

Frank then admitted he had a quart of whiskey which he, Pitts, and Bob drank before going into the bank. Cole and I never touched liquor in our life, and were shocked to hear that Bob had indulged. Had we known about the whiskey the whole ghastly affair never could have occurred.

Cole asked what had gone wrong inside the bank that caused the two shots to be fired. At that time we did not know that anyone had been fatally shot.

Frank said, 'There was a lot of shooting and yelling going on outside and I thought I better do as the boys said and get out of there. When I started toward the door the man on the floor stood up, he was pointing a small revolver at me. I still had my gun in my hand so I aimed for his shoulder and fired. His gun went off as he dropped to the floor. His bullet was high, I guess, it didn't come anywhere near me. I don't know how badly he was wounded or if at all.

This man did not do what I told him. He was the one who said there was a time lock on the vault, but he was lying. I then ran across the floor as Pitts yelled for us to run for it.'

No one spoke after Frank finished talking. We mounted and rode on. Later in the day we stopped again to rest. A cold steady rain had set in and it was miserable."

But the robbers had to keep going. Posses from Northfield and elsewhere were in pursuit, and those officials at the state capitol were also asked to aid. Governor John S. Pillsbury offered $1,000 as a reward for the surviving bandits. He later raised this offer to $1,000 each, dead or alive. The bank and various corporations also offered cash rewards.

Grief over Heywood's untimely death was widespread. He had been greatly liked and respected and was a member of the Board of Carleton College. President Strong of Carleton placed Heywood's body in a carriage and drove it to his residence. Mrs. Heywood showed herself worthy of the occasion. When she learned how her husband had been killed, she said, "I would not have had him do otherwise."

On Sunday, September 10th, two funeral services were held in honor of the murdered bank employee. During the morning the large auditorium of the high school was filled despite the prevailing rain and mud. The funeral eulogy, given by the Rev. D. L. Leonard, pastor of the Congregational Church, was so magnificent that people talked about it for months.

Later the funeral service at Mr. Heywood's home, conducted by President Strong, paid equal testimony as to the character of the deceased who was then buried in the Northfield Cemetery at the southern end of the city. It was marked with an appropriate headstone.

Coroner Waugh of Faribault held an inquest on the bodies of the dead outlaws. He said, "The two unknown men came to their death by the discharge of firearms in the hands of our citizens in self-defense and in protecting the property of the First National Bank of Northfield."

The bodies of the dead outlaws were carried to the open square, which was soon overcrowded with the morbid curious. Bill Chadwell was described as five feet nine inches tall, with auburn hair, slim and muscular. People tried to cut off pieces of his clothing or locks of hair. What happened to the compass and gold watch that were in his pockets at the time of his death is anyone's guess. Clell Miller was taller, about six feet three inches tall, with auburn hair and fair skin.

That night in an obscure corner of the cemetery two boxes were buried. No one took the trouble to determine if the boxes were empty or not, but we know that Clell Miller's body found its way back to Missouri where it was claimed by his father.

It was usual in those days for the bodies of dead criminals to be given to medical colleges to further the cause of anatomical science. Young medical student Henry M. Wheeler, who had shot and killed Bill Chadwell, thought this was a good idea. When Bill's body was taken off the street at Northfield, Wheeler asked for it. His request was granted, and he took the corpse to the University of Michigan at Ann Arbor. It was missing an ear, which someone must have whacked off. Today this same ear is on display under a glass case in the museum at Northfield.

After his graduation, Dr. Wheeler took the skeleton of Chadwell with him to Grand Forks, North Dakota, where it hung from a hook in his office, in line with the custom of that day. When a young reporter learned of this he made a good newspaper story about it. One day an elderly gentleman came to Dr. Wheeler's office and asked to see the skeleton. After some questions it was determined that this man was the father of Bill Chadwell, alias Bill Stiles. The old man was visibly shaken when he learned the truth of the matter. The skeleton at this time would have been difficult indeed to verify as that of his son, but the caller was willing to accept as fact that it really was. The skeleton remained in Dr. Wheeler's office until it was destroyed in a fire.

Joseph Lee Heywood

CHAPTER 18

Captured

WHILE TRYING TO ESCAPE, the remainder of the outlaw group traveled only fifty miles in five days. The original plan had been to go west and to stop at the telegraph office and destroy the instruments so as to avoid an immediate alarm. However, in fear of close pursuit they dashed their horses along any escape route which presented itself. At the same time the wires were humming the news of the invasion of Northfield by Missouri bandits.

At Millersburg they were recognized by the farmer who had served them a meal on the day before the robbery attempt. Fortunately for them the news of the trouble had not yet reached him, so they were able to ride on unmolested. At Shieldsville, fifteen miles west of Northfield, a number of men arrived from Faribault to join in the hunt. A cold, drizzling rain began to fall and continued for almost two weeks. The outlaws found themselves just a little distance from the cabin where the posse members had taken refuge from the weather. Due to their loss of Chadwell the outlaws did not know where they were, but they had seen the men enter the cabin. In a ravine several miles from Shieldsville some long-range shooting took place, but no one was injured.

By Friday morning 500 men were out in search of the outlaws. The most prominent leaders in the pursuit groups were Mayor Solomon P. Stewart of Northfield, Sheriff Ara Barton, George Baxter of Faribault, and the chiefs of police of St. Paul and Minneapolis. That morning two of the bandits rode to the home of Mrs. George James where they obtained some food and actually participated in "searching for the outlaws" with five other men.

Later on Friday the outlaws moved eastward in the direction of Waterville. At a ford of the swollen Cannon River they encountered several poorly armed guards. Shots were exchanged, and the robbers turned back to the protection of the woods, an old guerrilla trick. Later the guards had left that point, and the bandits swam the river and fled to the forest beyond. Late that same day they ate supper at the isolated farmhouse of John Kohn, between Elysian and German Lake. They told Kohn they were deputies in search of the bandits.

On Saturday morning the outlaws abandoned their horses and continued their journey afoot in that land of lakes and swamps. Their progress was slow and painful. Cole was wounded in the thigh and Bob in the elbow, but they received no medical treatment until their capture. That evening they spent some time on an island in the swamp. On Sunday morning they halted near the town of Marysburg. Their next stop was at a deserted farmhouse a few miles from Mankato. There they spent Monday night, Tuesday, and Tuesday night. They had advanced less than fifty miles in five days!

After the discovery of the abandoned outlaw camp and the half-starved horses, the possemen assumed that the outlaws were many miles away from the area. As a result, most of the pursuers returned to their homes. However, later news aroused fresh interest in the chase, and many men took to the trail again.

On Tuesday the outlaws ate breakfast at the home of a man named Ben Williams. He did not suspect their identity. On Wednesday morning they captured a man named Dunning, whom Cole Younger set free on his word that he would not report their whereabouts. Dunning hurried into Mankato, where he reported the matter to his employer. A new pursuit campaign was then organized under the direction of General Pope of Mankato.

Early Thursday morning Jesse James, in a high state of agitation, said he wanted to leave Bob and Jim Younger because they

Posse members who captured Youngers

would be treated well when found. In fact, he said to Cole, "Either leave your brothers or kill them, for they are making a trail of blood and slowing down our fight."

"You're a no-good bastard, Jesse James, to make such a suggestion," Cole exclaimed. "I ought to kill you for it. I have no quarrel with your brother Frank — he and I have always been friends. But now you and I have come to the parting of the ways."

"No killing," Bob Younger pleaded. "Jesse promised me there would be no killing on this raid."

Jesse's never-resting eyes flashed with a dangerous light at being called a bastard. He wondered if Cole knew something about him that he himself only suspected. George Shepherd had said on several occasions that Jesse and Frank were only half-brothers, that Jesse's real father was a certain Clay County physician.

Now, with a pretense at nonchalance Jesse said, "That's fine by me. We'll just let Frank make up his own mind."

This incident has been vouched for by those who knew the facts of the Northfield escape but were long reluctant to speak. Jim Younger later said it was absolutely true. Frank James, of course, never entertained any such an idea. He and Cole remained firm friends, but now it was agreed that Frank should accompany his brother. So the Youngers and Charlie Pitts parted company with the James brothers near Mankato.

That same morning the Youngers and Pitts crossed the Blue Earth River on the railroad bridge. At seven o'clock they were near the town of Madelia, a small village in Watonwan County, twenty-five miles southwest of Mankato. Not far from the bridge was the farmhouse of a farmer named Sorbel. Young Asle Oscar Sorbel spent many hours talking with the guards who were posted there. Colonel Vought told Oscar (as he was called) to keep a sharp lookout in the vicinity of the bridge and report to him any suspicious looking men who might be seen.

On Thursday morning, September first, while Oscar was milking the cows, two men walked by, bidding him the time of day. The boy was sure these two men were some of the robbers, so he hurried to tell his father about it. He persuaded his father to allow him to ride the old plow horse into Madelia to spread the news.

Oscar, mud from head to foot from falling off his horse into a mudhole, rode to the Flanders House where he imparted the information to Colonel Vought. Soon a company consisting of the colonel, Sheriff James Glispin of Watonwan County, Dr. Overholt, W.R. Estes, and S.J. Severson were en route to the Sorbel house. On the way they were joined by C.A. Pomeroy, G.A. Bradford, and Captain W.W. Murphy. From St. James came G.S. Thompson and B.M. Rice, most of their friends and neighbors being too indifferent to join them or perhaps placing no stock in the boy's story. (In subsequent reports the boy's name was always listed as Oscar Oleson Suborn in case members of the band might seek revenge against him. Sorbel died July 11, 1930, in Webster, South Dakota.)

While en route to the Sorbel place Sheriff Glispin was informed that the outlaws were on foot, making their way through Hanska Slough. Colonel Vought and Dr. Overholt sighted them. Dr. Overholt took careful aim at Cole Younger and fired. The bullet broke the walking stick that Cole was using. The bandits retreated into the dense brush along the Watonwan River.

Finally the outlaws were driven into an area of some five acres of a triangle covered with willows, grapevines, and underbrush of all sorts. Sheriff Glispin called for volunteers to attack this hiding place, but not many of the crowd responded. Those who did were the sheriff himself, Colonel Vought, Captain W.W. Murphy, B.M. Rice, S.J. Severson, G.A. Bradford, and C.A. Pomeroy.

These seven men, four paces apart, advanced in a line across the eastern side of the triangle, from the bluff to the river. They soon discovered the outlaws crouched in the thicket. There followed a violent gun battle, but it was of short duration.

Pitts was killed. [1] Jim Younger received five wounds, the most dangerous being the one that shattered his jaw, the bullet lodging under his brain. [2]

Bob Younger was wounded twice and Cole was badly shot up, having received eleven wounds.

Jesse James, Nebraska City, Nebr., 1876

Charlie Pitts, killed near Madelia, 1876

Jim and Cole Younger after capture, 1876

They were all taken in a farm wagon to Madelia under heavy guard. As they rode into town, the always gallant Cole, despite his wounds, managed to stand up in the wagon and bow to the ladies. The captives were all treated and fed at the Flanders House while a crowd of curious citizens milled outside the hotel. Cole and Bob confessed their identities to the authorities, but Jim at first claimed his name was Cal Carter. Many reporters invaded Madelia and many thousands of words were written about the Youngers and the Northfield affair. Here is the report that appeared in the *St. Paul Pioneer Press:*

I first called on Cole and James Younger, who occupy a bed together. Both are terribly wounded, and their faces are disfigured. They certainly do not look like such desperadoes as they are. Cole, who has bright red whiskers, had his right eye bandaged, and he was suffering from seven wounds. James has a fearful-looking mouth, the lower jawbone being shattered. I told them I represented the *Pioneer Press*, and asked if they wished to say anything to the public. Cole was much obliged, and asked if I could kindly express their thanks to the citizens of Madelia, who had treated them with such wonderful kindness. He expressed his surprise at such treatment, and was grateful for it. The doctor did not allow them to talk much, and as curious people were passing by, I left them to call on Bob.

These men suffer much, and their talk is sometimes delirious. Both are brave men, never moaning, and are receiving every possible attention. I found Bob, as he asked to be called for short, lying in bed, shackled and suffering from a wound in the arm received at Northfield, and from a wound in the breast he got yesterday. He was pleasant, cheerful, and communicative. He is a six-foot boy, twenty-three years old, and as fine looking a specimen of manhood as I ever saw. He has a kind expression, and speaks in a low, gentle tone, using the best of language, no oaths or slang. He was willing to talk of himself, but positively declined to say anything of the movements of the other men. I gave him a cigar, for which he was very grateful, and he arose to smoke while we conversed. He said he had tried a desperate game and lost. They are rough boys and used to rough work, and must abide by the consequences. He was inclined to think Heywood was more frightened than brave. He was in the bank, and said the shooting of the cashier was an impulse of passion on the part of the man who shot him. He said they all deeply regretted it.

They could have picked off many citizens, as they all were dead shots, but did not desire to do murder. He would not say who shot Heywood. He said the witnesses in Northfield undoubtedly knew. This was in answer to the question as to whether or not the outlaw killed yesterday shot Heywood. Of course, he regretted the situation, but all the chances were weighed before starting it. He had looked over the other banks before deciding, and knew all about those in the large places, and wished now he had undertaken one of them, as the chance to retreat was much better in a small place. At Shieldsville they frightened the boys, but did not shoot to kill anybody. They could have easily shot several. They stayed in the woods about Kilkenny Thursday night, when they crossed the ford at Little Cannon. They knew the guards had run, but did not know how many. They moved back into the woods, but started soon to make a crossing before the guards were reinforced. They camped Friday night where the horses were found. They left at daylight, made a little headway, stopped on a sort of peninsula, probably a half mile from the German church, but part of a day. They made a fire and took comfort. They shot a pig and a calf, both in the head, but they refused to die, and they did not dare fire much. They pushed on Sunday night until midnight, and camped in Marysburgh. They heard the church bell strike six, and thought it was a mile away. They made a fire there and had a good meal of corn and potatoes. Monday they made good headway. At night they camped in a field in the bushes. Twice they were alarmed by people passing by, though they did not go to Indian Lake, as supposed by Sheriff Davis.

When they took Dunning prisoner they said he made a solemn oath not to reveal having seen them. They would not shoot him under any circumstances, and did not tie him in the woods from human feelings, as they feared he would not be found and would die there. When passing through Mankato the steam whistle of the oil mill blew midnight and startled them. They hid a while and then passed on, and did not hear or see the guards at the bridge. After crossing, they got four watermelons and had a feast. They said they intended to call around someday and pay the gentleman for them. They got two old hens and one spring chicken at a house nearby, and in fifteen minutes would have a good breakfast, but they were alarmed by shouting, either of men on the railroad train or by pursuers. They saw one man looking for boot tracks, but did not think they were pursuers, but ran up a bank. It was the closest call they had. They did not cross the Blue Earth River then, but did during the day. They then kept on through the woods. Two men then left, and as the pursuit was directed at them, they had an easier time. He blamed himself for the capture, as he was overcome by drowsiness and insisted on remaining in the field, while the others wished to keep on. They would not leave him; if they had gone a half mile they would have been caught. He declined to say anything about his previous life. He said they had no regular leader. Every man was expected to do his work, whatever it was.

His wound was in the elbow of the right arm, the joint being fractured, and he cannot straighten the arm nor control the fingers. He is very polite; talks when questioned, but not obtrusive, and is so mildmannered that he would make a good impression on anybody. He shows much gratitude for his good treatment, and fears to give trouble. He says they were all tough, and could have endured much longer. He insisted that it was his own fault that they were captured, as his lagging gave them away. He says the men who captured them were brave fellows.

The dead bandit is a man of very marked physiognomy, coal black hair, whiskers, moustache, and eyebrows. His face shows great determination. He must have been killed instantly. On his body were found a compass, state map, and pocketbook with five dollars. Two of the others had the same amounts, and James Younger had $150. Cole had a pocketbook and compass. None had watches. Their clothing was terribly used up. All well supplied by the citizens. Boyd says the coats found in the camp belonged to him. They were making due west as near as possible, he would not say where to. Around the face of the dead man flowers had been placed by some lady, and others were scattered on his breast. The swollen features present a horrible sight. Barton has agreed to take the prisoners to St. Paul, but since arriving he has changed his mind, and will proceed directly to Faribault by way of Mankato, leaving here at 5:45 A.M. The body of the dead robber goes by the same train to St. Paul to be embalmed. The trip will be hard on the wounded men, particularly the one shot in the jaw. He suffers much. The doctors here object to moving him, but the men are plucky and will go all right. The town is full of people, but all quiet. No one is admitted to the hotel, which is strictly guarded. When found, the robbers had pieces of under-clothing tied on their feet in place of stockings. Cole Younger's toe nails fell off when his boots were removed. He told the doctor he did not care for himself, if dead all would be over in five minutes; was anxious about his brother, and told him to cheer up. He asked the doctor if he would die. While his wounds were being dressed he did not flinch nor move a muscle. He says that when the two comrades left they gave them most of the money, watches, rings, and valuables, thinking their chances best.

The prisoners denied that the two men who escaped were the James brothers, and would give no further information concerning them. Frank and Jesse escaped to Fort Dodge, Iowa, where they rested at the farm of Mr. Armes, telling the man they were cattle buyers. Later, they rode through Kingsley, Iowa, where they accosted Dr. S. Mosher of Sioux City, making him change clothes with one of them and taking his horse. The final escape from the area was with the aid of G.W. Hunt, editor of the *Sioux City Democrat*, who accompanied the robbers to the confluence of the Little Sioux and Missouri Rivers. The editor had found the James boys riding in the vicinity of Woodbury and explained his desire to help them. Since they were not acquainted with the area, they were glad to have his cooperation. The editor knew James Wall intended to patrol the Missouri River with four skiffs, close in to the shore, for it was thought the outlaws might try that avenue of escape. The editor had discouraged this plan; later he used it himself in helping the Jameses obtain a skiff to escape."

[1]On an order from the Surgeon-General Dr. Frank W. Murphy, the remains of Charlie Pitts were shipped to the Rush Medical School in Chicago. The young man who had asked for it did not want the body after all. It had been whacked in several places by medical students in St. Paul. Dr. Henry Hoyt of St. Paul took the body, as he wanted a skeleton to hang in his office. In order to whiten the bones to a desired color, Dr. Hoyt placed it in a box and submerged it in Lake Como after carefully marking the spot and placing a number of heavy stones in the box with the body.

Dr. Sidney Mosher

In March of 1877, Dr. Hoyt took a position in Las Vegas, New Mexico, where he had once sold a horse to Billy the Kid. He forgot all about Pitts' bones whitening on the bottom of Lake Como. One day a friend handed him a newspaper clipping which reported the story of the discovery of the remains of a murdered man found in Lake Como. The news article stated that a young muskrat trapper named August Robertson had found the box in the lake. This was reported to the St. Paul police who labeled it a foul murder. It was almost a year before Dr. Hoyt returned to St. Paul, where he informed the Chief of Police about what had happened. The story was verified and the puzzle solved.

When Dr. Hoyt moved to Chicago from New Mexico he took along the skeleton of Charlie Pitts. One day it disappeared, never to be seen again. Thus ended the career of Charlie Pitts, a Missouri lad long known as Sam Wells. Some people claim that the skeleton of Sam now hangs in a western historical museum in Savage, Minnesota.

[2] Because of the intense pain that ensued, the prison surgeon, after three years, tried to remove the bullet by making an incision in the roof of Jim's mouth and trying to pry loose the leaden bullet. His efforts were futile, but some days later Jim pleaded with a hospital intern, who made a careful investigation and finally dislodged the bullet from where it was embedded near the salivary gland and the muscles of the throat, working at intervals of two days. Jim was happy to give the intern the bullet as a keepsake.

CHAPTER 19

The Dark Road

ON SATURDAY, SEPTEMBER 23, 1876, the three Younger brothers were taken from the Flanders House at Madelia by Sheriff Barton of Rice County and transported to the county jail at Faribault. So strongly was the jail guarded that one night a city police officer approached the guard, but when he failed to respond to the challenge of the guard he was shot and killed.

The Grand Jury in the case of the Youngers, on Thursday, November 16, 1876, came in with four indictments:

1. Accessory to the murder of J. L. Heywood
2. Attacking of A. E. Bunker with intent to do great bodily harm
3. Robbery of the First National Bank of Northfield, Minnesota
4. Coleman Younger as principal, and Robert and James Younger as accessories to the murder of Nicholas Gustavson, a citizen of Northfield while the three defendants were participating in the bank robbery.

Their legal counsel, G. W. Batchelder, advised them to plead guilty, thus escaping capital punishment, since the death penalty was not very probable according to the then Minnesota law.

At 1:00 P.M. court convened, the presiding judge was Samuel Lord, and the building was jammed to capacity with only standing room available. Crowds also amassed in lines from the jail to the courthouse of Rice County. The crowd was unruly and unfriendly, to say the least. The people hurled insults and curses upon the Youngers in no uncertain terms, calling them killers, robbers and murderers. At the end of the crowd walked their faithful sister Henrietta and the boys' aunt, Mrs. L. W. Twyman of Blue Mills, Missouri. They were heavily veiled in order to escape detection, but the treatment given the Younger boys was anguish hard for them to bear.

Cole, Jim, and Bob Younger were neatly dressed and were cool and calm, betraying no signs of nervousness as they walked toward the courtroom. When court was called to order Sheriff Barton ordered the crowd to find seats, while County Attorney G. N. Baxter stood before the bench and read the indictments against the Younger brothers.

The prisoners, their shackles now removed, rose to listen to Mr. Baxter as he read the indictments against them. Their physical condition appeared very good, since most of their wounds had healed. Bob still carried his wounded arm in a sling. A recent operation had been performed to cut away the cords from the elbow joint to prevent permanent stiffening.

After the reading of the indictments the prisoners were told to approach the bench individually. Each man pleaded guilty to the murder of cashier Heywood.

"I shall move," said Mr. Baxter, "for the impaneling of a jury to ascertain the degree of the guilt of the prisoners and, as I understand the counsel for the defense desired to argue the motion, I shall ask that it be postponed until this afternoon."

"Very well, I will hear the argument at two o'clock," said Judge Lord. "Court adjourned to that time."

The irons were replaced upon the wrists of the prisoners, the guards took their places, and down the back stairs prisoners and escort marched, while the crowd surged forward to learn what the pleas had been.

Mr. Batchelder, counselor for the defendants, requested to defer his argument until Saturday. Judge Lord granted the request, but due to the need of one of the witnesses to travel to Madelia on Saturday, the answer to the indictments was postponed until Monday, November 20, 1876.

At ten o'clock on Monday morning the prisoners were again taken into court, followed by a large crowd who wondered what pleas actually would be made. Perhaps the defendants might now plead not guilty. Suspense was ended when the Youngers stayed by their plea of guilty to the first indictment for the murder of Joseph Lee Heywood. Mr. Baxter gave notice that he would move to impanel a jury to fix the penalty for the offense. Counsel for the defense desired to argue the question, so the matter was postponed until that afternoon.

The court fixed the time 2:00 P.M. for hearing arguments. The prisoners were returned to the jail. There Cole said he guessed they did the best thing they could. They might have spent large sums of money in legal fees, and still be found guilty of murder in the first degree. The punishment for that would be the same as if they pleaded guilty.

At two o'clock a crowd assembled in the courtroom to witness the closing scenes of the legal drama. The number of spectators exceeded all former gatherings and included a number of ladies.

At 2:15 P.M. the prisoners were brought in without the attendance of armed guards, and were seated in chairs within the bar. Their sister Henrietta sat next to Jim and Mrs. Twyman sat at the end of the bench.

That afternoon, after a lengthy debate over the Minnesota law concerning murder cases by County Attorney Baxter and Attorneys Rutledge and Batchelder for the defense, Judge Lord delivered his opinion:

"The practice of the courts in construing criminal statutes was universal in favor of giving them a strict construction. Where any doubt existed as to the true construction, the interpretation was always given in the manner most favorable to the defendant. As to the question now presented, there seems to be no statute to construe upon this particular point. The statute states that when a jury is impanelled to try a case of murder in the first degree it may pass upon whether the death penalty shall be imposed. The court does not consider that it strictly belongs to the functions of a jury to affix the punishment for an offense. If it were so the jury would be bound to agree, and a judge would be justified in keeping the jury until they agreed either to find in favor of the death penalty or nothing. I deem it clear beyond a question that a jury cannot be impanelled for the sole purpose of passing on that question."

Mr. Batchelder then announced that the prisoners were ready to receive their sentence. The county attorney asked that the court proceed to rend judgment.

Judge Lord asked the prisoners if they had any reason to urge why sentence should not be pronounced and each replied in the negative. The judge then entoned:

"You have been indicted by the grand jury and have acknowledged your guilt. There remains nothing for me, then, but to pass the sentence customary and usual in such cases. I have no words of comfort for you, nor do I desire to reproach or deride you. While the law leaves you life, it leaves but the empty shell; all that goes to make it desirable, its pleasures, hopes, ambition, being gone. You, Thomas Coleman Younger, listen to your sentence: It is that you be punished by confinement in the State's Prison at hard labor during the remainder of the term of your natural life; and you, James Younger, that you be confined in the State's Prison at hard labor for the term of your natural life; and you, Robert Younger, that you be confined to the State's Prison to the end of your natural life."

The sentence was received by the three brothers without a movement of a muscle or a change of expression. Miss Henrietta, seated next to Jim, was completely overcome, and leaned her head upon his shoulder and wept bitter tears. Jim also tried to comfort Mrs. Twyman who was also much affected emotionally. The prisoners then arose and left the courtroom, followed by the two women supported by the defense counsel. No vindictive feelings were manifested by a large crowd of the curious who followed them.

In their cells the brothers returned to their usual good spirits. They resigned themselves to the fate in store for them. Cole said it was what they had expected. Their wounds gave them no trouble except that Bob was unable to use his right arm. It was generally thought that it would always be partially disabled, and

Bob Younger in prison, 1889

Jim Younger in prison, 1889

Minnesota State Prison at Stillwater, Minn.

so it turned out. They expressed gratitude for the humane treatment they had received at the jail, and they had no complaint to
make at their sentence.

The Youngers were taken to the prison at Stillwater on the
morning of November 22, 1876, under guard of Sheriff Ara
Barton, John Passon, Thomas Lord, W. H. Dill, and Phineas
Barton. Henriette Younger and Mrs. Twyman also accompanied
the group.

At the Minnesota State Penitentiary Warden A. J. Reed assigned each brother a cell several cells from the other. Each cell
measured only 5 x 7 and contained a Bible, two cups, one small
mirror, a spoon, face towel, dish towel, a comb, blankets, sheets,
pillowcases, mattress, bedstead and springs, and a small piece of
soap.

The brothers were permitted to see one another once a month
until 1884. Cole was assigned to work in the factory where tubs
and buckets were made. Jim worked in the leather shop and Bob
was assigned to making baskets and straw carriers of various
types. Their special guard was a man named Ben Cayou.

From the tub factory Cole was a long time later elevated to the
job of librarian, where he was allowed to see visitors. One day a
young reporter was permitted to talk with Cole in the library.

"My visit is not to seek revelation of secrets deep within your
hearts, but to simply seek what information I can and what you
are willing to divulge," said the reporter.

"That sounds fair. Ask ahead."

"What do you think caused the birth of the guerrillas in
Missouri?"

"That would take a volume in itself. In Jackson County, where I
come from the people are born fighters. Joe Smith and Brigham
Young laid out Independence, Missouri. Even so, the people
drove them out after several hard fights. The Mormons left and
went to Nauvoo, Illinois, but returned to Missouri and settled in
Platte County; at least, some of them did. Irate Jackson County
citizens, my grandfather Richard Fristoe, among them, again
determined to drive them out. While crossing the river the

ferryman turned the boat over on a bribe from the Mormons. A large number of the men were drowned, fortunately not my grandfather and several others I knew.

"Independence was headquarters for Mexican freighters before the Mexican War, and freight passed between Mexico and Missouri on pack mules, and many Jackson County men engaged in that business. There Colonel Doniphan recruited his famous regiment for the Mexican War. Doniphan marched to Chihuahua and captured it, raising the American flag aloft; then he continued his march to the Gulf of Mexico. You know, Independence was also the headquarters and supply post for the gold seekers of '49. Majors, Russell & Waddell, the overland freighters and pony express people, also lived at Independence. I think the group of guerrillas was an outcome of the Kansas Wakarusa War of 1856 as Jackson County men went to fight in it. In 1855 Kansas was ripped by internal strife over the slavery question. Pro-slavery factions from Missouri actually invaded Kansas from time to time, carrying off anti-slavery advocates. When F. Coleman murdered an anti-slavery man named Charles Dow, pro-slavery elements from Missouri invaded the state and kidnapped Dow's neighbor, a man named Branson, to prevent him from testifying against Coleman. The result was the bitter struggle called the Wakarusa War. Later, Jim Lane, Quantrill's bitter enemy, finally drove the attacking Missourians across the border, ending the conflict.

"So, many Missouri men became guerrilla fighters, conducting a war of spoilation and reprisal, through the brush, trained to quick sorties and deadly ambuscades, thus becoming desperate men by an irresistible combination of circumstances. As this class of guerrillas increased, the warfare on the border became necessarily more cruel and unsparing. Where at first there was only killing in ordinary battle, there became to be no quarter shown. The wounded of the enemy next felt the might of this individual vengeance, acting through a community of bitter memories, and from every stricken field there began, by and by, to come up the substance of this awful bulletin: Dead, such and such a number — wounded, none."

The reporter replied: "Your response is most interesting and enlightening. Did Quantrill really carry a black flag as many writers stated? Some of the ex-guerrillas claim such a flag, is this true?"

"I know that Jim Lane carried a black flag until the fall of 1863, when we captured it, and later sent it to General Price. It may be that Quantrill carried such a flag at the very outset of the war, but not to any extent. It has been said that Annie Fickel made such a flag and gave it to Quantrill in 1862. I never saw it, but heard it was destroyed."

"Where is Quantrill buried?" asked the reporter.

"In a Catholic cemetery in Louisville, Kentucky. Some claim he was not killed, but that is false. Frank James saw him just a while before Quantrill died, and I think Jim did also." (Quantrill's bones were later exhumed and supposedly reburied in Canal Dover, Ohio, by his mother in 1882.)

"What is your opinion of the story that Frank and Jesse James were not full brothers?"

"Surely their mother is the same. I assume they had the same father. I did not know the family until years after that and never did know them well, other than Frank. I also heard this rumor that Jesse was the son of some doctor in Kansas City named Woods."

The reporter continued: "What were the circumstances surrounding the Northfield raid? I understand you were against it and some said Jesse was against it. I also recall that your brother Jim was so badly wounded in the mouth and leaving a trail of blood that Jesse wanted to kill him as he was impeding your escape. Is this true?"

"I will give no details of that robbery or any other that is laid at our door. I tell everyone the same thing. I do this not out of unkindly feelings for your question but not to say anything that might reflect upon our friends."

"After your capture in the swamps, how long did you require medical attention?"

"We are still receiving medical attention, and probably will be doing so for the rest of our lives."

"Can you tell me how often you and your brothers have been shot?"

"I have been wounded altogether twenty times. Eleven of these were received at Northfield and after. Jim was wounded four times at Northfield; six times in total. Bob was never wounded until the pursuit in Minnesota, at which time he was shot three times."

The inquiry continued: "Can you tell me the name of the officer at Independence who ordered all guerrillas captured not to be treated as prisoners of war?"

"It was Colonel Jennison, 15th Kansas Cavalry. But after the Centralia matter this order was countered by Generals Douglass and Fisk, who stated that henceforth all guerrillas would be treated as prisoners of war."

"Do you and your brothers have specific duties here?"

"No. Jim and I do very little as we are on the hospital list, but Bob performs various duties. I occupy much of my time in theological studies for which I seem to have a natural inclination. It was the earliest desire of my parents to prepare me for the ministry, but the horrors of war, the murder of my father, and the outrages perpetrated upon my poor old mother, my sisters and brothers, destroyed our hopes that any of us could be prepared for any duty in life except revenge."

"Do they treat you well here?"

"Yes. We have met with kindness from all corners. We are grateful for the consideration and kindnesses shown us by the various prison guards."

"Did you know Jesse James during the war?"

"No. I did not meet him until January of 1866 at Blue Spring, where we had gathered to discuss giving ourselves up to the State of Kansas which had requisitioned Missouri to do so. Our attorneys advised the lot of us that it would be foolhardy to do so as we would not be given a fair chance. I saw Jesse James again when I went to the Samuel home to visit with his brother Frank. There I saw him, a sort of handsome kid with a little turned up nose, brown hair, blue eyes, high cheekbones. I also saw that the tip of the third finger of his left hand was missing. I later learned he had done this with a pistol when a kid. After the Liberty affair I went to Tensas Parish, to our friend at the Amos place, near Fortune Creek. Later I went to East Carroll Parish, and hid for a spell at the Bass farm. After several months I went to Scyene, Texas, where some old Quantrillians had moved. There I met Myra Belle Shirley, later called Belle Starr, and I had seen her before in Missouri when she was running spy letters for Quantrill. Later it was claimed she had a child by me named Pearl Younger, but this is false. The child was that of Jim Read. She never meant anything to me, no one did, other than Lizzie Brown and Lizzie Daniels."

"What did you think of Frank James?"

"Frank was a thinker; Jesse the doer. He could execute plans well and effectively. He did not want to lead the band, but some of the men thought I should as I was older and more experienced than Jesse. But no gang can have two leaders. We were not bad men in the sense of the Old West where killers were concerned, swaggering into saloons and having shootouts in the street. Scaring citizens and breaking windows and such was not our cup of tea. We never did much of this, if any. We did not tramp into a saloon and demand drinks and attention. We tried to execute well laid plans, get it over with, and ride into hiding or to some other city. We seldom drank at all, and it was surprising to me when Bob Younger and Frank James nipped the bottle too much before the Northfield raid." (Possibly the drinkers had decided to celebrate Jesse's birthday, September 5.)

"What was your mode of operation after a robbery?"

"We seldom rode too many miles from a robbery to hide as we knew every nook and cranny in the area and it was easy to outwit a posse. We never hid in caves and seldom used bedrolls for that would have been a dead giveaway that we slept outdoors. It would create suspicion. Usually we ate our meals at the home of farmers, giving the woman of the house a $5 gold piece or something on that order. We usually approached a target in small groups, never riding in a big group to create suspicion. We posed as cattle buyers most of the time, or horse traders and buyers. I always wore a long linen duster and I suppose my appearance made me the logical one to act as 'buyer.' I was a convincing talker all right and always managed to get the grain sack fairly filled with money."

"Didn't you get tired of riding the outlaw trail?" was the next question.

"I tried to get out of being an outlaw and would have liked it. But it was like being in a marsh, taking one step and sinking deeper with the next. I guess it was fairly easy for us to get recruits up to the time of Northfield. After that Jesse had plenty trouble all the way up to when he was killed by Ford. Our method was simple when entering a bank. I always used the name of Chas. Colburn and asked for change for a big bill or to get a bill discounted. I remember one time that the man did not have change and I left the bank, believe it or not, but we came back in a few days and robbed it anyway.

"I liked riding with brothers Jim and Bob and our brother-in-law, John Jarrette, who later became a prosperous rancher in Arizona. The problem between me and Jesse got worse when he started writing letters to some newspapers claiming I was present at such and such a robbery, when I was not. When Jesse saw Bob and Jim come into the gang he resented it because it meant three Youngers, and only two Jameses."

"Did you ever have any real trouble over this situation?"

"It was just like Jesse to think of a scheme to get me killed. He told me that George Shepherd, another of the band from time to time, was going to kill me. I could not understand that as George and I had been fast friends all through the war. But I determined not to let George get the drop on me. I should have discussed it with him first, knowing Jesse as I did. One night I stopped at the home of Silas Hudspeth, as did most of the men on the run, and to my surprise, there was George Shepherd also. We exchanged cordial greetings. Nothing was said of the supposed trouble between us. Hudspeth told us he had only two beds and that we'd have to bunk together. I watched George closely as we prepared for bed. George got into bed without removing his pants and slept toward the wall. In his hand was a pistol. I did the same thing and we both lay there, face to face, each with a gun in his hand. Nothing was said, we just stared at each other.

"Next morning George asked me why I wanted to kill him. I could have dropped dead. I told him because he wanted to kill me. We talked it over, and it did not take long to determine that Jesse planned for us to kill each other, or at least for one to kill the other. Sometimes it was difficult to tell who was your friend and who was not."

That was the end of the interview.

A few days afterward another visitor sought permission from Warden Reed to speak with Cole Younger.

When asked the reason for this visit the young man stated Cole had once saved his life during the war; that he and his newly-acquired wife were visiting Minnesota on their honeymoon and he desired to speak with his old friend. Reluctantly, the warden allowed the man to see Cole, although his actions plainly showed his dislike for Missourians.

Of course, Cole did not remember the man. It had been years since the incident he mentioned had occurred.

"Do you remember me, Cole Younger?"

"Frankly, I do not, but if you will give me an opportunity to do so, I suppose I will."

"Remember the Battle of Lone Jack and a young soldier whose life you saved by steering him away from the direction of the Union troops?"

"Indeed I do, but your name I never knew."

"It is Captain Warren C. Bronaugh. I want to return the favor by working to get the Youngers released from this awful place."

"That indeed would be wonderful. I doubt, however, that it can be accomplished," said Cole in a soft and respectful tone.

CHAPTER 20

A Fight for Freedom

OTHERS ALSO FOUGHT for the release of the Youngers. The sweethearts of Cole and Jim, since married to others, did all they could to help. Most effective was the work of Cora Lee McNeill Deming (now a widow) who always remained in the background, allowing the limelight to fall on the efforts of Captain Bronaugh, who made Herculean efforts to collect letters of recommendation for the Youngers. He even traveled around the country expounding their virtues as he saw them.

Letters also came from Senator S. B. Elkins, Cole's old schoolteacher whose life he had saved when Quantrill wanted to hang him as a spy. There were also letters from Major Emory S. Foster of the Union Army whose life Cole had saved after the Battle of Lone Jack when another guerrilla wanted to kill the major.

In 1906, Bronaugh wrote a book entitled *The Youngers Fight for Freedom*, describing his work in their behalf from 1882 to 1902. This book is fairly reliable, listing letters he wrote to friends and his spending of private funds as well as his raising of funds from friends, his wide travels in the cause, his camping on the doorsteps of governors, pardon boards, and wardens. Nevertheless it was said that the most driving force behind all this was Cora Lee, Jim's former sweetheart.

On Monday evening, September 16, 1889, Bob Younger died of tuberculosis (called consumption in those days). He had spent thirteen long dark, dreary years inside the prison walls. During

Cora Lee McNeill as a girl

Cora Lee McNeill Deming and daughter Edwynne Neill

Cora Lee McNeill Deming with Cole Younger, 1901

all that time he had been a model prisoner, faithfully performing work assigned to him, always docile under the prison officials. His sister Henrietta, who had suffered for his sake during his dreadful mistakes (or, perhaps, gloried in his fiery spirit), was with him to close his eyes after their last look at the world. The funeral services were held in the prison chapel. Not long afterward the body was taken to Lee's Summit, Missouri, by his sister.

With Bob's death a new and more vigorous campaign was begun to liberate Cole and Jim. Captain Bronaugh went to the then governor of Minnesota, asking him to recommend a pardon.

The Governor replied, "Such a move would be political suicide. Furthermore, all those concerned with Minnesota politics have agreed that no candidate can run for nomination as governor and at the same time advocate the freeing of the Youngers."

This rebuff did not discourage Bronaugh, even though his family suffered by his efforts to free the Youngers. He became so poor that he was compelled to work as manager of the Confederate Home at Higginsville, Missouri (long since razed), from which point he continued writing letters to important people, expressing his view of the matter.

Another woman walked on to the stage of the Younger drama. She was Alix Muller (or Mueller) who stated that she was a longtime lover of Jim and that he had always loved her. Miss Mueller wrote many letters to Jim while he was in prison, letters which he may never have read and certainly did not keep. To him she was an embarrassment whom he thought to be seeking publicity by making a claim upon him.

Another person influential on behalf of the Youngers was George M. Bennett, then attorney for James J. Hill and the Great Northern Railroad. Mr. Bennett, a widower, interested in the Younger case offered his legal counsel to Cora Lee. He had heard of the Youngers but had never met them until he accompanied Cora Lee to Stillwater shortly after she had made his acquaintance. Cole was cordial and Jim was definitely cold, perhaps sensing that Mr. Bennett might take too much of a personal interest in the matter. It is true that later Bennett appointed himself general manager of Cora Lee's attempts to free the Youngers, and he seemed eager to take personal credit.

On Friday, October 18, 1901, Cora Lee married this Mr. Bennett and moved to South Dakota. She had seen Jim several times after his release, but under the terms of his parole he was not permitted to marry.

In the 1901 session of the Minnesota State Legislature a bill was introduced which would provide for the parole of any live convict who had been confined for twenty years, on the unanimous consent of the Board of Pardons. This bill was introduced by Representative P. C. Deming of Minneapolis. Among those who worked for its passage was Representative Jay W. Philips who, when a boy, had been driven from the streets by the outlaws on the day of the Northfield raid. Senator Wilson, who introduced the same bill in 1899, was again a staunch supporter of this bill, and he championed its cause in the chambers of the State Senate.

This bill, which permitted Cole and Jim Younger to be granted a conditional parole, was finally passed. The Board of Pardons did not appear ready to grant them a full pardon or full freedom at that time. Cole and Jim were not to exhibit themselves for any purpose; they would write the warden of the prison each month; they would abstain from the use of liquor and would avoid evil associates; they would not go outside the State of Minnesota; they would remain in the legal custody of the Board of Parole Managers.

On July 14, 1901, Jim and Cole Younger went out into the world for the first time in nearly twenty-five years. The first person to meet them was Captain Bronaugh. Cole was seemingly embarrassed, and neither did the captain know how to begin a conversation.

The younger man said, "I said I'd be the first Missourian to shake your hand, Cole," obviously trying to control his emotion.

"And that you are, captain," and the firm grip they exchanged told its own story.

Cole asked, "Did you send telegrams to any of the folks in Missouri?"

"I sure did."

"I sent one myself," said Cole, a glint of a tear in his eye.

"Who to?"

"Lizzie Daniels down at Harrisonville. You know she was always a dear friend from 'way back."

Bronaugh did not realize that Lizzie was the only one true love of Cole Younger. When Cole finally did return to Missouri his first social call was at the home of Mr. and Mrs Thomas Monroe. What a sad occasion that must have been! Lizzie was married to that prominent businessman and had raised a fine family during the years of Cole's incarceration.

The first employer of the Younger brothers was P. N. Peterson of St. Paul and Stillwater. Their job was to sell tombstones at a salary of $60 a month each, plus expenses. One day Jim was thrown from his buggy when his horse bolted. This accident started anew the physical problem he had in prison, due to the bullet that had lodged under his spine. Because of it Jim was compelled to seek other employment.

Cole worked for the Peterson Granite Company until the latter part of 1901. The change of living habits and working hours took a heavy toll on Cole's vitality. When he returned to St. Paul he went to work for Edward J. and Hubert C. Schurmeier, friends who had fought for his release. Cole also worked for James Nugent of the Interstate Institute for the Cure of the Liquor and Morphine Habits. He enjoyed St. Paul, and several months later he went to work for Chief of Police John J. O'Connor of that city as a personal investigator.

At that time Jim Younger was working for the Andrew Schoch Grocery Company in St. Paul. He also found employment with the Elwin Cigar Company, where he remained until a few days before his death.

In light of Jim's love for Cora Lee and his harsh experiences with Alix Mueller, it is hard to believe that he committed suicide because the Parole Board refused to allow him to marry Alix. The stories left by Miss Mueller probably were figments of her imagination. Jim Younger had never loved her. None of her alleged letters from Jim have ever been seen. Besides, Jim said he never did write any letter to Alix Mueller. The black cloak of despondency and ill health which shrouded poor Jim more than likely decided his final decision.

On October 13, 1902, Jim had requested a full pardon from the Parole Board, but he was refused. About that time Major Elwin sold his cigar store, and Jim planned to go to work for Yerxa Brothers in St. Paul. It was not to be.

On Sunday afternoon, October 19, 1902, Jim's dead body was found in his room at the Reardon Hotel, Seventh and Minnesota Avenues, in St. Paul. He had sent his trunk to friends, and there was every indication that he had carefully planned his death by his own hand. A bullet hole above his right ear and a pistol clutched in his hand told the grim story of suicide. Dr. J. M. Finnell, acting coroner, stated that Jim must have shot himself early in the afternoon. No one had heard the shot.

Cole Younger was ill at the time of Jim's death, and Dr. J. J. Platt, his physician, advised him not to attend the funeral. The body was prepared for burial by the O'Halloran & Murphy Undertaking Establishment, under the direction of Chief of Police O'Connor, who consented to act in Cole's behalf. No mourners were at the train depot except Mr. and Mrs. C. H. Hall, Henrietta Younger Rawlins, and her daughter and her husband.

The funeral services for Jim were held in the same little church in Lee's Summit, Missouri, where services had been held for Robert Younger in 1889. The pallbearers were C. W. Wiggington, O. H. Lewis, H. H. McDowell, Sam Whitsett, William Gregg, and William Lewis, all old neighbors and comrades in arms during the Civil War. Another Younger had come home to rest in the family plot at Lee's Summit.

Newspapers tried to play up the Alix Mueller story again. She told reporters that Jim had killed himself because he was not allowed to marry her. At the mortuary she created such a disturbance at not being allowed to select Jim's casket "as his widow" that the police were called upon to force her to leave. Later family members stated that she was too ill to attend the funeral. Perhaps she did love Jim in her own way — who knows? She later joined her brother in Oklahoma City, where she ran a land business. She died there in April of 1904.

Indeed the story of Jim and Cora Lee was a sorrowful one. Who knows but that if Jim had asked her to do so she might have refused to marry Mr. Bennett, but he would not have interfered with her life to that extent. No doubt she would have continued fighting for a full pardon for him, but that came only in time to benefit Cole.

Jim's tragic death had again brought the name of the Youngers into the limelight. Many people began to suggest that Cole should be allowed to return to Missouri. They claimed that Minnesota had already claimed two of the brothers — why not allow one to enjoy the life left to him? Letters making this suggestion came from many residents of Northfield itself, even from the attorneys who had prosecuted the Youngers. Of course Minnesota probably never had any regard for Cole's feelings, but the time came when the people generally were willing to give him a chance to get out of the state where he had so long suffered.

The time came when the Board of Pardons actually arrived at the decision to grant Cole a conditional pardon. Some of the conditions were similar to those contained in the original parole, with the addition of: "It is ordered that a pardon be granted to Thomas Coleman Younger, upon the condition precedent and subsequent that he return without unnecessary delay to his friends and kindred whence he came, and that he never voluntarily return to Minnesota."

Several days later Cole filed an affidavit with Governor Van Sant promising to keep the conditions of the pardon. He was actually free!

Cole crossed the Missouri-Iowa line via the Chicago-Great Northern Railway at 3:00 P.M. on Sunday, February 14, 1903. Five hours later the train rushed across the bridge at Lee's Summit, and Cole once more set foot upon his beloved Jackson County soil. He had started for Missouri much earlier than he had intended, because on receiving a wire from Lee's Summit that his sister Henrietta was very ill he had hurried to leave Minnesota. He made an effort to avoid publicity, but one reporter did discover his intended departure and made the long trip with Cole to his home town.

Cole was driven to the Midland Hotel for lunch when the train stopped at Grand Central Depot in Kansas City. Then he visited a barber shop, always trying to keep his identity unknown. His attempt to dine was futile, for several agents of an eastern brewery, who had been told not to bother Cole at Kansas City, were on hand to greet him. Frustrated, Cole was driven to the railroad depot, from which point he was to leave at 9:15 that evening for Lee's Summit on the Missouri-Pacific Line.

Cole Younger in 1903 was a well built, stalwart-looking man, clean-shaven and bald-headed, weighing about 220 pounds. His face beamed with smiles and his eyes sparkled, even though he had spent the last twenty-five years in prison. Now twenty-seven years had passed and he was back in Missouri again.

As the train chugged toward the historic Big Blue River, Cole spoke of the proximity of the stream which he said had been the scene of many a hard fight. What a story Cole could have written if he had chosen! The little autobiography which he did write did not shed much light on his varied activities during the war and after. He also still clung to his conviction of not naming Frank and Jesse James as being the two outlaws who used the names of Howard and Woods at Northfield.

The train reached Lee's Summit at 10:15 P.M. The platform was deserted, and a bitter cold north wind added to the conditions caused by a heavy snowfall the previous day. He went through the knee-deep snow to the Summit Hotel some 900 feet away. The hotel was an old fashioned one, owned by A. G. Donahue, the husband of Cole's niece, Nettie Hall, daughter of Mrs. Belle Hall, Cole's sister.

At the moment Cole walked into the lobby Donahue leaped to his feet, took Cole by the hand and loudly exclaimed, "Hey, ain't you Cole Younger?"

"No, sir, my name is Rockford, Dr. Rockford," said Cole, still determined to remain incognito until he had obtained his much needed rest.

It was no use. Donahue called his wife, and a short while later Cole was in the private apartments of the family, telling stories to his relatives until 3:00 A.M. It was now February 16, 1903, and Cole slept on an old-fashioned Missouri featherbed for the first time since 1876. He must have felt like a Rip Van Winkle.

When living at the hotel became too hectic for Cole he moved in with his niece, Nora Hall, and his nephew, Harry Younger Hall.

Later he bought the Halls a two-story white frame building where he resided with them until his death.

Time passed slowly for the old fighter as he sat around the stove or visited with his ex-guerrilla cronies. He realized that he should go to work, so he tried selling coal-oil stoves to the Missouri farmers. They were not interested in the newfangled product. They had plenty of wood to burn. All they wanted to do was to see Cole and talk with him. Cole soon gave up the idea of trying to sell the new invention.

The Wild West Show of Buffalo Bill was so successful that some Chicago brewers contrived the idea to have Frank James and Cole Younger travel around the country with a similar show, a show to include various acts depicting the frontier life, Indian warfare, and marksmanship. Frank James was to direct every performance, Cole to act as general supervisor. Of course, as one condition of his pardon Cole was not permitted to exhibit himself. Adhering to this stipulation to the letter, he simply walked about the grounds while Frank did all the shooting and riding.

Harry Younger Hall spent many hours in his big house at Lee's Summit listening to the stories Cole had told him. This nephew was the treasurer of their Wild West Show, and he kept close tabs on everything that went on.

At one point he said, "Uncle Cole gave up the Wild West Show and came home, just sitting around and gabbing with old friends. He loved children, and they loved him. As soon as he stepped outdoors a bunch of youngsters would crowd around him, calling his name and asking him to tell them stories. He liked that and always obliged them. Sometimes Frank James would visit Cole, but the children did not call him Uncle Frank. To the children Cole was always Uncle Cole."

Later Cole joined the Lew Nicholas carnival, but Frank James did not. It was with the money earned from this job that Cole bought Harry Younger Hall and Nora the two-story house on Market Street, the same house in which Cole died in 1916. This house was razed in recent years to make way for a bank parking lot.

After a time the carnival life began to tell on Cole, so he quit and returned to the Hall home at Lee's Summit. Now all he did

Cole Younger, 1912

Home in Lee's Summit, Mo. where Cole Younger lived until his death

Frank James

Mr. Dutton, Jim Campbell, Cole Younger, and Jeff Boggs

AMUSEMENTS.

"Younger Brothers."

A proposition to donate $10,000 to the charities of Minnesota has been made by the National Amusement Co. of Chicago, owners of the play "Northfield Band Robbery, or Younger Brothers" for a rescission of that part of Cole Younger's pardon which prohibits his appearance in a theatrical exhibition. The company had a play written to present the thrilling circumstances in the lives of the guerrillas with the intention of starring Cole Younger. When they offered the outlaw of former days $10,000 for 100 weeks of his time, the latter informed the theatrical managers he was prevented from making any exhibition of himself for the remainder of his life. Cole and Jim Younger were pardoned July 10, 1901, with the provision they were not to appear in a theatre or make any other exhibition. In 1902 Jim Younger committed suicide because he was unable to obtain suitable employment. He died a socialist and religionist after writing a note to William Jennings Bryan, asking the latter to espouse socialism and devote his gift of oratory to its advocacy. Cole Younger was recently made a partner of Senator Elkins in a street car company that is now being promoted by the former bandit. Cole Younger is a preacher, a penitent man, a humanitarian, and lover of his fellows with none of the wild desires for vengeance that prompted him to commission of his desperate deeds of days gone by. All he desires now is "to end his days in peace." The Minnesota board of pardons may not grant the privilege but if they fail, the theatrical company will engage Frank James and Colonel "Buffalo Bill" Lavelle, former notables in the exciting history of 1861-5 inclusive.

The Younger Brothers will appear at the Pattee opera house this evening.

"Younger Brothers."

"The Younger Brothers" was the attraction at the Pattee Opera House last evening. A small audience was present and they got disgusted before the stunt was over. The only characters that were at all creditable were Roy E. Weed as Eprum Green, and Susie Howard as Anna.

OCTOBER 25, 1905.

Five Coal Barges Sunk.

Ironton, O., Oct. 25.—The tow boat Ironsides in a fog struck the cofferdam of the new bridge here Tuesday morning, losing five barges of coal. The Ironsides left Pittsburg on Saturday night with 22 barges in command of Capt. Richardson bound for Cincinnati.

OCTOBER 21, 1905.

Pattee Opera House

MONDAY, OCTOBER 23.

The National Amusement Company

Presents the Northfield Bank Robbery, or

YOUNGER BROS.

Great, Grand, Graphic, Gigantic Production.

15 People, Singing and Dancing, 2 Loads of Special Scenery.

You must see the murderous assault upon the telegraph operator, wild flight of the midnight express (8 cars), hand to hand encounter at the frightful precipice, marvelous explosion scene, bold bank robbery.

$1,000 reward for the capture of Younger Bros.

A play written for ladies and children, telling a beautiful love story. No shooting

PRICES 25c, 35c and 50c.

Seats on Sale Saturday at Hodgen's Annex

Amusements: Younger Brothers performance, 1905

was sit each day in the lobby of the hotel or take a comfortable chair to the sidewalk outside his home and doze in the sunshine. Sometimes children came up to greet him or to ask for more stories. This pleased the old warrior. He never refused to comply with the wishes of children.

As might be expected, Cole Younger and Frank James had always been ardent democrats. When Frank James told Cole he was going to vote for Teddy Roosevelt on the Bull Moose ticket, Cole almost flipped. Teddy had taken a liking for Frank James, as was his custom with many old outlaws and gunfighters. He gave Frank several of his campaign buttons with his picture on them, and these buttons are still treasured by the family.

Cole loved to attend the ex-Quantrillians' annual get-together at Blue Springs or Independence, along with Bill Gregg, Hi George, Frank James, Jesse Edwards James (the outlaw's son), Harrison Trow, Benjamin Morrow, and many others. He was proud of the Quantrill ribbons each man wore at these picnics. The daughters of Ben Morrow and the son of Hi George, as well as the sons of Frank and Jesse James, were interviewed for material used in this book.

Some time later Cole wanted to go on a lecture tour around the country, telling the people of his experiences and especially his prison years. Many young boys crowded around him. Cole tried to tell them to be good citizens, but they were more interested in his outlaw career than in anything else. He went through a number of the states, expounding the virtues of a good life and stressing that "crime does not pay."

When his wartime buddy, Frank James, died at Kearney, Missouri, on February 18, 1915, Cole was too ill to attend the funeral. The news hit him hard. He went to his room and stared out the window for a long time. After that he seldom saw anyone except perhaps the last of the Quantrillians still around. They seemed to brighten the spark of life still in him.

A year later Cole followed Frank James to the grave. He passed away on February 21, 1916, at 8:45 P.M., at the age of seventy-two. Before his death he had told Jesse E. James and Harry Hoffman that the man who had killed Heywood at Northfield was the man who had ridden the dun horse.

Mr. and Mrs. Ben Morrow

Only three sisters survived Cole. They were Mrs. Helen Kelley of Amoret, Missouri, aged 84; Mrs. Martha Ann Jones, Dennison, Texas, aged 81; and Mrs. Sallie Duncan, Kansas City, Kansas, aged 71. None was able to attend the funeral due to advanced years.

The funeral was held in the Younger home, with the new edition Jesse James and Robert F. James acting as two of the pallbearers. Although every effort had been made to locate some of Cole's old war buddies, only two could be found who were able to make it to the funeral. The list of old Quantrillians was swiftly running out.

Cole Younger was buried in the Lee's Summit Cemetery beside his mother's grave. In the same plot rests two other brothers who chose the outlaw trail, Jim and Bob. John's grave remains near Osceola, Missouri.

A suitable marker was erected at the grave of Cole Younger: a simple headstone with the following inscription: "Cole Younger, 1844-1916, Rest in Peace Our Dear Beloved."

Later the Daughters of the Confederacy placed a marble plaque alongside the headstone. It reads: "Captain Cole Younger, Quantrill's Co., C.S.A."

The Youngers had come home — to the state which had suffered most of their depredations.

Grave of Cole Younger

APPENDIX A:

Quantrill's Guerrillas

Akers, Sylvester.
Anderson, James.
 Killed in Austin,
 Tex. after the
 war.
Anderson,
 William. Killed
 at Orrick, Mo. in
 1864.
Archie, Hugh.
Archie, William.
Asbury, A.E.

Baker, John. Or-
 derly Sergeant.
Barker, John.
Barnhill, John.
Basham, Sol.
Brasham, William.
 Surrendered at
 Smiley, Ky.
Berry, Dick.
Berry, Ike.
Bishop, Jackson.

Bledsoe, William.
 Killed on retreat
 from Lawrence,
 Kans.
Blunt, Andy.
 Wounded on
 April 16, 1862.
Blythe, ?
Bochman, Charley.
Brady, Mass. Cap-
 tured.
Brinker, John.
 Capt.
Broomfield, Ben.
Brown, John.
 Sheldon, Mo.
Bunch, Oliver.
Burns, Dick.
 Hanged on May
 27, 1867.
Burton, Pete.
 Killed at Lamar,
 Mo. on Nov. 5,
 1862.

Campbell, Doc.
Carr, Bill. Killed
    on April 16,
    1862.
Carter, Harrison.
Castle, Theodore.
Chatman, John.
Chiles, Bill.
Chiles, James
    Crow. Killed by
    a citizen at Inde-
    pendence, Mo.
Chiles, Kit.
Chiles, William.
Clarke, Jerome H.
    (Sue Monday).
    Hanged at Lou-
    isville, Ky.
Clarke, Sam C.
Clayton, George.
Chifton, Sam.
Clements, Arch.
    Killed at Lex-
    ington, Mo. on
    Dec. 1866.
Clements, Henry.
Coger, John.
Commons, Smith.
Corum, Al.
Corum, James.
Corum, John.
Crabtree, Joe.
Crawford, Riley.
    Killed in Jack-
    son Co., Mo.
Creek, Ereth.
Cummins, Jim.
    Died in Confed-
    erate home in
    Higginsville,
    Mo. ca 1928.

Cundiff, James.
Cunningham, Al-
    bert.

Dalton, J. Frank.
    Died in Grand-
    bury, Tex. in
    1951.
Dalton, Kit.
Dancer, Jim.
DeBonhorst, Paul.
DeHart, E.P.
Devers, Alva.
Devers, Art.
Donohue, Jim.
    Killed at Lamar,
    Mo. in 1862.

Edmundson, J.F.
Emory, Jeff.
Ervin, J.C.
Esters, Josh.
Estes, ?
Evans, Tom. Sur-
    rendered at
    Smiley, Ky.

Flannery, Ike.
    Killed by Jesse
    James after the
    war.
Flannery, John.
Flannery, Si.
Flournoy, John.
Fox, ?
Freeman, Will.
Frisby, John.
Fry, Frank.

Gaugh, Bill. Went to Ky. with Quantrill.

George, Dave.

George, Gabe. Killed at Independence, Mo. on Feb. 1862.

George, Hicks.

George, Hiram. Captain in Quantrill's band.

Gibson, Joe.

Gilchrist, Joe. Killed at Pink Hill, Mo. on April 1862.

Glasscock, Richard. Killed on May 10, 1865, in Ky.

Gordon, Silas.

Graham, John. Went to Ky. with Quantrill.

Gray, Frank.

Greenwood, William. Became prosperous Vernon Co., Mo. farmer.

Gregg, Frank J. Settled in Independence, Mo. after the war.

Gregg, William H. Adjutant of Quantrill's Guerrillas.

Guess, Hiram.

Haick, ?

Hall, Isaac. Went to Ky. with Quantrill.

Hall, Robert. Went to Ky. with Quantrill.

Hall, Thomas. Went to Ky. with Quantrill.

Haller, Abe.

Haller, Wash.

Haller, William. Quantrill's first recruit.

Hamilton, Sam.

Hamlett, Jess.

Hampton, John.

Harris, John.

Harris, Reuben. Harbored Quantrill's men.

Harris, Tom.

Harrison, Charles.

Hart, Joseph.

Hays, Perry.

Hays, William.

Hegan, Edward.

Helms, Polk.

Hendricks, James A.

Henry, Thomas.

Higbee, Charles.

Hildebrand, Sam. Killed March 21, 1865 at Pinckneyville, Ill.

Hill, Thomas.

Hill, Tucker.

Hill, Woot.

Hinds, James.

Hines, John.
Hink, Edward.
Hinton, Otto.
Hockinsmith,
   Clarke. Killed
   on May 10, 1865,
   in Ky.
Hollings, Washing-
   ton.
Holt, John.
Hotie, Richard.
Hoy, Perry. Exe-
   cuted at Fort
   Leavenworth,
   Kans.
Hubbard, John.
Hudspeth, George
   (Babe). Went
   part way to Ky.
   with Quantrill.
Hudspeth, Rufe.
   Went part way
   to Ky. with
   Quantrill.
Huffaker, Mose.
Hulse, William.
   Went to Ky. with
   Quantrill.
Hunt, Thomas
   (Guerrilla Tom).
   Mistaken for
   Jesse James.

Jackson, John.
James, Frank. Died
   in Kearney, Mo.
   in 1915.
James, Jesse Wood-
   son. Shot by Ro-
bert Ford in St.
   Joseph, Mo.,
   1882.
James, William.
Jarrette, John.
   Later owner of
   large sheep
   ranch in Ariz.
Jobson, Smith.
Johnson, Oll.
Jones, Jim.
Jones, Payne.
   Killed by Jim
   Crow Chiles.

Kelly, James.
Kelly, Tom.
Kennedy, Dave.
Kennedy, Steve.
Kennedy, Sterling.
Kerr, Nathan.
Ketchum, Al.
Key, Foster.
King, Willis.
Kinney, Dick.
Knight, ?
Koger, Ed.
Koger, John W.

Lea, Joe. Died in
   Roswell, N. Mex.
   in 1904.
Lee, Albert.
Letten, Ling.
Lilly, James. Went
   to Ky. with
   Quantrill.
Little, James. Went
   to Ky. with
   Quantrill.

Little, John.
Little, Thomas.
Hanged by a
mob at Warrens-
burg, Mo.
Long, Peyton.
Went to Ky. with
Quantrill.
Lotspeach,
William.
Luckett, ?

Maddox, George.
Chief scout; re-
tired to Nevada,
Mo.
Maddox, Morgan
T.
Maddox, Richard.
Killed by a
Cherokee In-
dian after the
war.
Marshall, Ed.
Marshall, James.
Maupin, John.
Maupin, Thomas.
Became a Texas
cattleman after
the war.
Maxwell, Ambros.
Maxwell, Thomas.
Miller, Edward.
Killed by Jesse
James after the
war.
Miller, McClellan
(Clell). Killed in
Northfield bank
raid 1876.

Monkers, "Red."
Moody, Jasper.
Morris, James.
Morrow, Bejamin
J.
Morton, Wade.
Murray, "Plunk."

McAninch, Henry.
McArtor, James T.
McCabe, James.
McCorkle, John.
McCorkle, Joseph.
McCorkle, Josiah.
McCorkle,
Thomas.
McCoy, Arthur.
McCoy, Richard.
McDowell, John.
McGuire, Andy.
Hanged in June,
1867.
McGuire, Bill.
McIlvaine, John.
McIvor, John.
McMurty, Lee.

Nicholson, Arch.
Nicholson, Joseph.
Noland, Edward.
Went to Ky. with
Quantrill.
Noland, Henry.
Went to Ky. with
Quantrill.
Noland, William.
Went to Ky. with
Quatrill.
Norfolk, John.

O'Donal, Patrick.

Owens, Thomas.

Palmer, Chris.
Went to Ky. with
Quantrill.

Palmer, Allen H.
Died at Wichita
Falls, Tex. 1927.

Parr, "Buster"
Mike.

Patterson, Hank.

Pense, "Bud."
Went to Ky. with
Quantrill.

Pense, "Donny."
Went to Ky. with
Quantrill.

Perkins, ?

Perry, Joab. De-
serted Quantrill
after Lawrence
raid.

Peyton, ?

Pool, Dave. Settled
in Sherman,
Tex. after the
war.

Pool, John.

Pope, Sam.

Porter, Henry.
Went to Ky. with
Quantrill.

Potts, Levi, Capt.

Pringle, John.

Privin, Hence.

Privin, Lafe.

Railly, Lon.

Ralston, Crockett.

Read, James.
Killed in Texas
in 1874.

Renick, Chatam.
Ordered Riley
Crawford exe-
cuted.

Reynolds, William.

Robertson, Gooley.

Robinson, George.

Robinson,
William.
Hanged in Ky.
in 1865.

Roder, William.

Rollen, ?

Rollen, ? (second).

Ross, John. Went
to Ky. with
Quantrill.

Rudd, John.

Rupe, Jackson.

Ryan, Volney.

Sanders, Tid.

Schull, Boon.

Scott, Ferando.

Shepherd, Frank.

Shepherd, George.
Spent time in
Ky. penitentiary.

Shepherd, Oliver.
Killed by police
in 1868.

Shores, Stephen.

Simmons, ?

Skaggs, Larkin
Milton. Killed in
Lawrence, Kans.

Smith, William.

Southwick, A.B.
Southwick, C.H.
Stewart, Charles.
Stewart, William.
Story, "Bud."
Stuart, William H.
Sturgeon, ?
Sutherland, Jack.
Sutherland, Zeke.

Talley, George.
Tarkington,
   William.
Tate, David.
Taylor, Charles
   Fletcher. Later
   in Mo. legisla-
   ture.
Thrailkill, John.
   Captain in
   Quantrill's band.
Tigue, Nat.
Todd, George.
   Killed at Inde-
   pendence, Mo.
   in 1864.
Todd, Thomas.
Toler, Bill.
Tooley, J.B.
Tolliver, Anse.
Toothman,
   William, Lt.
Traber, Thomas.
Trow, Harrison B.
   Identified body
   of Jesses James.
Tucker, James.
Tucker, Morris J.
Tucker, William.

VanMeter, John.
Vaughn, Dan.
Vaughn, James A.
   Wrote book,
   claimed to be
   Frank James.
Vaughn, Joseph.
Venable, Randall
   M. Went to Ky.
   with Quantrill.

Wade, Sam.
Walker, Andrew J.
Warren, John
   Thomas. Died in
   Colo. in 1932.
Wayman, F.
   Luther.
Webb, Charley.
Webb, George.
Webster, Noah.
Welch, Warren.
Wells, Polk.
West, Richard.
White, James.
White, John.
Whitsett, James Si-
   meon.
Wiggington,
   George.
Wilkinson, James.
Williams, Hank.
William, James.
Wilson, Dave.
Wood, Bennett.
Wood, Robert.
Wood, Hop.
Wyatt, Cave.

Yeager, Richard.

Young, Joseph.
Younger, Chris.
Younger, James.
Commited sui-
cide 1902 in
Minn.
Younger, John.
Killed by Pinker-
tons near Os-
ceola, Mo. in
1874.
Younger, Thomas
Coleman (Cole).
Died in Lee's
Summit, Mo.
1916.

APPENDIX B:

The Younger Family

THE ANCESTORS OF COLE YOUNGER came to this country from Europe, where they had helped to rule the Free City of Strasburg. The family settled in Crab Orchard, Kentucky, where Henry Washington Younger was born in 1812. He migrated to Missouri with his parents some time before 1830 and settled in a stretch of country known as Jackson County which included such towns as Kansas City, Independence, Lee's Summit, and Blue Springs.

Soon after his arrival in Jackson County Harry Younger met the pretty Miss Bursheba Fristoe of Independence. They were married in 1830 after a brief courtship and settled on a farm at Lee's Summit on Big Creek. He was eighteen, she thirteen, according to the family records. The 1850 census records Henry W. Younger being age 38 and Bursheba Younger being age 33. It also shows that Mr. Younger was a farmer worth $9,000 and that he owned six slaves. Also living with the family were two carpenters, Hardin and W. Shoemate.

Their first child was Helen Younger, born some time in 1832, followed by Isabella, born in 1834; Martha born in 1836; Richard, born in 1838; Josephine born in 1840; Caroline born in 1842; Thomas Coleman, born in 1844; Sarah born in 1846; and James born in 1848. The remaining five children followed after 1850.

Richard Fristoe, the father of Bursheba Fristoe Younger, had fought with General Andrew Jackson at the Battle of New Orleans, and it was chiefly through his efforts that Jackson County, Missouri, was named after his commander. Mrs. Bursheba Younger was descended from the Sullivans, Logans, and Percivals of

267

South Carolina, the Taylors of Virginia, and the Fristoes of Tennessee. Cole's grandfather Fristoe was the grandnephew of Chief Justice Marshall of Virginia.

Henry Washington Younger's family had always been politically prominent. Cole's great-grandmother, Mary Lee, the daughter of "Lighthorse Harry" (Henry) Lee of Revolutionary war fame, had married Logan Younger, born about 1754 in Kent County, Maryland. This marriage occurred in 1770. The family was also distantly related to General Robert E. Lee, the third son of Lighthorse Harry Lee by his second wife, Anne Hill Carter.

The records indicate that Logan Younger married a second time to Catherine Yates in 1786. By his first wife he had the following children: Elizabeth, Charles Lee, and Isaac Younger. By his second wife he had Steven, Polly, Nimrod, Sally, Mary, Joan, Garret, and Lewis Younger.

Charles Lee Younger, the son of Logan Younger and the grandfather of Cole, married Sarah Sullivan Percell in Clark County, Missouri, August 21, 1807. Charles Lee Younger was born in Missouri about 1789 and died there on November 12, 1854. The only record that can be found earlier in the Younger family is that of Lewis Younger, born about 1725, and who no doubt was the father of Logan Younger.

There were fourteen children born of the union of Henry Washington Younger and Bursheba Fristoe Younger; three of them died at an early age, and in 1860 Richard, the eldest son passed away.

Thomas Coleman Younger, the seventh child, was born on January 15, 1844, at the Younger plantation about five miles south of Lee's Summit, Missouri. He was named in part after his uncle Coleman Younger. When Cole later turned to outlawry this uncle moved to California, where he operated a large country-type mercantile store. Cole visited the area from time to time when he was on the run. Members of this Younger family later became prominent in California political circles, as did Drury Woodson James, an uncle of Jesse and Frank James.

James Henry Hardin Younger was born on January 15, 1848, John in 1851, and Robert Ewing Younger in 1853. Thus it was that Cole, being the eldest of the four Younger brothers destined to ride prominently through the pages of history of the Missouri territory was to play the most important role in this drama of death, friendship, and political hatred.

Several writers have denied the existence of other Younger families in Missouri. They claim that Cole did not have a cousin in the Missouri Enrolled Militia (the one he killed). Two of Cole's uncles we know of were Thomas Jefferson Younger and Benjamin Franklin Younger who, at one time, was sheriff of St. Clair County, Missouri.

Adeline Younger, Cole's aunt, married Louis (or Lewis) Dalton on March 12, 1851, according to the records at Independence, Missouri. She was fifteen, he thirty-six years of age. Adeline Younger Dalton bore fifteen children in the counties of Cass, Clay, or Jackson. Among these there were the notorious Bob, Emmett, and Grattan, two of whom were killed while trying to rob two banks at the same time at Coffeyville, Kansas.

Louis Dalton was a Kentuckian, a farmer and stockman, and a lenient parent. Adeline was the disciplinarian of that family due to her early years when she was taught never to shirk her responsibilities in any regard.

In 1882 Louis Dalton moved his family to the Indian Territory of Oklahoma, where he settled near Vinita, about a hundred miles east of Guthrie. From that point the Dalton boys launched their crime spree.

Cole always denied being a cousin of the Dalton boys and refused to discuss the matter. He once hinted that they were related to Jesse and Frank James, but this is not true.

Cole Younger's Speech, given many times between 1905 and 1912

Looking back through the dimly lighted corridors of the past, down the long vista of time, a time when I feared not the face of mortal man, nor battalions of men, when backed by my old comrades in arms, it may seem inconsistent to say that I appear before you with a timidity that almost overwhelms me; not that timidity born of cowardice, but perhaps you will understand better than I can tell you that twenty-five years in a prison cell fetters a man's intellect as well as his body. Therefore I disclaim any pretentions to literary merit, and trust that my sincerity of purpose will compensate for my lack of eloquence; and, too, I am not so sure that I care for that kind of oratory that leaves the points to guess at, but rather the simple language of the soul that needs no interpreter.

Let me say, ladies and gentlemen, that the farthest thought from my mind is that of posing as a character. I do not desire to stand upon the basis of the notoriety which the past record of my life may have earned for me.

Those of you who have been drawn here by mere curiosity to see a character of a man, who by the events of his life has gained somewhat of notoriety, will miss the real object of this lecture and the occasion which brings us together. My soul's desire is to benefit you by recounting some of the important lessons which my life has taught me.

Life is too short to make other use of it. Besides, I owe too much to my fellow men, to my opportunities, to my country, to my God, and to myself, to make any other use of the present occasion.

Since I am to speak to you of some of the important lessons of my life, it may be in order to give you some account of my ancestry. It is something to one's credit to have an ancestry that one need not be ashamed of.

But I am proud to say, ladies and gentlemen, that no loop of stronger twine sometimes referred to ever plagued any relation of mine. No member of our family or ancestry was ever punished for any crime of infringement of the law. My father was a direct descendant from the Lees on one side and the Youngers on the other. The Lees came from Scotland tracing their line back to Bruce. The Youngers were from the City of Strasburg on the Rhine, descending from the ruling family of Strasburg when that was a free city.

My sainted mother was a direct descendant from the Sullivans, Ladens, and Percivals of South Carolina, the Taylors of Virginia and the Fristoes of Tennessee. Richard Fristoe, mother's father, was one of three judges appointed by the governor of Missouri to organize Jackson County, and was then elected one of the first members of the Legislature. Jackson County was so named in honor of his old general, Andrew Jackson, with whom he served in the Battle of New Orleans.

My father and mother were married at Independence, the county seat of Jackson County, and there they spent many happy years, and there my own happy childhood days were spent. There were fourteen children of us; I was the seventh. There were seven younger than myself. How often in the dark days of the journey over the sea of life have I called up the happy surroundings of my early days when I had a noble father and a dear mother to appeal to in faith for counsel. There had never been a death in the family up to 1860, except among our plantation Negroes. Mine was a happy childhood.

I do not desire to pose as an instructor for other people, yet one man's experience may be of value to another, and it may not be presumptuous for me to tell some of the results of experience, a teacher whose lessons are severe, but at least, worthy of consideration. I might say, perhaps, with Shakespeare, 'I have bought golden opinions from all sorts of people.'

The subject of my discourse tonight is the index of what is to follow. I believe that no living man can speak upon his theme with more familiarity. I have lived the gentleman, the soldier, the outlaw, and the convict, living the best twenty-five years of my life in a felon's cell. I have no desire to pose as a martyr, for men who sin must suffer, but I will punctuate my remarks with bold statements, for the eagle should not be afraid of the storm.

It is said that there are but three ways by which we arrive at knowledge in this world: by instruction, by observation, and by experience. We must learn our lessons in life by some one or all of these methods. Those of us who do not, or will not, learn by instruction or by observation are necessarily limited to the fruits of experience. The boy who is told by his mother that fire burns, and who has seen his brother badly burned, surely does not need the fact still more clearly impressed upon his mind by experience. Yet in the majority of cases, it takes experience to satisfy him. By a kind of necessity which I cannot at this point stop to explain, I have had to learn some very impressive lessons of my life by the stern teacher, experience. Some people express a desire to live over again, under the impression that they could make a better success of it on a second trip; such people are scarcely logical, however sincere they may be in a wish of this kind. They seem to forget that by the unfailing law of cause and effect, were they to go back on the trail at the point from which they started and try it over again, under the same circumstances they would land about where they are now. The same causes would produce the same effect.

I confess that I have no inexpressible yearnings to try my life over again, even if it were possible to do so. I have followed the trail of my life for something over fifty years. It has led me into varied and strange experiences. The last twenty-six years, by a train of circumstances I was not able to control, brought me to the present place and hour. Perhaps it may be proper for me to say, with St. Peter, on the mount of transfiguration, it is good to be here.

The man who chooses the career of outlawry is either a natural fool or an innocent madman. The term outlaw has a varied meaning. A man may be an outlaw, and yet a patriot. There is the outlaw with the heart of velvet and a hand of steel; there is an outlaw who never molested the sacred sanctity of any man's home; there is the outlaw who never dethroned a woman's honor, or assailed her heritage, and there is an outlaw who never robbed the honest poor. Have you heard of the outlaw, who in the far-off Western land, where the sun dips to the horizon in infinite beauty, was the adopted son of the Kootenai Indians? It was one of the saddest scenes in all the annals of human tragedy. It was during one of those fierce conflicts which characterized earlier frontier days.

The white outlaw had influenced the red man to send a message to the whites, and for this important mission the little son of the Kootenai chief was selected. The young fawn mounted his horse, but before the passport of peace was delivered the brave little courier was shot to pieces by a cavalcade of armed men who slew him before questioning his mission. The little boy was being stripped of the adornments peculiar to Indians when the outlaw rode upon the scene.

"Take your hands off him, or by the God, I'll cut them off," he shouted.

"You have killed a lone child · the messenger of peace · peace which I risked my life to secure for the white men who outlawed me."

Taking the dead body tenderly in his arms, he rode back to face the fury of a wronged people. He understood the penalty but went to offer himself as a ransom, and was shot to death.

This, however, is not the class of outlaws I would discuss, for very often force of circumstances makes outlaws of men, but I would speak of the criminal outlaw whom I would spare not, nor excuse. My friends, civilization may be a thin veneer, and the world today may be slimy with hypocrisy, but no man is justified in killing lions to feed dogs. Outlawry is often a fit companion for treason and anarchy, for which the lowest seats of hell should be reserved. The outlaws, like the commercial freebooter, is often a deformity on the face of nature that darkens the light of God's day.

I need not explain my career as an outlaw, a career that has been gorgeously colored with fiction. To me the word outlaw is a living coal of fire. The past is a tragedy — a tragedy wherein danger lurks in every trail. I may be pardoned for hurrying over a few wild, relentless years that led up to a career of outlawry — a memory that cuts like the sword blades of a squadron of cavalry. The outlaw is like a big, black bird, from which every passerby feels licensed to pluck a handful of feathers.

My young friend, if you are endowed with physical strength, valor, and a steady hand, let me warn you to use them well, for the God who gave them is the final victor.

Think of a man born of splendid parents, good surroundings, the best of advantages, a fair intellectuality, with the possibility of being president of the United States, with the courage of a field general. Think of him lying stagnant in a prison cell. This does not apply alone to the highway outlaws but to those outlaws who are sometimes called by the softer name 'financier.' Not long ago I heard a man speak of certain banker, and I was reminded that prisons do not contain all the bad men. He said: 'Every dog that dies has some friend to shed a tear, but when that man dies there will be universal rejoicing.'

I am not exactly a lead man, but it may surprise you to know that I have been shot between twenty and thirty times and am now carrying over a dozen bullets which have never been extracted. How proud I should have been had I been scarred battling for the honor and glory of my country. Those wounds I received while wearing the gray, I've ever been proud of, and my regret is that I did not receive the rest of them during the war with Spain, for the freedom of Cuba and the honor and glory of this great and glorious republic. But, alas, they were not, and it is a memory embalmed that nails a man to the cross.

I was in prison when the war with Cuba was inaugurated, a war that will never pass from memory while hearts beat responsive to the glory of battle in the cause of humanity. How men turned from the path of peace, and seizing a sword, followed the flag. As the blue ranks of American soldiery scaled the heights of heroism, and the smoke rose from the hot altars of the battle gods and freedom's wrongs avenged, so the memory of Cuba's independence will go down in history, glorious as our own revolution —

'76 and '90 — twin jewels set in the crown of sister centuries. Spain and the world have learned that beneath the folds of our nation's flag there lurks a power as irresistible as the wrath of God.

Sleep on, side by side in the dim vaults of eternity, Manila Bay and Bunker Hill, Lexington and Santiago, Ticonderoga and San Juan, glorious rounds in Columbia's ladder of fame, growing colossal as the ages roll. Yes, I was in prison then, and let me tell you, dear friends, I do not hesitate to say that God permits few men to suffer as I did, when I awoke to the full realization that I was wearing the stripes instead of a uniform of my country.

Remember friends, I do not uphold war for commercial pillage. War is a terrible thing, and leads men sometimes out of the common avenues of life. Without reference to myself, men of this land, let me tell you emphatically, dispassionately, and absolutely that war makes savages of men, and dethrones them from reason. It is too often sugarcoated with the word 'patriotism' to make it bearable and men call it 'National honor.'

Come with me to the prison, where for a quarter of a century I have occupied a lonely cell. When the door swings in on you there, the world does not hear your muffled wail. There is little to inspire mirth in prison. For a man who has lived close to the heart of nature, in the forest, in the saddle, to imprison him is like caging a wild bird. And yet imprisonment has brought out the excellencies of many men. I have learned many things in the lonely hours there. I have learned that hope is a divinity; I have learned that a surplus of determination conquers every weakness; I have learned that you cannot mate a white dove with a blackbird; I have learned that vengeance is for God and not for man; I have learned that there are some things better than a picture on a church window; I have learned that the American people, and especially the good people of Minnesota, do not strip a fallen foe; I have learned that whoever says there is no God is a fool; I have learned that politics is often mere traffic, and statesmanship trickery; I have learned that the honor of the republic is put upon the plains and battled for; I have learned that the English language is too often used to deceive the commonwealth of labor; I have learned that the man who prides himself on getting on the wrong side of every public issue is as pernicious an enemy to the country as the man who openly fires upon the flag; and I have seen mute sufferings of men in prison which no human pen can portray.

And I have seen men die there. During my twenty-five years of imprisonment, I have spent a large portion of the time in the hospital, nursing the sick and soothing the dying. Oh! the sadness, the despair, the volcano of human woe that lurks in such an hour. One, a soldier from the North, I met in battle when I wore the gray. In '63 I had led him safely beyond the Confederate lines in Missouri, and in '97 he died in my arms in the Minnesota prison, a few moments before a full pardon had arrived from the president. The details of this remarkable coincidence were pathetic in the extreme, equalled only by the death of my young brother Bob.

And yet, my dear friends, prisons and prison discipline, which sometimes destroy the reason, and perpetuate a stigma upon those who survive them, these, I say, are the safeguards of the nation.

A man has plenty of time to think in prison, and I might add that it is an ideal place for a man to study law, religion, Shakespeare, not forgetting the president's messages. However, I would advise you not to try to get into prison just to find an ideal place for these particular studies. I find, after careful study, that law is simply an interpretation of the Ten Commandments, nothing more, nothing less. All law is founded upon Scripture, and Scripture, in form of religion and law, rules the universe. The infidel who ridicules religion is forced to respect the law, which in reality is religion itself.

It is not sufficient alone to make good and just laws, but our people must be educated, or should be, from the cradle up, to respect the law. This is one great lesson to be impressed upon the American people. Let the world know that we are a law-loving nation, for our law is our life.

Experience has taught me that there is no true liberty apart from the law. Law is a boundary line, a wall of protection, circumscribing the field in which liberty may have her freest exercise. Beyond the boundary line, freedom must surrender her rights, and change her name to 'penalty for transgression.' The law is no enemy, but the friend of liberty. The world and the planets move by law. Disregarding the law by which they move, they would become wanderers in the bleak darkness forever.

The human mind is its normal condition moves and works by law. When selfwill, blinded by passion or lust, enters her realm, and breaks her protecting laws, mind then loses her sweet liberty of action, and becomes a transgressor. Chaos usurps the throne of liberty, and mind becomes at enmity with law. How many, many times the words of the poet have sung to my soul during the past twenty-six years:

> Eternal spirit of the chainless mind,
> Brightest in dungeon's liberty thou art,
> For there thy habitation is the heart,
> The heart, which love of thee alone can bind.

Your locomotive with her following load of life and treasure is safe while she keeps the rails, but suppose that with an insane desire for a larger liberty, she left the rails and struck out for herself a new pathway: ruin, chaos and death would strew her course. And again let me impress the fact upon you. Law is one of humanity's valiant friends. It is the safeguard of the highest personal and national liberties. The French revolution furnishes a standing illustration of society without law.

There are times when I think the American people are not patriotic enough. Some think patriotism is necessary only in time of war, but I say to you it is more necessary in time of peace.

When the safety of the country is threatened, and the flag insulted, we are urged on by national pride to repel the enemy, but in time of peace selfish interests take the greater hold of us, and retard us in our duty to country. Nowhere is patriotism needed more than at the ballot box. There the two great contestants are country and self, and unless the spirit of patriotism guides the vote our country is sure to lose. To be faithful citizens we must be honest in our politics. The political star which guides us should be love of our country and our country's laws. Patriotism, side by side with Christianity, I would have to go down to future generations, for wherever the church is destroyed you are making room for asylums and prisons. With the martyred Garfield, I too, believe that our great national danger is not from without.

It may be presumptuous in me to proffer so many suggestions to you who have been living in a world from which I have been exiled for twenty-five years. I may have formed a wrong conception of some things, but you will be charitable enough to forgive my errors. I hope to be of some assistance to mankind and will dedicate my future life to unmask every wrong in my power and aid civilization to rise against further persecution. I want to be the drum-major of a peace brigade, who would rather have the good will of his fellow creatures than shoulder straps from any corporate power.

One of the lessons impressed upon me by my life experience is the power of which we call personal influence, the power of one mind or character over another. Society is an aggregate of units. The units are related. No one lives or acts alone, independently of another. Personal influence plays its part in the relations we sustain to each other. Do you ask me to define what I mean by personal influence? It is the sum total of what a man is, and its effect upon another. Some one has said, 'Every man is what God made him,' and some considerably more so. That which we call character is the sum total of all his tendencies, habits, appetites, and passions. The terms character and reputation are too often confused. Character is what you really are; reputation is what someone else would have you.

Every man has something of good in him. Probably none of us can say we are all goodness. I have noticed that when a man claims to be all goodness, that claim alone does not make his credit any better in business, or at the bank. If a man is good the world has a way of finding out his qualities. Most men are willing to admit, at least to themselves, that their qualities are somewhat mixed. I do not believe that the good people of the world are all bunched up in one corner and the bad ones in another. Christ's parable of the wheat and the tares explains that to my satisfaction. There is goodness in all men, and sermons even in stones. But goodness and badness is apt to run in streaks. Man, to use the language of another, is a queer combination of cheek and perversity, insolence, pride, impudence, vanity, jealousy, hate, scorn, baseness, insanity, honor, truth, wisdom, virture, and urbanity. He's a queer combination all right. And those mixed elements of his nature, in their effects on other people, we call personal influence. Many a man is not altogether what he has made himself, but what others have made him. But a man's personal influence is within his own control. It is at the gateway of his nature from which his influence goes forth that he needs to post his sentinels.

Mind stands related to mind, somewhat in the relation of cause and effect. Emerson said, 'You send your boy to school to be educated, but the education that he gets is largely from the other boys.' It is a kind of education that he will remember longer and have a greater influence upon his character and career in life than the instructions he gets from the teacher.

The great scholar, Elihu Burritt, has said, 'No human being can come into this world without increasing or diminishing the sum total of human happiness.' No one can detach himself from the connection. There is no spot in the universe to which he can retreat from his relations to others.

This makes living and acting among our fellows a serious business. It makes life a stage, ourselves the actors — some of us being remarkably bad actors — and imposes upon us the obligation to act well our part. Therein all honor lies. And in order to do this it behooves us to stock up with the qualities of mind and character, the influence of which will be helpful to those who follow the trail behind us.

Another plain duty my experience has pointed out is that each of us owes an honest, manly effort toward the material world's progress. Honest labor is the key that unlocks the door of happiness. One of the silliest notions that a young man can get into his head is the idea that the world owes him a living. It does not owe you the fraction of a red cent, young man. What have you done for the world that put it under obligation to you? When did the world become indebted to you? Who cared for you in the years of helpless infancy? Who built the schoolhouse where you got the rudiments of your education? The world was made and equipped for men to develop it. Almighty God furnished the world well. He provided abundant coal beds, oceans of oil, boundless forests, seas of salt. He has ribbed the mountains with gems fit to deck the brows of science, eloquence and art. He has furnished earth to produce for all the requirements of man. He has provided man himself with an intellect to fathom and develop the mysteries of His handiwork. Now He commands that mortal man shall do the rest, and what a generous command it is! And this is the world that owes you a living, is it?

This reminds me of a man who built and thoroughly equipped a beautiful church, and presented it as a gift to the congregation. After expressing their gratitude, a leading member of the church said to the generous donor: 'And now may we request that you put a lightning rod on the church to secure it against lightning?' The giver replied: 'No. I have built a church wherein to worship Almighty God, and if He sees fit to destroy it by lightning, let Him strike.'

There was a church struck by lightning in New Jersey, where the big trust magnates met for worship, and the Lord is excused for visiting it with lightning. No, the Lord is not going to strike down your good works at all. He has laid out an earthly Paradise for each of us, and nothing is due us except what we earn by honest toil and noble endeavor. We owe the world a debt of gratitude we can never repay for making this a convenient dwelling place. We owe the world the best there is in us for its development. Gerald Massey put it right when he said: 'Toil is creation's crown, worship is duty.'

Another important lesson life has taught me is the value, the priceless value, of good friends, and with Shakespeare I say: 'Grapple them to they soul with hooks of steel.' Some sage has said: 'A man is known by the company he can not get into.' But truly this would be a barren world without the association of friends. But a man must make himself worthy of friends, for the text teaches us that 'A man who wants friends must show himself friendly.' What I am today, or strive to be, I owe largely to my friends — friends to whom I fail in language to express my gratitude, which is deeper than the lips; friends who led us to believe that 'stone walls do not a prison make, nor iron bars a cage;' friends who understand that human nature and sincerity are often clothed in prison garb; friends who have decreed that one false step does not lame a man for life. Oh, what a generous doctrine! And, although unwritten, I believe God has set His seal upon it. Honest friendship is a grand religion, and if we are true to ourselves, the poet tells us, we cannot be false to any man.

However, I am forced to admit that there are many brands of friendship existing these days which had not birth in our time. For instance: A number of men have visited me in the prison, and assured me of their interest in a pardon, etc. They have talked so eloquently and earnestly that I thought I was fortunate to enlist the sympathies and aid of such splendid men. After the first or second visit I was informed as gently as possible that a price was attached to this friendship; how much would I give them for endorsing or signing a petition for a pardon? I remember how I glared at them, how my pulse almost ceased beating, at such demands. What injustice to the public to petition a man out of prison for a price! If a man can not come out of prison on his merits, let him remain there. I hold, too, that if there is honor among thieves there should be among politicians and pretentious citizens. I hate a liar and a false man. I hate a hypocrite, a man whose word to his friend is not as good as gold.

My friends, there is just one thing I will say in my own defense if you will so far indulge me. I do not believe in doing under the cover of darkness that which will not bear the light of day. During my career of outlawry I rode into town under the glare of the noonday sun, and all men knew my mission. Corporations of every color had just cause to despise me then. But no man can accuse me of prowling around at night, nor of ever having robbed an individual, or the honest poor. In our time a man's word was equal to his oath, and seldom did a man break faith when he had once pledged himself to another.

What I say to you, fellow citizens, I say not in idle boast, but from the soul of a man who reverences truth in all its simplicity. Think of it — a price for a man's proferred friendship. On my soul, I do not even now comprehend so monstrous a proposition, and, believe me, even the unfortunate creatures about me in prison looked more like men than your respectable citizens and professional men with a price for their friendship.

I should like to say something to the ladies who have honored me with their presence. But as I have been a bachelor all my life I scarcely know what to say. I do know, though, that they are the divine creatures of a divine Creator; I do know that they are the high priestesses of this land; and too, I say, God could not be everywhere, so He made woman. One almost needs the lantern of a Diogenes in this progressive age to find an honest man, but not so with a good woman, who is an illumination in herself, the light of her influence shining with a radiance of its own. You will agree with me that the following lines contain more truth than poetry, and I bow to the splendid genius of the author:

> Blame woman not if some appear
> Too cold at times, and some too gay and light;
> Some griefs gnaw deep — some woes are hard to bear.
> Who knows the past, and who can judge them right?

Perhaps you have heard of banquets for gentlemen only. Well, it was upon one of these occasions that one of the guests was called upon to toast 'The Ladies.' There being no ladies present, he felt safe in his remarks. 'I do not believe there are any real, true women living any more.' The guest opposite him sprang to his feet and shouted: 'I hope that the speaker refers to his own female relations.' I never could understand, either, when a man goes wrong it is called 'misfortune,' while if a woman goes wrong it is called 'shame.' But I presume, being in prison twenty-five years, I am naturally dull, and should not question a world I have not lived in for a quarter of a century. I tell you, my friends, that I know very little of women, but one thing I am morally certain of: If the front seats of Paradise are not reserved for women, I am willing to take a back seat with them. It seems to me that every man who had a mother should have a proper regard for woman-hood. My own mother was a combination of all the best elements of the high character that belong to true wife and motherhood. Her devotion and friendship were as eternal as the very stars of heaven, and no misfortune could dwarf her generous impulses or curdle the milk of human kindness in her good heart. Her memory has been an altar, a guiding star, a divinity, in the darkest hour when regrets were my constant companions. It is true that I was a mere boy, in my teens, when the war was on, but there is no excuse for neglecting a good mother's counsel, and no good can possibly result. I was taught that honor among men and charity in the errors of others were the chief duties of mankind, the fundamentals of law, both human and divine. In those two commandments I have not failed, but in other respects I fell short of my home influence, and so, my young friends, do not do as I have done, but do as I tell you to do — honor the fourth commandment.

There is no heroism in outlawry, and the fate of each outlaw in his turn should be an everlasting lesson to the young of the land. And even as Benedict Arnold, the patriot and traitor, dying in an ugly garret in a foreign land, cried with his last breath to the lone priest beside him: 'Wrap my body in the American flag;' so the outlaw, from his inner soul, if not from his own lips, cries out, 'Oh, God, turn back the universe!'

There is another subject I want to say a word about — one which I never publicly advocated while in prison, for the reason that I feared the outside world would believe it a disguise to obtain my freedom. Freedom is the birthright heritage of every man, and it was very dear to me, but if the price of it was to pretend to be religious, the price was too high, and I would rather have remained in prison. Some men in prison fly to it as a refuge in sincerity — some otherwise. But to the sincere it is a great consolation, for it teaches men that hope is a divinity, without which no man can live and retain his reason.

But now that I have been restored to citizenship I feel free to express my views upon religion without fear that men will accuse me of hypocrisy. I do not see why that word 'hypocrisy' was ever put into the English language. Now, I am a lecturer, not a minister, but I want to say that I think it is a wise plan to let the Lord have his own way with you. That's logic. The man who walks with God is in good company. Get into partnership with Him, but don't try to be the leading member of the firm. He knows more about the business than you do. You may be able for a time to practice deception upon your fellow men, but don't try to fire any blank cartridges at the Author of the Universe. There are a great many ways to inspire a man with true Christian sentiment, and I must say that the least of them is sitting down and quoting a text from Scripture. Religious men and women have visited me in prison who have never mentioned religion, but have had the strongest influence over me. Their sincerity and conduct appealed to one more strongly than the bare Scripture. I can see in imagination now one who I have so often seen in reality while in prison. She was a true, sweet, lovely, Christian young lady. I remember once asking her if all the people of her church were as good as she was. She replied, honest and straightforwardly: 'No, you will not find them all so liberal toward their unfortunate brothers, and every church has its share of hypocrites — mine the same as others. But God and the church remain just the same.'

There are some don'ts I would call to your attention. One of them is, don't try to get rich too quickly by grasping every bait thrown out to the unwary. I have been in the society of the fellows who tried to get rich too quickly for the past twenty-five years, and for the most part they are a poor lot. I do not know but that I would reverse Milton's lines so as to read:

> 'Tis better to sit with a fool in Paradise
> Than some of those wise ones in prison.

Don't resort to idleness. The boy who wears out the seat of his trousers holding down dry goods boxes on the street corners will never be president of the United States. The farmer who drives to town for pleasure several days in the week will soon have his farm advertised for sale. An idle man is sure to go into the hands of a receiver. My friends, glorious opportunities are before us, with the republic's free institutions at your command. Science and knowledge have unlocked their vaults wherein poverty and wealth are not classified — a fitting theater where the master mind shall play the leading role.